# Integrated Learning for
# ERP
# SUCCESS

## A Learning Requirements Planning Approach

# Integrated Learning for

# ERP

# SUCCESS

## A Learning Requirements Planning Approach

## Karl M. Kapp
### with William F. Latham
### and Hester N. Ford-Latham

The St. Lucie Press/APICS Series on Resource Management

$S^t_L$

**St. Lucie Press**
Boca Raton • London
New York • Washington, D.C.

**APICS**®

**THE EDUCATIONAL SOCIETY
FOR RESOURCE MANAGEMENT**
Alexandria, Virginia

## Library of Congress Cataloging-in-Publication Data

Kapp, Karl M.
    Integrated learning for ERP success : a learning requirements planning approach / by Karl M. Kapp ; with William F. Latham and Hester Ford-Latham.
        p.   cm. — (The St. Lucie Press/APICS series on resource management)
    Includes bibliographical references and index.
    ISBN 1-57444-296-1 (alk. paper)
    1. Organizational learning. 2. Business planning. 3. Employees—Training of. 4. Organizational change. I. Latham, William F. II. Ford-Latham, Hester. III. Series.
HD58.82 .K36 2001
658.4′012—dc21                                                                                      00-067360
                                                                                                          CIP

### Visit the CRC Press Web site at www.crcpress.com

© 2001 by CRC Press LLC
St. Lucie Press is an imprint of CRC Press LLC

No claim to original U.S. Government works
International Standard Book Number 1-57444-296-1
Library of Congress Card Number 00-067360
Printed in the United States of America  1  2  3  4  5  6  7  8  9  0
Printed on acid-free paper

# Dedication and Acknowledgments

*Dedicated to **Marshall A. Kapp**, my father, who instilled in me persever-ance, thoughtfulness, and patience. Thanks.*

Thanks also to my wife, Nancy, and to Nicholas and Nathan who had to live with an author for six months. Also, a sincere thank you to Peggy Bross, Tyrone Howard, Christine Richards, Kathleen Boyd, and especially to Gregory Walsh, who all contributed to the development of the predecessor to the social simulator used in this book. Thanks to Debbie Karako, Pete Ferraro, and David Mueller for their help with the Lilly Software screen captures and to Scott Dawson for his contribution to the concept of the software training plan. Thanks to the CRC Press team of Carol Whitehead, Joette Lynch, and Drew Gierman who all helped make this book possible. Thanks also go to my colleagues at the Bloomsburg University Instructional Technology Department who bantered with me concerning the LRP model and to my students who have given their insights and ideas to the model. And a special thanks to my mother ... for everything.

# Contents

# Foreword

What do you get when you combine a team of a practitioner, a consultant, and an academic, with their own extensive backgrounds in enterprise management and the use of technology? You get this exceptional book on how to implement management software within the enterprise. *Integrated Learning for ERP Success: A Learning Requirements Planning Approach* provides both the theory and the practice on how to be successful with implementing an ERP system or any other technology that requires business transformation. Bill, Karl and Hester provide a real-world holistic approach to implementing ERP and leveraging the human capital in the enterprise. There may be new technology and new approaches, but the bottom line for success is still people.

Learning requirements planning (LRP) is an innovative look at how an appropriate education and training plan can be developed to ensure ongoing ERP success. The logic behind this approach is well proven through years of MRP and ERP implementations.

Bottom-line return from technology is not possible unless the technology removes or expands a current business constraint. Current business rules are inextricably linked to technology. When the business rules are changed without changing the appropriate technology, suddenly the technology becomes the constraint. When technology is installed without changing necessary business rules, then the business rules become the constraint. Only when the business rules are changed synergistically with the technology and the focus is on improving the holistic enterprise will technology drive real bottom-line results. Awareness of and motivation to change these business process constraints is only possible in a learning enterprise. Technology is changing at an increasing rate and continuous learning and process change are necessary for a company to compete in today's fast-paced global business world.

Continuous improvement is not just about business processes. Continuous improvement must leverage the current process, transform those processes that are constraining the enterprise's performance, build or install systems that support those improved processes, and run this technology in a secure scalable environment. This cycle repeats itself over and over to provide the enterprise a competitive advantage. The crank that turns this cycle and drives real bottom-line results is people — well-trained and educated people. *Integrated Learning for ERP Success: A Learning Requirements Planning Approach* brings out the question that many executives ask, "What happens if education is provided for company personnel and they leave?" This book clearly answers how education can actually enhance retention. With so many career changes and the lack of job security, employees will gravitate to the companies that provide them the opportunity to develop their personal value in the market — those that provide lifelong learning. This lifelong learning provides long-term success both for the employee and the company as these motivated learners continuously improve processes and practices and successfully install the required technology to support them. In addition, this book provides excellent insights on how to best measure that learning has occurred through this educational investment in the company's human capital and shows how retention can be improved through this investment.

Too many executives believe the sales pitch of the software companies that all they need to do is simply purchase the software and they can be successful. They are disappointed when they find that the promises were empty and the results are just not there. Technology is necessary but not sufficient to drive positive ROI. The real improvement to the bottom line comes from people. This book outlines in great detail the process by which necessary skills can be identified and developed to ensure the maximum return on investment from the investment in technology. Not only does the book claim that education is needed, the right education is needed at the right time in the right way to really achieve the desired bottom-line result.

If you think education and training are expensive — try ignorance. Even the smallest ERP implementation requires significant dedication of financial and human resources. Would you want the pilot on your last flight to have just been given the latest aircraft with no training on that specific model? Although the pilot may understand in general how to fly, extensive training and education are required on that particular aircraft before he is allowed into the cockpit. The same reasoning exists for your employees trying to utilize the latest and greatest software — even assuming they understand what is expected and why they should use it, training is still needed on how to effectively utilize the new software. Far too many implementations fail because people did not understand what was expected, where they fit into the whole picture and why this is so important. *Integrated Learning for ERP Success: A Learning Requirements Planning Approach* covers in depth how to improve the acceptance of ERP in the enterprise through leveraging key personnel. Education is the key to understanding. These three expert authors bring real-life examples to their learning requirements planning (LRP) model on how to ensure ERP acceptance and success.

The organization of the chapters clearly covers the concepts and application of learning requirements planning (LRP). The ready-to-use checklists provided at the ends of many chapters allow this material to be quickly adopted into any size company. The LRP model consisting of Analysis, Diagnosis, Design, Implementation, Evaluation, and Continuation provides an excellent model for implementing the ERP system on time and within budget. This LRP model is clear and easy to understand and provides an excellent framework for the chapters. More importantly, the overall LRP approach has a focus on how it contributes positively to the bottom line. These six concepts are described in good depth with real-life examples to aid in the overall understanding.

The master learning plan and skills inventory approach provide a framework that the implementation project manager can leverage to ensure that each person affected by the system implementation does not get too much education thereby wasting their time, too little education thereby risking the success of the implementation, or the wrong kind of education. The learning plan in conjunction with the discussion on learning styles ensures that individuals can get just the education they need, how they best learn it, and ensure that they will retain it. A one-size-fits-all approach docs not fit in clothing and it most certainly does not fit in education. *Integrated Learning for ERP Success: A Learning Requirements Planning Approach* also provides an excellent overview of e-learning and how it can best be used to support the project needs and ongoing educational requirements.

This is not a book that is meant to be read cover-to-cover in one weekend. It is a book that you will keep close at hand on your shelf and refer to often. Attempting to implement ERP without integrating the concepts in this book would be like bungee jumping without a bungee cord — you may think you will get there quicker, but long-term survival is unlikely. Don't attempt any major business system implementation without this book.

Carol A. Ptak, CFPIM, CIRM, Jonah
Author of *ERP, Tools, Techniques and Applications for Integrating the Supply Chain* and coauthor of *Necessary But Not Sufficient*

# Preface

The purpose of this book is to describe a systematic method for implementing an Enterprise Resource Planning (ERP) system with a focus on training and education. This book provides a road map for achieving organizational change through effective, targeted education. Too often, educational initiatives associated with organizational change are treated as a "warm and fuzzy" something that is nice to do — something that "keeps the troops happy" — but not something that supports enterprisewide strategic goals.

Organizations can no longer survive this mentality. If an organization is not continuously learning, it will fail. The current rate of change is too fast. Yet, developing an enterprisewide plan for organizational learning is not a familiar process. Few executives, middle managers, consultants, supervisors, or project team leaders have ever considered organizational training efforts and fewer still have attempted to implement a strategic educational initiative.

Training and education are the last bastions of untamed "wilderness" within a manufacturing organization. Accounting departments have been formalized for decades. Widespread use of reorder point inventory control was eliminated long ago because of the efficiencies of Material Requirements Planning (MRP). Statistical Process Control brought stability and predictability to thousands of processes. Sales and Operations Planning has helped to lower inventories, provide better customer service, shorten customer lead times, and stabilize production rates. Formalized customer/vendor relationships have even "tamed" the wild world of customer demand. Process improvement initiatives have reached into every operation that impacts the ultimate customer of a manufacturing organization except the training department.

Training and education programs within many manufacturing organizations are still ill structured, poorly planned, and horribly executed. The results of training are not properly measured, records are not audited, and the process is rarely examined. One-size-fits-all training is applied universally, with poor results.

Every other functional area within the manufacturing organization has applied a systematic approach toward process improvements. These functional areas have developed and implemented processes aimed at operational efficiencies, reduction of nonvalue-added time, and increased productivity. The goal is to maximize the resources of the organization. Ironically, the most expensive resources an organization possesses — human resources — have not had the same systematic approach applied toward keeping them productive and efficient.

One of the reasons for this is because no integrated model for undertaking such a formal approach to organizational training and education has previously existed. Yes, there are many excellent books on the individual pieces of this model, and many academic theories on organizational learning, and even well-defined concepts such as learning organizations, but a step-by-step model detailing the design, development, and delivery of training and education to support a strategic implementation of a new technology initiative like an ERP system has been absent. Practitioners, executives, managers, consultants, supervisors, and team leaders are often left to "fend for themselves" when attempting to integrate the different theories, ideas, and techniques into one comprehensive enterprisewide solution.

Just as MRP formalized materials handling, Learning Requirements Planning formalizes the educational process. As ERP integrated the silos of information within an organization, LRP integrates learning into the organization. LRP makes it possible to apply a systems approach to enterprisewide educational initiatives.

This book describes the LRP process and provides examples of how the process is applied and how it can be utilized within any organization. The primary purpose of this book is to provide a comprehensive, integrated model of enterprisewide training and education that supports an ERP implementation.

However, the LRP model is not limited to ERP implementations. The LRP process can be used to formalize training and educational initiatives in organizations implementing supply chain concepts, Just-In-Time procedures, e-learning systems, and e-commerce web sites. Any strategic initiative requiring employees to learn new skills is a LRP candidate.

# About the Author and Co-Authors

**Karl M. Kapp, Ed.D., CFPIM, CIRM** is a leading trainer, educator, scholar, consultant, and expert on the convergence of learning, technology, and manufacturing. His background in implementing ERP systems, knowledge of adult learning theory, and experience in training CEOs and shop floor personnel provide him with a unique perspective on organizational learning.

Karl understands how people learn and how to promote effective learning within an organization. He received his Doctorate of Education in the Instructional Design program at the University of Pittsburgh in Pittsburgh, PA. The field of Instructional Design focuses on the systematic design, development, delivery, and evaluation of instruction in a corporate environment.

Currently, as Assistant Director of Bloomsburg University's Institute for Interactive Technologies, Karl helps organizations such as CIGNA Healthcare, the Pennsylvania Department of Public Welfare, and AT&T understand how e-learning technologies impact employee productivity and learning. As Assistant Professor of Instructional Technology at Bloomsburg University, Karl teaches a unique class in which students are formed into "companies," write a business plan, receive a Request for Proposal (RFP) in the field of e-learning, respond to the RFP in writing and by developing a working prototype, and then present their solution to representatives from various corporations. Typical companies represented include click2learn.com, Booz·Allen & Hamilton, Verizon, and many boutique e-learning development firms.

In addition, Karl understands manufacturing. He is Certified as a Fellow in Production and Inventory Management (CFPIM) and is Certified in Integrated Resource Management (CIRM). His articles on learning, technology, and manufacturing have appeared in *APICS~The Performance Advantage, Manufacturing Systems, National Productivity Review, Hospital Materials Management Quarterly, The EDI Forum,* and the *Production and Inventory Management Journal.* He is co-author along with Gary Langewalter of the APICS Education and Research Foundation's white paper titled "Assessing the True Cost of Implementing an ERP System."

Karl spent five years as training manager at an ERP software development and implementation company where he developed a document detailing the step-by-step process necessary for implementing an ERP product. During that development process, he realized that most tasks were not software related, but were "people" related. This focus on people is the cornerstone of his workshops, academic research, and training presentations. He is frequently sought for interviews concerning his knowledge of the convergence of learning, technology, and manufacturing. He has been interviewed by *Software Strategies, Knowledge Management, Distance Learning,* and *TRAINING* magazines.

Karl has vast experience speaking to large groups. In addition to presenting to his students every week, he has spoken to local APICS Chapters, the Pittsburgh Chapter of the American Society of Training and Development (ASTD), the Allegheny County United Way, ASTD's TechKnowledge 2000, PNC Bank, and the Joseph M. Katz School of Business. In addition, he has spoken at the last four APICS International Conferences.

Karl is committed to helping organizations develop a strategic, enterprise-wide approach to organizational learning. He believes that effective education and training are the keys to increased productivity and profitability. His goal is to transform manufacturing organizations into learning organizations. He can be reached at kkapp@bloomu.edu.

# Co-Authors

**William F. Latham, CFPIM, CIRM** is an educator, trainer, seminar presenter, and management
consultant with experience in implementations
and customer support for customers around the
world. His rich and diverse professional experience provides a solid foundation for understanding business and manufacturing processes. With
over 24 years of hands-on experience as a practitioner in Purchasing, Production Scheduling,
and Materials Management, Bill has attained a
high level of expertise.

One of the APICS nationally recognized "Qualified Instructors," Bill has
demonstrated a mastery of the training and education process. He brings his
knowledge of a broad range of manufacturing environments and industries
to his classes, seminars, and clients.

Bill has served as an MRP II implementation consultant, applications
trainer, and educator for people from companies as diverse as Alcoa Fujicara,
Intel, Aviat Aircraft, Boeing, General Motors, Mitsubishi Heavy Industries,
Intermec, Rockwell-Collins, Siemens Medical, Starbucks Coffee, and Weyer-
hauser. He was the Technical Advisor for two books: *MRP and Beyond: A
Toolbox for Integrating People and Systems* and *ERP: Tools, Techniques, and
Applications for Integrating the Supply Chain.*

Bill is a regular presenter at APICS dinner meetings, classes, and seminars.
He has been an invited presenter at three APICS International Conferences,
two Volunteer Leadership Workshops, one ASTD Technowledge Conference,
The Global Quest for Competitiveness in Puerto Rico, and Congress for
Progress, and has presented seminars and training sessions in Indonesia and
Thailand.

William Latham graduated summa cum laude from Quinnipiac College
in Hamden, CT in Financial Management. He is Certified at the prestigious
Fellow level in Production and Inventory Management (CFPIM), and is also
Certified in Integrated Resource Management (CIRM) by APICS. Bill is also
listed as an APICS "Qualified Instructor" and is a qualified "Train the Trainer"
Instructor. Bill is a past president of the Commencement Bay Chapter and
is the Region 10 vice president for APICS. He is also a member of the
American Society of Training and Development (ASTD).

Bill Latham is the founder and head of Leading Principles for Dynamic
Management, a consulting and training firm focused on improving efficiency

in materials and production management and processes by educating, training, and guiding the people who make it happen.

**Hester Ford-Latham, CPIM** is a project manager for the Boeing Airplane Company. Her largest project to date is a companywide training management system implementation. Other positions include instruction of master scheduling, material requirements planning, and application-specific training in support of the Boeing Company's ERP system. She has held positions of MRP Planner, Planner/Buyer, and Production and Inventory Control Manager in a variety of manufacturing environments.

Hester has an AA Degree in Industrial Technology, and a Vocational Certification in Instruction. She has attended courses on instructional design and has completed a Train the Trainer course. She has designed and delivered instructor-led courses, lesson plans, and enhancements.

Hester served the Commencement Bay Chapter as a Director of Education for two consecutive years. Hester has presented at two APICS Region 10 July Officers' Training Workshops, and has co-presented at the APICS International Conference Volunteer Leadership Workshop and the ASTD Tech-Knowledge Conference.

# About this Book

## Book Audiences

This book has been written to satisfy a diversity of audiences interested in the concept of Learning Requirements Planning (LRP) and how it relates to successfully implementing an ERP system. Each audience will approach the book from different angles and viewpoints and each will read the book with different goals in mind.

One audience for this book is comprised of the consultants, implementation managers, training decision makers, and ERP project managers faced with the difficult task of implementing monumental change within an organization through the introduction of an ERP system while simultaneously maintaining the normal level of productivity.

For these readers, the best approach to the book is to read it in a linear fashion in the order in which the information is presented. This reading strategy provides a holistic view of LRP and the "big picture" insight missing from many implementation plans.

These readers should pay close attention to the concepts and explanations for each particular element within the model. The temptation may be for these busy readers to quickly obtain the checklist for LRP and begin to implement LRP without a clear understanding of the methodologies or concepts behind the checklist items. LRP cannot merely be implemented in a checklist fashion without a deeper understanding of the underlying, fundamental principles upon which it is founded. LRP is best understood as an integrated process for implementing ERP or any other large-scale, strategic-level technology-based change within an organization.

Another important audience reading this book is ERP implementation team members representing the various functional areas of a company including inventory, production, quality, finance, engineering, human resources, sales and marketing management, information technology, and supply chain management. These readers should pay particular attention to the detailed examples and methods explained in the text. Often, it is the managers of a particular functional area within an organization who are tasked with designing and delivering instruction to co-workers. Many of these individuals are not professional trainers and some don't even like to stand in front of co-workers and conduct training.

These readers can learn from the instructional approaches outlined in the various sections of the LRP model and apply those approaches to their own situations. The readers in this category may want to focus primarily on the Design chapter (Chapter 6). The Design chapter describes methods of classifying information to be learned as well as methods of presenting the information to co-workers.

One effective method for the implementation team members is to read the book as a team. Each member of the ERP implementation team should read the LRP Overview chapter (Chapter 3) and one of the other chapters describing an individual element of LRP. The team can then get together and compare notes and exchange information from each chapter. The team should discuss how the information contained in each chapter fits into the organization. This approach is highly effective in opening dialogue between and among team members and in encouraging them to actively think about the process of implementing the ERP system. ERP implementation project leaders may want to obtain multiple copies of the book and distribute them to "book clubs" within the organization that can benefit from understanding how learning impacts an entire organization.

A further audience for the book is instructional designers and course developers who are tasked with developing effective instruction, either for internal or external clients. The art and science of instructional design is often segmented into two opposite ends of a continuum. On the one end are the highly theoretical aspects of right-brain/left-brain interactions, cognitive structures, and constructivistic learning strategies. On the other end are the down and dirty, throw-it-out-and-see-if-it-sticks methods of developing and delivering instruction. The LRP process is firmly in the middle of this continuum.

Designers leaving highly theoretical instructional design graduate schools need to learn how theory and practice are combined to enhance the learning opportunity for corporate employees. Proper instructional design should not become a time-consuming, resource-draining process.

In addition, self-taught instructional designers who have been working within organizations for five or more years need to be aware of the theories supporting the instruction they are developing. In many organizations, instruction is developed and delivered and seems to be effective, but no one knows for sure. Much internal training has never been empirically validated. Organizational developers and trainers need to approach instructional development with some knowledge of the theoretical concepts that have made the development of effective training more of a science and less of an art.

The instructional designers will want to refer to the book as a reference source. They will look up information they need to obtain insight into a particular element of the LRP model. The checklists at the end of the chapters, the extensive use of actual examples, and the inclusion of a number of ready-made job aids provide a wealth of resources for the busy but dedicated instructional designer.

Another audience for the book is the executives overseeing the ERP implementation process. It is important for the executives to understand the interrelatedness of learning and technological innovation. It is difficult, if not impossible, to implement any new technology without some degree of training. Executives who are aware of the training/technology connection are prepared to lead their organizations into the future. These readers will want to pay particular attention to the Overview (Chapters 2 and 3) and Continuation (Chapter 9) chapters of the book.

Individuals who are tasked with training others will also find value in this work. Individuals who want to be trainers (or who are requested to become trainers) often look to experienced individuals within the field for advice and ideas on how to become a good trainer. Trainers of trainers can benefit from reading this work because it provides a solid road map for explaining to others what is required to make training successful — not only for an individual but for an organization as well.

Another audience is the faculty members in operations and human resource programs who are teaching students how to lead organizations. For this audience, many case studies and practical examples have been included to bring the information from a theoretical perspective down to the practical level. When gaps occur between pure instructional design theory and the application of the theory, the application is discussed and highlighted. The intent is to provide a theoretical foundation for organizational learning, but to temper that theory with actual practice and plenty of examples.

The checklist approach provides "talking points" for faculty to begin or conclude a class or lesson on a particular element of the model. One effective method for teaching the LRP model is to explain the model to the students and then ask them, in turn, to explain the model to each other in small groups. This tactic is at first seen as "silly" by students because they think "What new information could possibly be gained?" or, "We just learned this." However, this method is effective because the students embellish on the model and add their own insights. The students learn and teach each other the importance and relevance of the model.

It is suggested that as each element in the model is discussed and explained, students be encouraged to develop examples and sample items related to LRP. One of the best ways to learn new information is to view or collect examples of the new concept or idea and to study how those examples impact each other.

Another audience interested in Learning Requirements Planning is the students who will be entering into organizations faced with an unprecedented learning challenge. The speed of technological change requires a constant learning and re-learning within organizations. Current students need to be aware of how their learning will continue in the future and how they must be prepared to support, implement, or develop instruction for themselves and their co-workers. These readers should approach the book with interest in the interconnectedness of the LRP model's elements. Students should attempt to incorporate what they know about operations and instructional design into the LRP model to create a robust paradigm for leading change through learning.

Learning Requirements Planning appeals to many audiences in both the instructional design and resource management fields. The universal appeal of the concept is that it applies a systematic method for simultaneously implementing technology and enhanced human potential into an organization. While reading the book, think of how this method can be applied to the variety of technological innovations introduced into your organization on a regular basis.

## Chapter Outline

This book breaks the LRP model into distinct elements or steps. Each step is carefully examined and explained with case studies and examples. This allows the reader to understand the theories, ideas, and techniques supporting each step within the LRP model. Readers can also observe how organizational learning theory is put into practice within an actual manufacturing organization.

Anyone who has studied cultural change within an organization, or has been involved with an ERP implementation — successfully or unsuccessfully — understands that an implementation is not always a step-by-step, systematic process. There are far too many random events, unexpected delays, and "human factors" for an implementation to be strictly linear. An ERP system by its very nature is integrated and requires an integrated approach. The authors do not anticipate that any organization would approach an ERP system with an unwavering LRP approach.

Effective organizational change comes from adopting and adapting models to the unique needs of an organization. To be most effective, LRP must be modified within the organization to achieve success. The underlying principles and concepts must not be altered, but some of the methodologies and techniques can be adapted.

However, for the purpose of helping readers understand the LRP model and how each element of the model functions, we have taken the approach of parsing the LRP model into easily identifiable steps. This step-by-step explanation of the model provides readers with a tool for understanding how one part of the system impacts others. The final chapter unifies the process and explains how all the pieces can work together to achieve success.

Each chapter and its contents are explained below to provide the reader with a quick reference guide to the contents of the book and to help the reader identify which aspect of the model he or she should first examine. However, it should be noted that LRP works most effectively when the flow from analysis to continuation is followed. The variations should occur in the implementation of the model not in its sequence.

## *Chapter 1 — Why You Need Learning Requirements Planning*

This chapter contains a brief discussion of the economic impact of poor or nonexistent ERP educational initiatives. It includes a number of actual ERP implementation horror stories as related to failures in educational efforts. This is important to understand because millions of dollars a year are wasted on misguided training/education efforts.

Companies implementing ERP systems cannot afford to waste money or time in the area of ERP education. The largest ERP implementation expense is education and training. Investing in learning-focused ERP implementations will provide a substantial competitive advantage.

## Chapter 2 — Overview of ERP Systems

Chapter 2 discusses the fact that an ERP system is not a computer system. This is a common misconception that must be addressed prior to successfully implementing a system. This chapter stresses the fact that ERP encompasses a methodology for running an organization and is not a specific type of software. The overall learning requirements and training efforts needed to implement a large, totally integrated manufacturing management system are discussed in this chapter.

This chapter also addresses five different perspectives of an ERP system. These include the view of ERP as a basic storage facility for data all the way up to the view of an ERP system as a knowledge management system. Organizations that combine ERP with knowledge management will have a large advantage in the future. Technology will be used more and more to develop two-way communication with customers concerning everything from indicating the best time for stocking up on an item to assisting with the design and development of a new product.

Chapter 2 also discusses the most common mistakes that organizations make when implementing an ERP system. These mistakes are classified into different categories to assist the reader with understanding their severity and magnitude as well as describing how to prevent those mistakes from occurring in the first place.

## Chapter 3 — Overview of LRP Model

This chapter serves as an introduction to the LRP model and generally describes the elements and what the reader can expect from implementing LRP within the organization, especially in relationship to an ERP implementation. Chapter 3 lays the foundation for the next five chapters outlining the elements that comprise the LRP model. The format for these chapters is as follows.

The authors first define and discuss the element of the model. Next, examples of how the element can be applied to both a manufacturing and service-based ERP implementation is explained. Finally, individual employee development strategies are discussed from the perspective of an ERP implementation. An educational checklist appears at the end of each subsequent chapter listing the steps a company must take to implement this particular phase of the model.

Also in this chapter, types of learning within an organization are discussed as well as e-learning and the five disciplines of a learning organization.

## Chapter 4 — Analysis

The first element of the LRP model discussed is *Analysis*. This portion of the book discusses the type of organizational analyses that must take place prior to beginning the ERP educational initiative (internal analysis, external analysis, and cultural analysis). The analyses ask questions related to learner characteristics; environmental conditions; knowledge level of employees, vendors, and customers; and level of commitment to educational initiatives. Examples of this process are discussed. In this chapter, cascading learning objectives are discussed (development of learning objectives from corporate strategic objectives).

## Chapter 5 — Diagnosis

The next element covered is *Diagnosis*. This chapter discusses the need to design instruction related to different employee learning styles and preferences. This portion of the book discusses various educational strategies appropriate for different types of ERP education. For example, inventory accuracy training is taught using instructional strategies different from master schedule interpretation training.

The discussion of learning styles is designed to provide the reader with some insights into the different ways in which people learn. Many times organizations do not even consider the fact that different people learn using a variety of techniques. Often the ERP training, or any training within an organization, is designed only to appeal to one or two types of learners. The other learners are left without any good way to acquire the new information except to learn it on their own. If employees are aware of their own learning styles, they can develop methods to learn more effectively using that style. If corporate ERP trainers learn about different learning styles, they can tailor their training to provide instruction in each of the different learning styles, allowing the maximum number of their students to receive benefit from the instruction.

## Chapter 6 — Design

This chapter discusses the importance of designing instruction appropriate for the environment and corporate culture that will implement the ERP system. In some organizations, small group discussions are great methods for conveying information while in other organizations, lecture or computer-based learning is more appropriate. This chapter also discusses techniques for ensuring that the instruction is designed in a manner congruent with the objectives determined in the analysis phase of the model.

The designer or designers of an ERP training plan must not only provide technical training but soft skills training as well. The most successful ERP implementations are those that provide the users with a variety of training not necessarily directly related to ERP. The skills of leadership, communication, teamwork, and negotiation are all heavily used during an ERP implementation and should be an integral part of the ERP training plan.

## Chapter 7 — Implementation

An ERP system is an innovation within an organization and the acceptance of that innovation requires buy-in and credibility. This chapter outlines specific methods for obtaining buy-in for successfully implementing LRP within the organization. Also discussed are the different types of people in an organization in terms of their ability to adapt to technology. Understanding the different rates of technology adoption within an organization helps the implementation and executive teams to more effectively target their training and educational efforts.

In addition, this chapter addresses the most common methods of implementing an ERP system. It discusses the Big Bang, Phased, Parallel, and Pilot approaches toward implementation. The pros and cons of these methods are discussed. Each method has been used successfully in certain organizations. The trick is to match the organization's culture with the appropriate implementation method.

## Chapter 8 — Evaluation and Measurement

This chapter discusses four levels of evaluation for ERP training effectiveness as well as formative and summative training evaluations. The chapter also discusses formulas for determining training ROI and how to define measurement criteria as they relate to training accountability.

An organizational training plan cannot be effective if it is not measured properly. The old saying "you get what you measure" is as true in an ERP implementation effort as it is anywhere else. The training efforts supporting the ERP implementation must be measured and evaluated to ensure that the training program is helping the organization meet its goals. If the training program is not meeting the organization's goals then it must be redesigned.

## Chapter 9 — Continuation

This chapter explains how to keep a focus on learning even after the ERP implementation is considered complete. Organizations need to appoint a Chief Learning Officer responsible for administration of training across the enterprise as well as developing an internal focus on learning. Organizations that continue to learn are able to remain competitive. Organizations that fail to learn are doomed to repeat mistakes, constantly reinvent the wheel and lose precious time relearning what they already should have known.

This chapter highlights the steps needed to transform the enterprise from a manufacturing organization into a learning organization through LRP. This chapter also discusses the planning, resources, and incentives that must be in place to continue a focus on learning long after the ERP implementation is done. The chapter concludes with a discussion of the five learning disciplines as defined by Peter Senge.

## Chapter 10 — e-Learning/ERP Connection

Chapter 10 explores the concepts of using the Internet or a corporate Intranet to distribute ERP training to employees. In fact, revenues for web-based ERP training in the U.S. were $915 million in 1998 and estimated to reach the $2.8 billion mark by 2003.[1]

e-Learning has many advantages over traditional instruction and can provide a tremendous cost saving to an organization implementing an ERP system if it is handled correctly. This chapter explores web-based training. It defines basic e-learning terms and provides a look at the advantages and disadvantages of web-based instruction.

The use of e-learning is gaining popularity among ERP software companies for a variety of reasons. The chapter discusses how BAAN, SAP, PeopleSoft, and others are using web-based training to assist with ERP implementations.

## Chapter 11 — Conclusion

This chapter handles the conclusion in a unique manner by tying all of the instruction in the book to a case study of Marshall Manufacturing. This chapter highlights how Marshall implemented its ERP system using the LRP process and achieved success.

The chapter summarizes the book and explains how ERP implementations and LRP can work hand-in-hand for a variety of e-technology implementations including e-commerce, e-supply chain, and business-to-business information exchanges. Any enterprisewide initiative that requires that employees learn new skills can be enhanced through the use of the LRP model.

This book contains a comprehensive glossary with many terms related to the LRP process and the basic design of instruction for ERP implementation success. The appendices provide a complete LRP checklist, a job description for a Chief Learning Officer, and a blank Learning Diagnosis Chart. The material at the end of the book is designed to provide tools to the practitioner to help implement LRP and for the academician to teach the steps of the model to students in a manner in which they can apply the information when they enter the field.

## Summary

The best way to read this book is to team with others and study how the information can relate to your specific situation. Each of the various readers can learn something from the chapters. However, it is the comprehensive, holistic view of LRP that makes it such an effective tool for delivering instruction within an organization. The model is most powerful when the individual elements are combined to provide a learning advantage to an enterprise.

## Reference

1.  Wheatley, M., ERP training stinks, *CIO Magazine* [online], http://www2.cio.com/archive/060100_erp_content.html, June 2000.

# About APICS

APICS, The Educational Society for Resource Management, is an international, not-for-profit organization offering a full range of programs and materials focusing on individual and organizational education, standards of excellence, and integrated resource management topics. These resources, developed under the direction of integrated resource management experts, are available at local, regional, and national levels. Since 1957, hundreds of thousands of professionals have relied on APICS as a source for educational products and services.

- **APICS Certification Programs** — APICS offers two internationally recognized certification programs, Certified in Production and Inventory Management (CPIM) and Certified in Integrated Resource Management (CIRM), known around the world as standards of professional competence in business and manufacturing.
- *APICS Educational Materials Catalog* — This catalog contains books, courseware, proceedings, reprints, training materials, and videos developed by industry experts and available to members at a discount.
- *APICS—The Performance Advantage* — This monthly, four-color magazine addresses the educational and resource management needs of manufacturing professionals.
- *APICS Business Outlook Index* — Designed to take economic analysis a step beyond current surveys, the index is a monthly manufacturing-based survey report based on confidential production, sales, and inventory data from APICS-related companies.
- **Chapters** — APICS' more than 270 chapters provide leadership, learning, and networking opportunities at the local level.

- **Educational Opportunities** — Held around the country, APICS' International Conference and Exhibition, workshops, and symposia offer you numerous opportunities to learn from your peers and management experts.
- **Employment Referral Program** — A cost-effective way to reach a targeted network of resource management professionals, this program pairs qualified job candidates with interested companies.
- **SIGs** — These member groups develop specialized educational programs and resources for seven specific industry and interest areas.
- **Web Site** — The APICS Web site at http://www.apics.org enables you to explore the wide range of information available on APICS' membership, certification, and educational offerings.
- **Member Services** — Members enjoy a dedicated inquiry service, insurance, a retirement plan, and more.

For more information on APICS programs, services, or membership, call APICS Customer Service at (800) 444-2742 or (703) 354-8851 or visit http://www.apics.org on the World Wide Web.

# 1 Introduction: Why You Need Learning Requirements Planning (LRP)

*What lies behind ERP Disasters? And behind the rather long list of costly-but-underwhelming implementations ... the smoking gun: Poor Training.*

— Malcolm Wheatley, *CIO Magazine*[1]

## Introduction

The list of companies who have had problems with ERP implementations is long and illustrious. It includes Dow Chemical, Dell Computer, Apple Computer, Hershey Foods, Waste Management, and Whirlpool. What is the problem? It's not that these companies haven't spent hundreds of thousands or even millions of dollars on employee training. They have! The problem is that many Enterprise Resource Planning (ERP) training plans are haphazard, ill conceived, and focused on the wrong topics — if they exist at all.

During the implementation process, training is treated like a poor second cousin. Training classes are isolated events not relevant to employee jobs. The training offered by the vendor fails to help employees understand the integrated nature of the ERP system. The focus is on technical training, not integration. Training for the system is too early, other times it's too late. No one knows who attended which training class. Educational sessions are missed because of more important priorities. Employees do not understand their new roles and responsibilities. In the final analysis, most organizations spend more time planning the company picnic than they do devising an ERP training plan.

The unfortunate result of this lack of planning is failed implementations. Lots of them! Managers in organizations implementing ERP systems don't need technical training presented in a piecemeal fashion. They need an understanding of the underlying flow of information through the business itself. Managers, executives, and rank and file employees need an understanding of the integrated nature of ERP. They also need a direct tie between the strategic objectives set by the executives and the daily tasks they are asked to perform on the ERP system.

A systematic training plan tied directly to the strategic needs of the organization is required for ERP implementation success. Anything else is a gamble — a very expensive gamble.

Fortunately, a model exists for incorporating training into the ERP implementation process. The model is Learning Requirements Planning (LRP). LRP is a model for managing training and education initiatives at an enterprise level to achieve ERP implementation success. LRP is an exciting, innovative methodology for integrating people and systems through increased knowledge and focused education while implementing an ERP system.

Prior to the development and widespread implementation of ERP systems, each department within a manufacturing organization had its own software for performing its daily functions — silos of automation. Mission-critical production, marketing, and accounting information was hidden away in disparate databases, spreadsheets, and word processing documents with no easy way for sharing information. Departments within an organization didn't have to know how other departments functioned. Employees did not need to know what other departments did with this "hidden" information. And they didn't care. Understanding the integrated nature of the organization was the job for senior managers and executives, not for rank and file employees. All the average employee needed to worry about was his or her data — no one else's.

In the early 1990s all that changed. ERP systems merged production management spreadsheets, marketing databases, and accounting documents into a single electronic system. Now everyone was working with everyone else's data. Not just their own. This was a "culture shock" for many employees, senior managers, and executives. The inventory clerk was now directly affecting the general ledger with his inventory transaction data. The employee on the shop floor impacted overhead calculations by how she reported against a work order. The purchasing clerk could skew accounts payable numbers by entering the wrong "purchasing" code on a purchase order. An engineer could cost a company thousands of dollars worth of wrong inventory by leaving a prototype material in the middle level of a production bill of material.

This culture shock and new level of information sharing and integration led to problems. Industry surveys have shown that 40% of all ERP installations achieve only partial implementation and close to one in five are scrapped as total failures.[2] This means that not only is the investment in the software lost but the investment in implementing the software is lost, as well. And that investment is expensive. ERP implementation costs range from three to ten times the actual software purchase price.

Why all the failures? While the software and hardware technology for the new ERP system was impressive, people were not ready for the integrated nature of ERP. Instead of spending money training employees to work together as an integrated unit, share data among departments, or learn from each other's knowledge, investments were made in technology.

Senior executives, bolstered by the promise of an unprecedented technological advantage over competitors, purchased and continue to purchase ERP systems in record numbers. From 1995 to 1998 the ERP market grew at a compound annual rate of 35% and was still described as "poised for enormous growth."[3] And there is no sign of it slowing down. The ERP software market is projected by Advanced Manufacturing Research (AMR) to expand to $50 billion by 2002.

Yet this ERP buying frenzy has not led to the promised results. The industry magazine, *Midrange ERP*, reported that, "Companies have spent fortunes on ERP software and implementation only to find that business performance has not improved at all." *Midrange ERP* goes on to say that, "Nine out of ten companies don't get it right the first time."[4]

However, the companies that do "get it right" reap tremendous advantages. Oil giant Chevron Corporation estimated that its $100 million dollar investment in an ERP system pays back $50 million dollars in cost savings alone in one year, not to mention productivity improvements and streamlined processes.[5] Compaq Computer Corporation uses an ERP system to monitor order backlogs on a daily basis. Compaq's ERP system helped slash inventories from $2.2 to $1.2 billion, even as revenue rose 23%.[5] When ERP systems are implemented correctly, companies can expect vast improvements in managing sales, controlling operations, and utilizing assets.

With such a wide variation among ERP implementations — some successful and some disasters, the question becomes, "What is the difference between ERP success and ERP failure?" Clearly, purchasing better and faster ERP hardware and software technology is not the answer. ERP technology is available to everyone but does not, by itself, result in success. The answer is deceivingly simple — education and training.

However, the correct implementation of that answer is extraordinarily difficult. Manufacturing companies spend very little energy, time, resources, or dollars on formal, systematic ERP training and education. Traditionally, manufacturing organizations do not place a high priority on training and education. The average production worker in the U.S. receives less than 30 hours of formal training a year.[6] Many companies have no formal plan for regularly updating the skills of their workforce or a method of forecasting future skill needs.[7]

The problem is that companies do not follow a model for managing the training and education processes within their organizations. When it comes time to implement an ERP system the same pattern continues: little or no training for employees on the functionality and, more importantly, the integrated nature of ERP.

When training does occur, it is often focused in the wrong areas. Much of the literature concerning ERP implementations is based upon the needs of the ERP system — accurate inventory, good sales and operations procedures, accurate bills of material, a well-functioning master schedule — little has been written on the strategies and tactics of providing a solid educational foundation for the ERP implementation. Education is the single most important indicator of successful ERP implementations, yet it receives little attention in many manufacturing organizations.

Every major presentation, book, or article discussing an ERP implementation success story includes a section on the need for quality education and training. Without proper training, the article, book, or presenter asserts success could not have been achieved. Yet, these same books, articles, or presenters spend little time explaining in clearly understood terms how to develop a proper ERP training program. No wonder companies implementing ERP systems are confused.

This confusion and lack of an internal focus on training have turned into a huge market opportunity for providers of ERP training. More and more, companies that do not internally retain the expertise required to support training for ERP implementations have partnered with third-party training service providers. The ERP education and training services market is valued at $1.15 billion and is projected to hit $3 billion by 2002.[8]

Yet, improper or misguided training efforts are not effective. If the training does not follow a systematic plan integrated tightly with the ERP implementation, training dollars are wasted. External providers are an excellent source of ERP training provided the company implementing the system approaches the training in a systematic integrated way. Simply conducting training for the sake of training is not effective.

ERP systems are powerful, but without savvy employees who know how to take advantage of that power, the full benefits are not realized. Training and education are critical elements for ERP success, yet can cost organizations hundreds of thousands of dollars. Therefore, a systematic approach is needed. Companies that gain the most from ERP system implementations realize the high value of systematic, targeted education and training.

## ERP Implementation: Case Studies

One of the most effective tools for understanding the impact of systematic training on an organization implementing an ERP system is to examine actual companies to see what made them successful and what should be avoided. A look at three different companies reveals the impact a systematic, focused training effort can have on an ERP implementation and how its absence causes problems. The first two case studies are examples for the same industry. One company was unable to successfully execute its ERP implementation and ran into some serious financial difficulties as a result. The other company was able to successfully implement its system and gain the results it desired. The third case study highlights the importance of educating top management to gain their support and understanding of the obstacles involved with successful ERP implementations.

First, an examination of two different companies in the candy industry illustrates how a focus on training helped one company achieve success while the other encountered problems so severe, profits actually dropped.

**Hershey Foods Corporation,** a North American manufacturer of quality chocolate and nonchocolate confectionery and chocolate-related grocery products, ran into massive ERP implementation problems in the late summer of 1999.[1,9,10] The implementation of the ERP system was so bad that during Halloween, big customers like WalMart and Kmart were loading up on candy from competitors.[10]

One of the many mistakes made during the SAP R/3 software implementation was Hershey's failure to allow enough time for the employees to learn how to use the new ERP system and to understand how the integrated processes of an ERP system impacted the daily roles and responsibilities of the workers. Hershey Foods learned the importance of integration training the hard way.

Original plans to support a 4-year implementation of SAP's R/3 were compressed into 2.5 years. Hershey Foods met its July 1999 "go live" date to have the software turned on and running; however, by mid-September order processing problems resulted in a 19% drop in third-quarter earnings.[1,9,10]

Hershey's upper management, like so many other executives have done, pointed the finger at SAP and asked the software company to address perceived software problems and bugs. The fact of the matter was that there were relatively few software bugs or fixes required. Instead, the bigger problem was that Hershey employees needed to correctly follow the business processes built into the SAP software. The employees needed to understand how the various models of SAP R/3 interacted with one another. This required training not just in how the system functioned, but training in "why" the system functions in a certain manner.

In addition, Hershey employees were suffering from information overload. Hershey was not only implementing SAP's R/3 software, but also a customer relations-management program from Siebel Systems and a logistics package from Manugistics. Employees had a difficult time trying to learn the new systems, revise their procedures and policies, and still produce and ship product during the accelerated implementation process.

*Computerworld* describes Hershey Food's ERP implementation as a "catastrophic failure" resulting in "lost market share."[10] While not all of the problems at Hershey were related to a lack of a systematic approach to training the workforce, managers, and executives in ERP integration and functionality, many problems could have been avoided by a training-focused implementation.

In contrast, **Russell Stover Candies** is a company that focused on training during its ERP implementation and the results were more favorable. Russell Stover Candies, the largest manufacturer of fancy boxed chocolates in North America and a family-owned company, implemented BaanERP and BaanSCS Planner with impressive results.[11]

Russell Stover Candies chose a phased implementation strategy with a focus on aligning key business processes to the functionality of the software. The implementation strategy also focused on a systematic and focused training plan. For Russell Stover Candies, the training was ongoing and initiated shortly after the implementation began. This training focus made a tremendous difference for Russell Stover and led to a successful conclusion.

Russell Stover's ERP implementation resulted in reduced inventory checks, lowered vendor lead times, and improved resource utilization. The successful ERP implementation gave Russell Stover Candies' employees access to real-time information and greater visibility of the entire supply chain.[11] The employees know how to use the system to gain the desired results.

It doesn't take much analysis to see that two companies in the same industry can have dramatically different results when one focuses on training and education and the other does not. The need for a systematic training approach during an ERP implementation is acute. Employees, managers, and executives all need to take part in a step-by-step training and education plan for the implementation.

The **Barden Corporation** case study clearly illustrates the impact the training can have on an implementation and how education of the top executives is a key to success.[12] The early efforts to educate top management on ERP paid off for the corporation. In fact, Graham Sterling, the Managing Director of the Barden Corporation, was "delighted" just after the cutover to the new system.[12] In October of 1998 the Barden Corporation, a German manufacturer of high-precision bearings, successfully implemented SAP R/3.

The implementation started in 1995 with education targeted toward Barden's top management team. Seven high-level managers attended a two-day seminar to learn what a well-implemented system could do for a company. Under the direction of a consulting firm specializing in implementing manufacturing management systems, Barden took the approach of training company employees to become experts in the ERP implementation process. This process gave Barden employees ownership of the project.

In 1997 Barden's top managers attended a more detailed implementation course. The course topics included discussions on various aspects of ERP implementations and ensured that the high-level managers of Barden knew what to expect during the implementation process.

Following this implementation course, an education program was designed and planned to teach employees new and better ways of running the business using the ERP software as a tool for improvement, as opposed to simply focusing just on the implementation of new software.

As part of the educational plan, the consulting firm recommended a minimum of 15% of indirect employees attend external ERP and system integration education to achieve a true culture shift. A significant factor in this implementation was that Barden did more than the minimum education on both the business principles as well as the ERP software. Education of employees began in May 1997, with cutover to the new system in October 1998.[12]

The 18 months of planned training paid off with a "delightful" ERP implementation. By implementation time the company could boast about

98% inventory records accuracy, 99% bill of material accuracy, and improved purchasing processes.

When asked how the implementation had gone, Graham Sterling, the Managing Director, commented that the "implementation went extremely well and they were already getting tremendous benefits as well as a reduction in costs. The whole culture of the company had changed, everyone was focused on working together and living off the same database."[12]

Richard Offer, a Business Unit Manager and project leader, attributed Barden's success to education and training. He said, "You cannot do too much education and training."[12] The importance of effective training can not be overemphasized. Many examples exist which illustrate the importance of developing an enterprisewide training and education plan to assist the ERP implementation.

## ERP Lessons

Success is achieved when organizations take the time to develop a training and education plan prior to beginning the ERP implementation. However, what does a company do if it has already implemented an ERP system but is not receiving the desired results? The answer is to develop and execute a training plan. Tortube Inc. is an excellent example of that situation.

**Tortube Inc.** is a European company in the forefront of tube manipulation technology. It originally supplied precision manipulated tubes and fabrications used in domestic gas cookers and boilers. Once the company expanded into manufacturing precision manipulated tubes for heating, motors, aerospace, and leisure industries, it realized that quality had to be of utmost importance. Continuous improvement became a company focus.

In 1996 Tortube Inc. implemented an ERP system called FourthShift. The implementation was not a complete failure but the company was not getting the results it expected. "They felt like they were carting around a full set of golf clubs, but only using the 7 iron and the putter!"[13]

What was missing? An understanding of how to use ERP as a tool for Tortube to reach its full potential within its respective supply chain. An extensive education program was designed, planned, and delivered. The result of this systematic re-education of the workforce was dramatic.

Upon completion of the education program, inventory accuracy shot up to 100% and improved master production scheduling cut cumulative order lead time significantly. The software didn't change, but the ability of the users to understand and exploit the features of FourthShift did. The training effort made it seem as if the company implemented a new ERP system. It hadn't. The only change was that users simply learned how to use their existing system more effectively.

## LRP Is the Solution

Just as manufacturing and service organizations need to follow a systematic model for counting, tracking, and planning inventory and services, these organizations also need a systematic model for designing, planning, and delivering training. That systematic model is Learning Requirements Planning (LRP).

LRP is a formal, enterprisewide training and education planning process that is time-phased to meet the long- and short-term ERP learning objectives of an organization based upon its stated strategic goals. LRP uses the concepts of "explosions," bills of learning, master learning schedules, gross-to-net logic, all in a framework of a six-step enterprise-level instructional design model.

The LRP process combines formulas, techniques, and concepts from two different but related bodies of knowledge. The first is the manufacturing body of knowledge that provides the MRP concepts of gross-to-net logic, master production scheduling, bills of material, explosions, and time phasing. Applying these familiar concepts to the training and education efforts within a manufacturing organization directly ties the LRP process to the ERP process. This tight integration and sharing of concepts are what makes LRP so appealing to manufacturing organizations implementing an ERP system.

The second body of knowledge is from the field of instructional systems design (ISD). The field of instructional design focuses on the systematic design, development, and delivery of effective instruction using a systems approach for the entire process. The systems approach ensures that the training is effective and accomplishes the desired outcome.

LRP uses the ISD concepts of analysis, design, implementation, and evaluation. These concepts are familiar to human resource (HR) and training personnel. They provide a systematic and proven methodology for designing and delivering effective instruction. ERP systems are only as good as the people using the systems and the people can only be as good as the instruction they receive. The ISD elements of LRP ensure that the employees receive effective training.

LRP actually evolved from the ISD model. Traditionally, ISD is focused on an individual training event or, at most, a training curriculum for an organization. LRP moves training from the curriculum level to the organization or enterprisewide level. This shifting of the ISD model means that the techniques and concepts behind ISD are now applied at a much higher enterprisewide level. This enterprise focus provides an organization with a proven methodology to achieve the implementation success of any e-technology, from ERP systems to e-commerce applications to e-supply-chain initiatives.

The combination of the two distinct disciplines into the LRP framework provides a common language that can be shared among the employees of the organization and used to discuss the techniques required for successful ERP implementation.

LRP provides a learning architecture upon which to base an ERP system and its implementation. It is a framework for teaching employees about the integrated nature of the organization and how to optimize that integration. LRP teaches employees to use the knowledge within the ERP system to make informed, intelligent, and effective decisions on a daily basis and it ensures that those decisions are tied to the strategic goals of the organization.

Developing a framework for successful ERP implementations is an important process. Many companies appoint an implementation staff who have had little time to work together as an integrated team. They receive no teamwork training, change management training, or other types of "soft skills" training required to bring about cultural change within an organization. If the team receives any training, it is typically in the area of MRP formulas and software functionality.

Implementation teams need to understand how to develop a sound structure for conducting the training required to make ERP a success. The first step toward success is to determine how best to train employees within an organization. These employees have diverse needs, backgrounds, learning styles, and levels of interest.

Throughout the years, many techniques have been developed based upon sound, empirical research. Unfortunately, many of these ideas are doomed to stay in academic limbo because they are not presented in clear, concise terms and they are not applied to practical ERP implementations.

An academician wrote this book with input from a practitioner in the field and an ERP implementation and training consultant. This unique blend of expertise means that the concepts laid out in this book are based on sound theory as well as practical experience. Understanding the LRP process will help employees within a company gain insight into common implementation training problems and their fellow employees. Understanding the LRP process will help companies avoid training-related problems and, more importantly, reap the rewards from a successful ERP implementation.

The implementation process is never easy and it is typically not the first priority of implementation team members. Therefore, tensions are high. Project team members would love to have a guidebook for assisting them through the implementation process. The more educated the project team, the higher the likelihood of a successful ERP implementation. The implementation team can receive a number of positive benefits by understanding the LRP process. Understanding the LRP process can:

- Help the implementation team avoid common ERP implementation and training mistakes that can sink careers.
- Help save the company money by implementing the ERP system on time and on budget.
- Position the team as being knowledgeable of the ERP implementation process and LRP when speaking with management and external consultants.

The concept of Learning Requirements Planning is simple, yet effective. It clearly illustrates the need for education and analysis prior to action. This book helps implementation teams understand LRP because of its systematic approach, interesting real-world case studies, and its simple, effective message.

## Summary

The emerging consensus concerning ERP training is that the important training is in business operations and integrations and not in understanding the fields and functionality of the software. If ERP training is not tied to corporate objectives and to the employee's daily tasks, it is not effective.

Learning Requirements Planning provides the architecture for effective training and education by furnishing a logical structure to develop the appropriate set of skills, knowledge, and abilities in an organization. Just as material requirements planning helped to revolutionize manufacturing because of its ability to minimize inventory and provide projected on-hand balances, LRP will revolutionize how organizations implement ERP systems and approach organizational learning.

# References

1. Wheatley, M., ERP training stinks, *CIO Magazine* [online], http://www2.cio.com/archive/060100_erp_content.html, June 2000.
2. Trunick, P. A., ERP: Promise or pipe dreams, *Transp. Distribution*, 40, 23, 1999.
3. Shepard, J., Sound off! Is ERP in trouble? If this is trouble, where can I get some? *Computerworld*, 32, 63, 1998.
4. Donovan, M.R., Successful ERP implementation the first time, *Midrange ERP*, Aug. 1999.
5. White, J.B., Clark, D., and Ascarelli, S., This German sofware is complex, expensive — and wildly popular, *The Wall Street Journal*, Friday, March 14, 1997, Vol. IC, No. 51.
6. Industry report: Who gets trained, *Training Magazine*, 35(10), 1998, pp. 55–62.
7. Kapp, K.M., How to develop a learning requirements plan (LRP) for your manufacturing organization, in *APICS 1998 Int. Conf. Proc.*, Falls Church, VA, 1998, pp. 193–195.
8. Crowley, A., Third parties step up with training options (Industry Trend or Event), *PC Week*, 15, 134, 1998.
9. Osterland, A., Blaming ERP, *CFO Magazine* [on-line], http://www.cfonet.com/html/Articles/CFO/2000/00Jablam.html, January, 2000.
10. Stedman, C., Failed ERP gamble haunts Hershey; candy maker bites off more than it can chew and 'kisses' big Halloween sales goodbye, *Computerworld*, Nov. 1999.
11. Supply chain system sweetens bottom line, *Prepared Foods*, http://www.prepared-foods.com/archives/1999/9902supplychain.htm, February, 1999.
12. Robinson, P., The Barden Corporation, a SAP R/3 success story, *BPIC Homepage*, http://www.bpic.co.uk, Case Studies.
13. Robinson, P., Tortube, Getting the most from FourthShift, *BPIC Homepage*, http://www.bpic.co.uk, Case Studies.

# 2 Overview of ERP Systems

## Introduction

The first step in implementing an Enterprise Resource Planning (ERP) system is to understand the definition, purpose, and functionality of ERP. Unfortunately, that task is not as easy as it sounds. ERP systems represent different things to different organizations, vendors, and individuals. Defining ERP is difficult because there are many variations of the term within the manufacturing literature. In addition, a wide variety of software companies advertise various versions of "ERP systems" with different modules and functionality configurations. To further complicate the matter, the concept of ERP is quickly merging with e-commerce, e-supply chain, and knowledge management.

In spite of these difficulties, an understanding of the various components of an ERP system is necessary for comprehending how to best teach the ERP system to executives, managers, office workers, and shop floor personnel. Employees must understand the nuances of ERP to adopt it quickly and integrate it into the organization. Without an understanding of the ERP system by the people in the organization, a successful implementation is difficult ... perhaps impossible. One place to start is to look at a traditional definition of an ERP system.

*APICS~The Educational Society for Resource Management* offers a traditional definition of an ERP system. The APICS dictionary, 9th edition, defines ERP as "a method for effective planning, and control of all resources needed to take, make, ship and account for customer orders in a manufacturing, distribution or service company."[1] This concise definition, while accurate, does not describe the depth and breadth of the impact that an ERP system can have on an organization. A more in-depth analysis of the definition of an ERP system is needed.

A complete understanding of an ERP system requires that the concept of an "ERP system" be examined from five different perspectives. The first is that of a data management system. The second is simply that all the software modules in the organization are sharing the same database. The third is that of a manufacturing philosophy. The fourth is that of a business philosophy communication tool. Finally, ERP can be viewed as a knowledge management system. However, in the final analysis, it is the people who make or break the ERP system.

## ERP Sophistication Hierarchy

The different levels of the ERP system move up the hierarchy from the least sophisticated view (that of a data management system) to the most complex and strategically advantageous view (that of a knowledge management system). Progressing through the hierarchy, an organization receives increasing degrees of value as it moves to the top level. As a company works to implement its ERP system, it needs to focus on achieving the highest level in the hierarchy. Figure 2.1 illustrates the levels in the ERP sophistication hierarchy and shows how the bottom levels work toward the top level of knowledge management. The five levels or perspectives must be

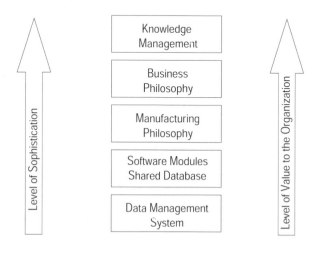

**Figure 2.1   ERP Sophistication Hierarchy — showing the five perspectives of an ERP system.**

understood by an organization in order to achieve the desired level of implementation success.

The first perspective of an ERP system is that of a simple data management system. Computers are excellent tools for managing large quantities of data. In today's connected environment, companies are able to capture vast quantities of data, ranging from market demand to sales information and on through production and distribution, stopping along the way to track product configurations, processing information, contractual data requirements, and even human resources activity. From that viewpoint an ERP system is largely a business results reporting system.

In essence the ERP system can be viewed as a large repository for organizational data. These data can be printed on reports, distributed to managers, and shared with vendors and customers. The data can be analyzed for trends and reviewed for inconsistencies. From this perspective, the ERP system is used simply as a large place to store data. While storage of company data is important, this is a limited view of an ERP system. It overlooks the integration potential of the data. Data alone do not have value; information and knowledge have value. Companies that implement an ERP system and view it simply as a means of centralizing data do not receive the full return-on-investment (ROI) from their ERP systems.

The second perspective is that ERP is a group of modules all connected onto a central database. This is perhaps the most common perception of an ERP system and the most straight-forward. Yet, it fails to capture the integrated nature of the system. Without knowing the integrated nature of the modules within the system it is difficult to understand how effective ERP can be.

The third perspective is that of viewing an ERP system as a manufacturing philosophy and not simply a software program. An ERP system is a collection of rules and procedures used for planning and reporting on various aspects of an organization. The heart of almost every ERP system is the material requirements planning process or MRP. This process uses a simple time-phased, gross-to-net logic process that compares on-hand inventory with expected inventory and then determines how much product to build. This methodology is quite different from a Just-in-Time philosophy, Theory of Constraints philosophy, or the order point philosophy. When an organization determines that it should purchase an ERP software system, the implementation and executive teams need to understand that a manufacturing philosophy is also being purchased. While many ERP systems have made modification to be compatible with other philosophies, it is the responsibility of the employees within the purchasing organization to make sure they understand the manufacturing philosophy of the ERP software that will now be supporting their organization.

Unfortunately, many executives and managers overlook this perspective of the ERP system and are rudely reminded of philosophical differences during the implementation process. One effective method for avoiding philosophical problems is to provide extensive training and education to employees on the new philosophy and its potential impact on the organization.

The fourth view of an ERP system is more conducive to receiving the desired ROI. This perspective is one in which the ERP system is viewed as a business philosophy communication tool. The process works as follows. First, management defines the strategic direction of the company in its business plan and strategic plans. Then, in all but the smallest of businesses, this information must be communicated to and adopted by employees who were not involved in the creation and acceptance of the plans. A hierarchy consisting of planning information at the top and execution information at the bottom can be used to illustrate the communications aspects of an ERP system.

The general flow of information as shown by the arrows in Figure 2.2 is top down, general to specific. From this perspective the ERP hierarchy is a communication tool to translate the business strategic plans and directions into tactical plans and ultimately into operational activities. As an execution tool, the hierarchy provides a mechanism for communicating details of operations and deployments back up through the organization. This closed-loop communication allows for corrections in resource allocations and other adjustments to the plans at higher levels.

In many respects this upward communication is a reflection of the power of the ERP system to be a business results reporting tool. With the increasing complexity of business and concurrent sophistication of data collection equipment, it is quickly becoming apparent that huge data warehouses are required to store and catalog the data and turn it into information and knowledge. This transformation of data into information occurs during the closed-loop communication from shop floor operations to higher-level planning activities. The ERP system either acts as the data warehouse or interfaces with a separate data warehouse to convert mass data into meaningful management information.

The fifth perspective is that of a knowledge management system. This view elevates the information found in the ERP system into knowledge that can be used by executives, managers, and employees to more effectively produce product, interface with customers, and navigate through competitive markets. This perspective balks at the thought of automating existing, old,

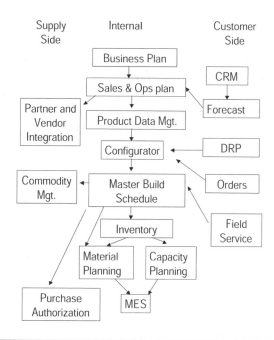

**Figure 2.2 Business Planning and Communication Hierarchy — showing the information flows for communicating business philosophy throughout the organization.**

nonfunctional, bureaucratic procedures with the brand-new million-dollar ERP system. Instead, this perspective revels in the "almost anything is possible" view of the ERP system. With all of this knowledge at each employee's fingertips, many former barriers are broken and new horizons are opened.

The knowledge contained within an ERP system can include customer buying habits, reliability of vendors, effectiveness of a particular manufacturing technique, productivity levels of particular product lines, historical requests for configured items, customer service issues, and a variety of other knowledge that can be used to develop new products and services. An ERP system can literally house all of the transactions that occur within the company and between the company and any outside organization. If this knowledge is properly managed, analyzed, and distributed, it can be extremely valuable. In fact, some knowledge within corporate ERP systems is so valuable that it can be repackaged and sold as a product. Viewing an ERP system as a knowledge management system is a powerful perspective and one that can lead to huge strategic gains for an organization.

An ERP system is many things to many people, but most importantly it is a means to assist the employees who run the business to coordinate and integrate their actions in an informed and effective manner. The knowledge management level provides the greatest degree of competitive advantage and can only be achieved if the ERP system is used as a catalyst for the organization to achieve its goals. Learning, innovation, and quick decision making must be tied into the use of an ERP system. Anything less is simply not going to be as effective or advantageous for the organization. Understanding the five different perspectives of an ERP system provides a basis for understanding how to best implement an ERP system and the goals an organization should strive to achieve during the process.

In the final analysis, an ERP system is not simply a computer program or a manufacturing or business philosophy. An ERP system is a framework for organizing, defining, and standardizing the business processes necessary to effectively plan and control an organization so the organization can use its internal knowledge to seek external advantage. As such, an ERP system is a people system. People run businesses, people make decisions, people need reliable information to do so, and people create and capitalize on knowledge. An ERP system provides the organized communication mechanism for ensuring that the high-level operating philosophies and strategies are followed during the tactical operation of the business.

To gain an additional understanding of ERP and how it impacts the people within an organization, it is important to place the history of the development of such systems into context. Understanding the growth and evolution of ERP capabilities and functionality helps to place the use of ERP systems into perspective. In addition, defining and describing the major components of ERP is of tremendous benefit in understanding how all the pieces fit together and how ERP systems can be used as knowledge management systems.

## History of Enterprise Resource Planning (ERP)

The groundwork for today's ERP systems was laid during the industrial revolution. As far back as Eli Whitney's (1765–1825) cotton gin, people were thinking of building consistency of product for interchangeability and efficiency. During the management science era, people were searching for mathematical solutions to optimize use of material, equipment, and people resources. The predecessor to even the earliest MRP systems was a class of software called Bill of Material Processors (BOMPs). BOMPs would calculate from a bill of material the extended quantities of all the components based on an order quantity. From this output, planners and buyers would coordinate the supply of materials. These material plans were then transferred to the expeditors who attempted, with varying degrees of success, to get all the right pieces in the right place at the right time so production departments could focus on producing.

BOMPs had significant shortcomings in many businesses. First, they usually did not check for any inventory of the materials, subassemblies, or finished goods already on hand. This resulted in excess inventory in many situations. In addition, BOMPs did not consider the lead times of manufacture. Material was frequently brought in well in advance of the time the production facility actually required it. Thirdly, BOMPs did not take into account lot sizing. While the management scientists were attempting to derive the best lot-sizing algorithm, using various techniques to balance the ordering cost against the carrying cost, BOMPs did not consider these algorithms in their statement of demands.[2] This added to the difficulties of coordinating materials for production.

About 1960, Joseph Orlicky and others pioneered the use of computers to calculate Material Requirements Planning (MRP) electronically.[3] MRP systems expanded on the capabilities of BOMPs by considering such things as inventory on hand, incoming replenishment orders, lot sizes, and lead times. MRP used gross-to-net logic and lead-time offsets to make plans for materials.

The gross-to-net logic calculation involves subtracting total requirements for materials (gross requirements and allocations) from all the available inventory (on-hand and scheduled receipts of material) the net result is a projected on-hand inventory.[2] If the projected on-hand is negative, then a net requirement is generated. The net requirement indicates that material needs to be ordered. If the projected on-hand is positive, no material needs to be ordered for that part.

The MRP reports provided time-phased schedules for materials to purchase and parts to manufacture. Early adopters often had to subcontract the computing processes to colleges and universities. The colleges and universities were the only organizations, at that time, with enough computing power to run the MRP calculations. This resulted in batch updates to the material plans. After each batch update the information was assumed to be accurate. Between MRP runs, the data became more and more suspect — there was no mechanism to update the plan with actual activity reports until the next subcontracted MRP run. In addition, the runs usually took hours and hours. The MRP process was usually run once a week, or even less frequently.

The term regenerative MRP was appropriate at this time because each MRP run was essentially a reloading of all the pertinent data on customer orders, purchase orders, and manufacturing orders. A complete pass through of the data was required and resulted in an entirely new set of requirements and schedules.

As systems gained acceptance and use, exception reporting was developed to ease the burden of an overwhelming amount of data generated from the MRP run. Imagine the amount of new "raw data" created every time regenerative MRP was run. Exception reports were the first attempt at turning data into information.

Over time, the price of computers and MRP software began to decline and companies began implementing MRP on in-house mainframe computers rather than outsourcing it to a university. This change made it possible to have more frequent updates of the inventory and planning information. This led to the development of "closed loop MRP."

With "closed loop MRP" actual purchase order and work order information were input to the computer to reflect the actions that were being taken by Buyers and Planners. These were input regularly into the one or two in-house computer terminals hooked to the mainframe. Depending on the volume of these inputs, net change MRP was often run to reflect these actions. These inputs closed the loop on the action messages that the MRP system had generated. During the net change runs these actions were compared with the plans created by the last regenerative MRP run and exceptions were noted and reported on.

This began the ability for Planners and Buyers to use the MRP system to communicate with each other regarding the viability of the planned activity. Where MRP had provided information on what needed to be done, closed loop MRP brought into the picture the reality of what could be done. With this additional information, potential material and scheduling problems could be identified and actions could be taken to minimize them. Note that to this point MRP systems were strictly limited to the planning of materials in support of the customers' orders or in some cases the master production schedule.

The underlying logic of MRP is a straightforward math calculation. It is based on the concept of dependent demand and lead-time offsetting. Dependent demand for parts means that the demand for some parts is dependent on the manufacture of others. As an example, a company might be in the business of manufacturing pencils. The demand for wood and graphite to make the pencils is dependent on the quantity of pencils to be made. If the company decided to make a large quantity of pencils, then large quantities of wood and graphite will be required. If the company decides to not make pencils for a period of time, then no wood or graphite will be needed. The dependent quantity is defined on the bill of material for the pencil. Understanding this dependent demand logic allowed the next logical extension of MRP into MRP II.

MRP II took the MRP logic and extended it to include calculations of many resources in addition to materials. By this time many companies had embraced the concept of working to a master production schedule. During the master-scheduling process, resources required to produce the master scheduled items are identified. These resources include many things other than just raw material. Cash requirements, shipping containers, labor requirements, and warehouse volumes could now be calculated based on the content of the master production schedule. All these resource requirements have dependent demand characteristics like raw materials and lend themselves nicely to this calculation. Again, the systems expanded and became an enhanced set of tools for communicating these requirements to the people who manage the business. This communication capability increased efficiency and improved resource use in many areas of the businesses.

Along the way, it became apparent that many duplicate entries were being performed; some to keep the physical production and inventory information correct and at the same time other entries were made into a separate accounting system to reflect the financial value of these actions. MRP II systems soon incorporated accounts payable, accounts receivable, and general ledger functions into their capabilities. As a result, the same daily transactions made to keep track of products were now also tracking financial data. The MRP II systems had the capability of summarizing and posting the financial information associated with the transactions directly to the financial modules of the MRP II system. This eliminated a huge transaction load for the accounting department as well as substantially reducing the chance of rekeying errors.

Until the late 1970s and early 1980s, the production and distribution functions of an organization were handled separately, using two or more different systems, some of which were automated and some which were not. Software vendors, who at this time mostly did custom programming of MRP II systems, and companies with a good understanding of MRP, adapted the MRP logic to product distribution and named it Distribution Requirements Planning (DRP). The MRP II systems soon had modules for DRP that linked directly into the other modules of the system.

Then, in the late 1970s and early 1980s, companies became aware of the Just-in-Time (JIT) philosophy used by the Japanese.[4] Many thought that the JIT techniques would eliminate the need for MRP systems. Some companies eliminated or turned off the MRP functions in their systems. In most cases this simply made apparent how important the MRP system was as a communication and planning tool. After some trying times, the MRP systems were turned back on and efforts were made to understand how to integrate the planning functions of MRP with the JIT techniques that turned out to be primarily execution focused. Over the years many companies have found ways to use both MRP planning and JIT execution together in a very efficient fashion.

As an example, a large metal-stamping company in Michigan that is a first-tier supplier to Toyota runs their MRP II system primarily to forecast demand to vendors. On the shop floor, the MRP II system is not used at all. Instead, various JIT techniques such as Kanban cards and specially designed containers are used as build signals to upstream operations. This company has devised an effective methodology for combining the two manufacturing philosophies.

During the late 1980s and early 1990s, computer hardware and software capability continued to improve. Businesses worked to improve their efficiency and reduce their lead time to customers. This often called for faster and better communication, improved methods for custom-configuring of products, and promising delivery schedules with better accuracy. Software companies developed many standalone applications for product data management, detailed execution system support, final assembly configurations, and many other areas of business decision support. These decision support systems have been incorporated into the MRP II systems, resulting in what is referred to as an Enterprise Resource Planning (ERP) system.

By the 2000s ERP systems had grown into software capable of running every aspect of a manufacturing organization. The modern systems perform "What If" analyses for various processes, track human resource information, manage warehouses, and allow sophisticated analysis and tracking of customer buying habits and preferences. In fact, the term ERP has expanded out of the realm of manufacturing into other fields. In the banking, insurance, and medical fields they are discussing enterprisewide systems which all reside on one database and contain all the information needed to run a business in that field. Often, the software vendors in those fields are referring to their systems as ERP systems.

The changes over the years have expanded MRP into ERP and made it an integral element within an organization. Running an ERP system is no longer a competitive advantage; it is simply a cost of entry. Without an ERP system, organizations cannot effectively plug into the e-supply chain movement sweeping across the economy. The ability of ERP systems to track, monitor, and share data across companies has made it an integral tool in today's global fast-paced economy.

## Major Components of a Typical ERP System

Another method of defining and understanding ERP is to examine the individual elements or modules that make up the system. Each of the elements traditionally interfaces into one database and shares data with all the other modules. This allows an entry made on the shop floor to be examined at the executive level as well as the financial and inventory levels. While some ERP systems have more functionality than listed below and some have less, the basic building blocks of ERP systems are relatively static. Most of the major ERP systems on the market today contain the following components.

## Business and Strategic Planning Module

The first element in an ERP system actually occurs outside of the system. This is the process of developing a business and strategic plan. The strategic plan is a series of goals and objectives that will be utilized to drive the business forward. The strategic plan is then converted into the business plan. The business plan is a statement of the long-range revenue, cost, and profit objectives of the organization. From these, the business plan computes cash flow projections and other financial expectations.

The Business Plan is stated in terms of dollars, grouped by product family, and extends between one and five years into the future. The Business Plan is developed by the top executives of the organization to plan large capital expenditures, the acquisition of new business units, the feasibility of expanding capacity through new construction, and human resource issues such as training, hiring, and succession planning.

The Business Plan forecasts what an organization expects to receive for new customer orders, predicts what the company expects to ship, calculates what is expected in finished goods inventory, and determines profit projections in dollars.[5] This plan is the basis for determining the budgets for all the departments within the company. The Business Plan is input into the ERP system as a long-range forecast stated in dollars by product family. Many ERP systems have the capability of translating forecasting in terms of dollars into a forecast of units of inventory produced.

Many ERP systems have the capability to perform simulations by testing multiple versions of the business plan to determine possible outcomes and possible needs of the organization. The executives of the organization can run through different scenarios to determine how best to prepare for the future. Once the appropriate scenario is agreed upon for the upcoming fiscal year, the business plan can be used to drive demand within the organization through the ERP system.

It is important to note that the business plan is a not a one-time event within the fiscal year. The plan needs to be revisited monthly to adjust for market changes as well as any internal changes. Organizations that monitor the business plan and make simple adjustments based on various factors are more successful with their ERP systems than companies that don't conduct business planning or "forget" to update a plan once it is developed.

## Resource Planning Module

A business plan cannot work if the necessary capacity is not available. Capacity planning conducted at the Business Plan level is called resource planning. Resource planning is the process of establishing, measuring, and adjusting limits or levels of long-range capacity. Usually, this examination of capacity is tied to the "What If" functionality of the ERP system. This allows the executives to determine the capacity ramifications of various business plan decisions.

Resource planning addresses items that may take long periods of time to acquire or build, such as a new building or sophisticated new equipment. Resource planning decisions always require top management approval and input. In most cases, many of the resource planning decisions within an organization are made with input from the information or knowledge contained within the ERP system but ultimately are the responsibility of the executive team.

Often, the ERP systems have modeling and probability analysis capabilities to examine critical resource requirements such as bottleneck processes, equipment, or vendor capabilities. ERP systems also have the capability of determining how many units of key product families can be produced by a given production line based on known constraints.

## Executive Decision Support Module

Utilizing mathematical models and formulas, an executive decision support module within an ERP system provides simulation capabilities, business process modeling, and "trigger and alert" warning systems. This module can also be referred to as an "executive dashboard" or Executive Information System (EIS). It is color coded and highly graphic for ease of use and quick recognition of problems. For example, an executive can view the dashboard, see a red area highlighted on the factory floor, and double-click on the area to drill down to more detailed information.

These modules help executives to further see the impact of tactical decisions on profitability and long-term financial viability. The systems are typically displayed graphically and provide flexibility in terms of various views of the data with the ability to manipulate the data to represent various business cases. More sophisticated versions of executive decision support systems allow the users to establish several business models and compare the models in terms of units produced and value of profit margin.

The trigger and alert functions allow an executive to automatically receive notification of a problem or issue. The ERP system allows the user to establish limits and parameters and then to automatically notify the executive of a problem. Usually this is done through an e-mail alert or a flashing area on a computer screen. The most sophisticated decision support systems can actually send a message of the problem to voice mail or a pager.

While many resource planning modules perform "What If" analyses, the executive decision support systems conduct "What's Best" analyses. The decision support systems evaluate various options based on parameters and formulas and determine the best course of action, rather than simply reporting what would happen if a certain action was undertaken.

## Sales and Operations Planning Module

Sales and operations planning (S&OP) is a balance of supply and demand. Sales and operations planning integrates customer-focused marketing plans for new and existing products with the management of the supply chain. The process brings together all the plans for the business (sales, marketing, development, manufacturing, sourcing, and financial) into one integrated set of plans.[1] S&OP operates on a monthly cycle and culminates in an executive S&OP meeting. Prior to that meeting, three important phases take place within the organization. The first is demand planning, followed by supply planning, and then a pre-S&OP meeting. In the pre-meeting, middle management personnel formulate recommendations for the executive session.[6]

The S&OP process must reconcile all supply, demand, and new product plans at both the aggregate and detail level and tie them to the Business Plan. It is the definitive statement of the company's plans for the near to intermediate term. The horizon covered by the Sales and Operation Plan must be sufficient to plan for resources and support the annual business planning process. "Executed properly, the sales and operation planning process links the strategic plans for the business with its execution and reviews performance measures for the continuous improvement."[1]

While S&OP can be performed "outside" of the ERP system, the results must be input into the system to feed the other processes within the company. Once the executive group signs off on the sales and operations plan, it is used by the ERP system to guide and constrain the master schedule.

## Forecasting Module

Manufacturing organizations need to forecast future demand to make sound purchasing and production decisions. ERP systems are linked to a variety of forecasting modules using a variety of forecasting techniques. Some of the techniques include using moving averages, weighted moving averages, seasonality formulas, exponential smoothing, regression models, curve fitting, and other methods. Prior to using fully functional forecasting software modules, organizations had to choose a single method of forecasting because that was all the system was programmed to handle.

Today, most forecasting programs provide a variety of methods for forecasting future demand. The problem is no longer one of being tied to a single forecasting method; the problem is now determining which forecasting method is most appropriate for the organization. Many forecasting modules will even help with the problem of determining the best method by comparing data against historically forecasted data to find the best fit.

The forecast information can then be used to make decisions at the Sales and Operations Plan level, and sometimes at the purchasing and inventory levels. While forecasting can be automated to a large degree, employees still need to view the computer-generated forecast and make qualitative adjustments to it for things like competitor actions, changes in governmental regulations, or a shift in technology.

## Customer Relationship Management (CRM) Module

Customer relationship management software offers a variety of tools for managing the relationship with a customer. CRM can include notes on customer buying habits, payment history, contact information, service agreements, acceptable forms of payment, engineering or manufacturing preferences, and the ability to be electronically reminded to send a follow-up message to a customer. Basically, CRM is a history of the relationship between the company and the customer.

CRM software modules offer a method of building strong customer relationships. For example, a strong contact management system enables the sales staff to prioritize prospective and existing customers by pulling relevant information from the ERP system.[7] The marketing department can pull information from customer or prospect profiles to design more targeted advertising campaigns. Special programs and products can be developed to meet the needs of a particular group of customers.

Tying customer information from an order entry management module within the ERP system to a CRM system provides an organization with considerable information. This information can be used to better understand customer needs and to develop a method of communicating with customers on a regular basis. The proper use of CRM also provides a value-added service to customers by anticipating their needs in terms of purchases, product requests, and innovations.

## Order Entry, Quoting, and Product Configurator Modules

Demand enters an ERP system through actual customer orders. ERP systems even allow orders to be directly entered via Electronic Data Interchange (EDI) and through e-commerce business-to-business web sites.

"EDI is the paperless (electronic) exchange of trading documents, such as purchase orders, shipment authorizations, advanced shipment notices, and invoices, using standardized document formats."[1] For many years EDI was an integral part of the supply chain. It still plays a role within the supply chain but is quickly losing ground to the easier and less expensive e-commerce business web sites.

e-Commerce business-to-business web sites are applications that allow a customer to log onto a secure system through a browser with virtually any computer and place an order. This allows the customer to order whenever convenient and ensures that the customer order is entered correctly. The web-enabled ordering system is then tied to the ERP system for a seamless interface between externally entered orders, internally entered orders, and any EDI orders that are received.

Most order entry systems allow for multiple ship-to, bill-to, and buy-from addresses by individual line item on the order. They also have built-in quoting and pricing functionality based on the product purchased, the amount purchased, and the type of customer. Most order entry systems check with the accounts receivable module to determine the customer's current credit status. Order entry systems also have the capability to view inventory on-hand and even calculate estimated order delivery dates.

Another aspect of ERP order entry systems is the product configurator. In many instances, a manufacturer's product has a variety of options from which a customer can choose. Some of the options have price implications and some of the options are mutually exclusive. All of these various options and rules can be accounted for with the use of a product configurator. The configurator allows the order entry clerk or customer on a web-enabled configurator to enter in the various options desired. An example might be a computer manufacturer that offers three options for processor speed, four options for RAM, four hard-drive sizes, etc. A customer can pick and choose, but the configurator will not allow selection of parts that would not be compatible. The resultant total price will appear on the screen, as well as the price for each individual option. The system will also present warning messages when options conflict or when one option requires the purchase of another option. In addition, previous product configurations can be stored by the system so the user can retrieve and modify a previous configuration if necessary.

## Master Production Schedule Module

The Master Production Schedule (MPS) is a time-phased anticipated build schedule for manufacturing end products or product options.[2] The Master Production Schedule represents products the company plans to produce expressed in specific configurations, quantities, and dates. The master production schedule typically looks at manufacturing products from one of three alternatives: make-to-stock, make-to-order, or assemble-to-order. The choice determines whether scheduling should be based on end items, specific customer orders, or some group of end items and product options.[2]

The Master Production Schedule looks into the future and creates planned orders to satisfy demand. The Master Production Schedule provides messages indicating recommended actions that should be taken to maintain the schedule. The messages include indication of lead-time violations, orders that should be expedited or slowed down, and recommendations about when to release or cancel orders.[8]

An employee with the title of Master Scheduler typically controls the Master Production Scheduling process. The Master Scheduler is responsible for managing, establishing, reviewing, and balancing the information from the Sales and Operations Plan and other factors to provide realistic inventory planning and scheduling dates to the rest of the organization. Once the Master Scheduler develops the MPS, the demands for lower-level components are given to the rest of the organization through the Material Requirements Planning process.

The Master Scheduler has a series of specialized bills of material to facilitate the planning process and allow him to control, track, and monitor a large number of parts with minimal effort. These specialized bills of material can be grouped under the term "planning bill of material." One type of planning bill is the modular bill of material. The modular bill is arranged in product modules or options, "It is often used in companies where the product has many optional features, e.g., assemble-to-order companies such as automobile manufacturer."[1]

Another type of planning bill is the super bill. This type of planning bill is located at the top level of the planning process. It ties together various modular bills to define an entire product or product family: "The quantity-per relationship of the super bill to its modules represents the forecasted percentage of demand of each module. The master-scheduled quantities of the super bill explode to create requirements for the modules that are also master scheduled."[1]

The Master Production Schedule is translated into the MRP component requirements by exploding the bill of material for the manufacturing items throughout the plan. However, before the work orders can be printed and jobs prioritized, capacity must be considered to determine the "soundness" of the Master Production Schedule.

## Rough Cut Capacity Planning Module[2,3,8]

Once the Master Scheduler develops the Master Production Schedule, it is run through Rough Cut Capacity Planning (RCCP) to determine if the proposed schedule can actually be manufactured. Constraints must be examined and identified. Rough Cut Capacity Planning is the process of converting the Master Production Schedule into requirements for key resources, "often including labor, machinery, warehouse space, suppliers' capabilities, and, in some cases, money. Comparison to available or demonstrated capacity is usually done for each key resource."[1] This comparison assists the Master Scheduler in establishing a feasible Master Production Schedule and in identifying work cell overloads.

Rough Cut Capacity Planning only looks at the workload on critical work cells. It then determines whether or not the items planned in the Master Production Schedule can be processed through the known bottlenecks or constraints during the time frame allowed by the MPS. If too much capacity is required during a specific time frame at a particular work cell, it is assumed that the schedule would not be feasible for the less critical work cells either.

This process provides a quick and effective method to view over-capacity problems. When capacity is not available at the bottleneck work cells, the MPS is adjusted to alleviate some of the workload on the bottlenecks. The process is then re-run to determine the impact. The combination of master scheduling and rough cut capacity management is ofter referred to as the Master Scheduler's Workbench in ERP systems. If the MPS can be completed without undue problems, the next step is to run Material Requirements Planning (MRP).

## Material Requirements Planning (MRP) Module

Material Requirements Planning (MRP) is the basic framework for many functions of an ERP system. The foundation of these functions is that dependent demand can be calculated based on independent demand. MRP performs two primary processes: exploding demand from the parent items (independent demand) to the components (dependent demand) required to make that parent, and offsetting the lead time to determine the start time of the components. The result is a schedule with priorities and actions planned. This process requires several inputs and accurate data.

Inputs to the MRP process are generally grouped into four categories. The first input is the basic planning data. In the planning data are data to guide the MRP system in how to perform the calculations. These data are separated into system functions and item-specific decision rules. System decisions are such things as: how demand will be grouped for planning (planning bucket size), how far into the future to plan (horizon), and what will drive MRP to actually explode the demand (actual orders, master schedule, forecast).

These decisions are generally made at implementation time and are seldom changed unless a problem is discovered indicating that one of these items was incorrectly set. In the category of item-specific decision rules there are quite a few fields to enter to define how the MRP system should plan for that specific part. These items are usually entered in a screen referred to as a part master or item master. Data to input involve part lead times, unit of measure, safety stock levels, scrap/shrink and yield rates, and lot size rules.

One common error during implementation is to make generic decisions about parts and applying them almost globally. An example is to set all the lead times for purchased parts equal to four weeks. This makes the process of defining lead times in terms of the system very easy. One number can be imported into the lead-time field in an automated fashion. The problem is that most parts do not have a four-week lead time. As a result, MRP will recommend making some parts too soon and others will not get enough planned lead time and substantial expedite fees will be wasted.

While this decision to use a "standard" lead time feels like it saves time at implementation, what it really does is postpone making proper decisions and plants the seed for people to justify not believing the system output. This example is an error of intent. The intent is to ease the implementation: the result is thousands of erroneous planned orders and years of reworking each item's lead time to match reality.

Next in the area of inputs to MRP are the bills of material (BOMs). BOMs are listing of all the components required to manufacturer or assemble one of the parent item. BOMs must be properly structured to coincide with the manufacturing process and routing steps. While it would seem that BOMs would be accurate because a company has been building a product for some time, it is not uncommon for the BOMs to be incongruent with the routing or actual manufacturing process.

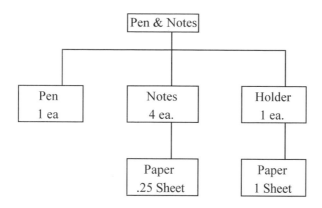

**Figure 2.3   Pen and Notes Bill of Material — (BOM).**

If incorrect BOMs are entered, MRP will drive demands for parts that are not needed and not drive demand for parts that are required. Figure 2.3 shows a BOM for a "Pen and Notes" item in graphical form. In this form it is easy to see that the Notes are made from a quarter of a sheet of paper and the holder is made from a whole sheet of paper. The pen is purchased and then the pen, notes, and holder are assembled together to make the "Pen and Notes."

The data inputs described so far are not subject to a great deal of change in the ordinary MRP management. These items, when incorrect, generate a number of errors.

The next category of inputs is the dynamic data that is subject to a great deal of change on a regular basis. These are open orders (sales, purchase, and work orders) and on-hand inventory balances. The MRP system makes plans for people to execute. These plans are based on the MRP process, using the decision rules and BOMs. As the business proceeds through time, these plans are converted to actions.

In some cases the plans can be executed exactly as planned, but in others those plans may need modification to match the reality of life. When these plans are converted to actual work orders and purchase orders, they must be modified to provide visibility in the system of the actual expectations. The MRP system will assume the dates and quantities on these orders will happen exactly as shown.

One common error of MRP users is to leave overdue orders scheduled in the past in the belief that this will underscore their true priority. These errors will cause the MRP process to make plans that are invalid. When reports are generated from these invalid plans, the staff will see action requirements that are not correct. In some cases they will follow these defective plans, in other cases they will ignore those plans and make other plans that might be better or worse — it is difficult to know since the data is defective. It is important that the data reflect reality. People are depending on it and making business decisions upon it.

The last category of input is the master schedule. The master schedule is a statement of the finished goods or product options the company intends to build. This schedule should be managed to provide a proper combination and sequence of product to support the company objectives in customer service, inventory investment, and production efficiency. From an MRP perspective, the master schedule becomes the driver for all materials and sub-assembly requirements. MRP explodes through the BOM of the master scheduled items and plans all the components to support that schedule.

Once all the inputs are available, MRP can perform its planning process. This process is a series of simple mathematical calculations. The reason a computer system is required in most companies for this process is that there are hundreds of thousands of calculations involved in an MRP run. People certainly could perform these calculations manually, but the results would not be timely enough to be meaningful. MRP performs two primary processes: balancing and exploding. Balancing involves analyzing future requirements for the item and planning replenishments to support those requirements. Figure 2.4 shows an MRP planning grid that is used in training.

This grid shows the gross requirements for 8 periods into the future. Starting with the on-hand (OH) balance, MRP will subtract gross requirements period by period until it projects a negative available quantity at some time in the future. In Figure 2.4 this negative condition occurred in period 6. Once MRP projects a negative available quantity it will make a planned order receipt to cover that negative quantity. In Figure 2.4 the negative quantity was 50 and MRP planned an order for exactly 50 to cover the negative quantity.

As noted, MRP will make a plan to replenish the item when it is needed. MRP will then look at the lead time to obtain the item and determine when that planned order should start. In Figure 2.4 the lead time of 1 week means

| Item ID: Pen & Notes | | | | | Lot Size: Lot for Lot | | | |
|---|---|---|---|---|---|---|---|---|
| OH=300,  Lead time 1 period | 1 | 2 | 3 | 4 | 5 | 6 | 7 | 8 |
| Gross Requirements | | | 100 | 150 | | 100 | | 200 |
| Scheduled Receipts | | | | | | | | |
| Projected Available | 300 | 300 | 200 | 50 | 50 | 0 | 0 | 0 |
| Planned Order Receipts | | | | | | 50 | | 200 |
| Planned Order Releases | | | | | 50 | | 200 | |

Figure 2.4   MRP Planning Grid for Pen and Notes.

that the first order must be started in period 5 to be available for the requirement in period 6. MRP will continue calculating into the future until it finds another negative condition or until the end of time as defined by the planning horizon of the system. In Figure 2.4 another negative projected available quantity occurred in period 8 and MRP planned another order, in this case for a quantity of 200. This grid is used in training to make the lead-time offset highly apparent. Figure 2.5 shows the MRP process being "exploded" down through the BOM to each subsequent level.

Some ERP and MRP systems still display MRP data in this fashion, although many have turned the page sideways so future needs run down the page rather than left to right. These grids help to illustrate the concept of the MRP explosion and how the requirements at the top level of an item master can drive the requirements for lower-level items in the BOM.

## Detailed Capacity Planning Module

Once MRP is run, the process of Detailed Capacity Planning is undertaken. Detailed Capacity Planning looks at the available capacity for every work cell in the manufacturing process. This information determines if the schedule of component items generated by MRP is feasible at each individual work cell.[2]

Detailed capacity planning uses the information produced by the MRP explosion process to determine required capacity at each work cell. The information utilized includes consideration of all actual lot sizes, routings, as well as the lead times for both open shop orders and planned shop orders. In addition, the ERP system will account for the current status of all work in process so only the capacity needed to complete the remaining operations is considered in calculating the required work cell capacity.[2] Today's systems also account for additional capacity that might be required — not only based on the MPS demand but also based on scrap or yield of the production process.

Detailed capacity planning uses either finite or infinite scheduling of work cells. Many systems can be run in either mode. Finite scheduling means scheduling no more work into a work cell than it can be expected to execute in a particular time frame. This process is used to level-load the shop floor and not overload a work cell with work that cannot possibly be completed by the required due date.

Infinite scheduling shows the work scheduled for a work cell in the time periods required, regardless of the capacity of the work cell to actually complete the work. While this may seem a setup for failure, one advantage of infinite scheduling is that it quickly alerts operators and supervisors to problems and can be used to determine shop floor constraints over time. Infinite loading makes it easy to determine how much a work center is overloaded.

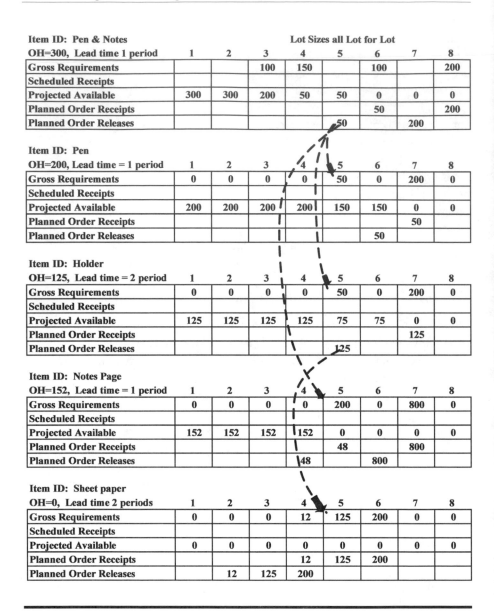

**Item ID: Pen & Notes** — Lot Sizes all Lot for Lot
OH=300, Lead time 1 period

| | 1 | 2 | 3 | 4 | 5 | 6 | 7 | 8 |
|---|---|---|---|---|---|---|---|---|
| Gross Requirements | | | 100 | 150 | | 100 | | 200 |
| Scheduled Receipts | | | | | | | | |
| Projected Available | 300 | 300 | 200 | 50 | 50 | 0 | 0 | 0 |
| Planned Order Receipts | | | | | | 50 | | 200 |
| Planned Order Releases | | | | | 50 | | 200 | |

**Item ID: Pen**
OH=200, Lead time = 1 period

| | 1 | 2 | 3 | 4 | 5 | 6 | 7 | 8 |
|---|---|---|---|---|---|---|---|---|
| Gross Requirements | 0 | 0 | 0 | 0 | 50 | 0 | 200 | 0 |
| Scheduled Receipts | | | | | | | | |
| Projected Available | 200 | 200 | 200 | 200 | 150 | 150 | 0 | 0 |
| Planned Order Receipts | | | | | | | 50 | |
| Planned Order Releases | | | | | | 50 | | |

**Item ID: Holder**
OH=125, Lead time = 2 period

| | 1 | 2 | 3 | 4 | 5 | 6 | 7 | 8 |
|---|---|---|---|---|---|---|---|---|
| Gross Requirements | 0 | 0 | 0 | 0 | 50 | 0 | 200 | 0 |
| Scheduled Receipts | | | | | | | | |
| Projected Available | 125 | 125 | 125 | 125 | 75 | 75 | 0 | 0 |
| Planned Order Receipts | | | | | | | 125 | |
| Planned Order Releases | | | | | 125 | | | |

**Item ID: Notes Page**
OH=152, Lead time = 1 period

| | 1 | 2 | 3 | 4 | 5 | 6 | 7 | 8 |
|---|---|---|---|---|---|---|---|---|
| Gross Requirements | 0 | 0 | 0 | 0 | 200 | 0 | 800 | 0 |
| Scheduled Receipts | | | | | | | | |
| Projected Available | 152 | 152 | 152 | 152 | 0 | 0 | 0 | 0 |
| Planned Order Receipts | | | | | 48 | | 800 | |
| Planned Order Releases | | | | 48 | | 800 | | |

**Item ID: Sheet paper**
OH=0, Lead time 2 periods

| | 1 | 2 | 3 | 4 | 5 | 6 | 7 | 8 |
|---|---|---|---|---|---|---|---|---|
| Gross Requirements | 0 | 0 | 0 | 12 | 125 | 200 | 0 | 0 |
| Scheduled Receipts | | | | | | | | |
| Projected Available | 0 | 0 | 0 | 0 | 0 | 0 | 0 | 0 |
| Planned Order Receipts | | | | 12 | 125 | 200 | | |
| Planned Order Releases | | 12 | 125 | 200 | | | | |

**Figure 2.5 MRP Explosion Process — showing how higher-level items drive the demand for lower-level items in the BOM.**

In a work center that can easily adjust its capacity (such as an assembly area) this can actually be better than finite loading.

The basis for monitoring the detailed capacity planning plan is input/output control. This is the process of comparing the planned input and planned output of a work cell with the actual input and actual output of the work cell. These data are usually expressed in hours. The input/output process also monitors backlog at work cells. Backlog is the cushion between input and output. The formula is simple: backlog is equal to the prior backlog plus or minus the difference between input and output. The monitoring of input, output, and backlog typically involves keeping track of the cumulative deviations and comparing them with present limits.[2] The best way to ensure the output from a work center is to monitor its output and then control the input to a rate that can be produced.

## *Production Activity Control (PAC) Module*

Once it is determined that the capacity is available at each work cell to meet the schedule, manufacturing orders are released to the shop floor. The production activity control (PAC) of an ERP system maintains and communicates status information on manufacturing orders (both discrete and repetitive). The PAC module assigns a priority to each order, maintains work-in-process quantity data, provides actual output data for feedback to detailed capacity planning, provides information for the accounting modules in terms of inventory and labor transactions, and provides measurements of efficiency, utilization, and productivity of manpower and machines.

In a discrete manufacturing environment, the ERP system plans the releases of shop orders or manufacturing orders. A manufacturing order is a document, group of documents, or a schedule conveying authority for the manufacture of specified parts or products in specified quantities.[1] Each shop order or manufacturing order has a discrete order number that is tracked and used for recording material usage and labor against the shop order.

Once on the shop floor, a scheduling algorithm is run to determine the sequencing of manufacturing orders. "For example, [a detailed capacity planning] ... procedure would examine the status of all open orders (scheduled receipts), estimate how long they will take (set up, run, wait, and move) at particular work centers, and thereby derive when they will arrive at subsequent work centers."[2]

The production activity control module of an ERP system releases work orders to the shop floor, provides the capability of recording production feedback by operation, and provides various production reports.

Most ERP systems are mixed-mode, meaning they contain functionality for both discrete manufacturers and process manufacturers. In the process mode, ERP systems release a flow order. A flow order is an order that is filled by production over time and checked by cumulative count until the flow order quantity is complete. Flow order functionality allows an organization to schedule work using JIT scheduling techniques like Kanban card creation and synchronized manufacturing. Kanban is a method of production which uses standard containers or lot sizes with a signal card attached to each. It is a pull system in which work cells signal, with a card, that they wish to withdraw parts from its upstream operation.

In a discrete environment, a dispatch list is issued to provide employees with a listing of manufacturing orders in priority sequence. The dispatch list contains detailed information on priority, location, quantity, and the capacity requirements of the manufacturing order by operation. These lists are normally generated daily and are visually oriented by work cell.

## Manufacturing Execution System (MES) Module

An element of shop floor control and monitoring incorporated into ERP packages is a Manufacturing Execution System (MES). MES is a factory floor information and communication system with several functional capabilities. The MES systems tie electronically into the machines on the shop floor and into the ERP system.

MES systems provide minute-to-minute input into an ERP system. These systems can be used to measure tolerances on material produced, shut off machines if they run too hot, report quantities to the ERP system, and send alerts to supervisors when they shut down.

In recent years, this term has been expanded to encompass many of the same functions as production activity control. The APICS dictionary defines MES as including functions such as resource allocation and status, operation-detailed scheduling, dispatching production units, document control, data collection and acquisition, labor management, quality management, process management, maintenance management, product tracking and genealogy, and performance analysis.[1]

## Issuing Material to Jobs Module

Once production has begun on the manufacturing orders, material needs to be applied to the order. Material can be issued to the manufacturing order or flow order as it moves through the shop floor or material can be backflushed. Backflushing is the "deduction from inventory records of the component parts used in an assembly or subassembly by exploding the bills of material by the production count of assemblies produced."[1]

ERP systems typically have several backflushing methods. One is post-deduct backflushing. This is the technique of inventory bookkeeping where component inventory is deducted from the on-hand balance in the computer system only after completion of activity on the components' parent item, based on what should have been used as specified in the bill of material.[1]

Another technique is pre-deduct backflushing, where inventory is deducted from the on-hand balance in the computer system at the time a scheduled receipt for the part or subassembly is created via a bill of material explosion.[1] Both of these methods can cause a difference between the computer on-hand quantity and what is actually physically in stock or in Work-in-Process (WIP). This occurs because of the lag time between the actual product movement and the computer transaction. This can cause a lot of problems for the people who rely on the computer on-hand quantities to make operational decisions. ERP systems can avoid these problems by having count points within the routings which allow for the backflushing of material multiple times at various steps within the routing.

## Advanced Planning and Scheduling (APS) Module

Advanced Planning and Scheduling Systems grew out of finite scheduling programs but have quickly moved to optimization systems that use advanced programming to help planners and schedulers recognize constraints and plan around them.

One of the criticisms of MRP systems is the fact that most systems calculate material requirements first and capacity is assumed to be infinitely available. Many infinite loading and scheduling systems were developed to import the open orders from the MRP system, then perform very detailed scheduling of work centers. These met with varying degrees of success due to both the complexity of the implementation and because they were attempting to calculate lead time with great precision using lead-time information that was only approximated for MRP purposes.

During its processing an APS system will use both material and capacity in its scheduling. Indeed, the company can define which to prioritize during the process. Rather than search for one optimum schedule, APS systems offer users good, achievable alternatives that consider multiple issues and factors. APS systems request that the user prioritize several factors such as material, capacity, and cash flow, so that in a situation where a bottleneck cannot be circumvented the system suggests changes to minimize impact to the production resources.

Most APS systems also include order promising tools such as "available to promise" and "capable to promise" to allow a user to simulate a proposed delivery or calculate the best delivery on a proposed order.[9]

The APS systems are designed to help planners create a feasible schedule within identified constraints. Once the optimal schedule is determined and confirmed, the APS information becomes the new schedule for the ERP system.

## Financial Modules

ERP systems support the financial goals of a company by creating and feeding transactional information to the general ledger as soon as the transaction occurs. For example, scrapping a finished product on the shop floor can immediately impact the value of inventory in the general ledger.

ERP systems allow for a single setup of the financial flow of data throughout the system. This recording, tracking, and monitoring of financial transactions within an ERP system occurs whenever a transaction is entered into the system. When material is received, a financial transaction is recorded. When material is issued to a manufacturing order, a financial transaction moving the inventory dollars into work-in-process is executed.

With ERP systems, financial transactions occur continuously, whether the user is aware of the correct accounting flow or not. This is why users must understand that the transactions they enter into the system have far-reaching ramifications. An error on a purchase order is not limited to the purchasing department — it now resonates throughout the company all the way into the general ledger.

The financial modules of an ERP system include accounts payable, accounts receivable, the general ledger, and often, a fixed assets and/or a payroll package. The financial modules allow for the analysis of key data and the creation of cash flow statements, income statements, and balance sheets along with a host of other financial analysis reports.

## Costing Modules

Because ERP packages track transactions and are fully integrated from the shop floor to the accounting modules, costing information can be easily obtained through the normal course of manufacturing activities. ERP systems provide the data necessary for both traditional costing methods (standard, actual) and Activity-Based Costing (ABC).

A standard cost system uses a cost unit determined for material, labor, overhead, and indirect costs before actual production. For management control purposes, the standards are compared to actual costs and variances are computed.[1] The idea is to track the variances and only take corrective action if the variances are too far from the standard.

An actual cost system collects labor, indirect costs, material, and associated overhead costs that are charged against a job as the job is produced.[1] This technique is frequently used in job shops and allows for the tracking of actual costs to the specific manufacturing order.

Activity-Based Costing (ABC) is a cost accounting system that accumulates costs based on activities performed and then uses cost drivers to allocate these costs to products or other bases, such as customers, markets, or projects. It is an attempt to allocate overhead costs on a more realistic basis than direct labor or machine hours.[1]

ERP systems typically are able to track both standard costing as well as ABC costing. Many times, the costing information is displayed graphically and can be seen in detail when needed.

## Engineering Modules

ERP systems have an Engineering module that allows for the design and development of new products without interfering with normal production. Many systems have engineering BOM interfaces that allow the company engineers to use actual parts and cost information to design new products without interfering with existing production BOMs. Many ERP systems even interface into Computer-Aided Drafting (CAD) programs so that they can design the entire product, virtually, and once the designs are complete, download the parts into a standard engineering BOM.

Once the engineering BOM is ready for release, the ERP program will move the engineering BOM to the production side of the ERP system and allow it to be used for manufacturing orders. The same process exists for engineering routings that become transformed into production routings on a computer-aided process planning (CAPP) module.

The engineering modules also typically handle drawing and item revisions as well as engineering change orders. These systems can become quite complicated and are able to link actual on-line documents to the information within the ERP system. This linkage allows an employee on the shop floor to view a BOM for an item and then, on-line, pull up the corresponding drawings, change orders, or notes input into the system by the engineering department. These systems also allow the operators as well as field maintenance personnel to feed back information to the engineers, who may use that information to make changes to future versions of that product.

Engineering modules can also have shop floor layout capabilities that allow the engineers to create "What If" layouts on the shop floor to optimize the manufacturing process. These programs provide actual capacity data on work cells, input/output information, and even offer suggestions based on product sequencing parameters.

## Human Resource Modules

Many ERP systems now contain information related to the most valuable asset in the organization — the employees. These human resource management (HRM) modules include: payroll, training management, performance review tracking, recruitment, retention and succession, compensation management, time and attendance tracking, and employee stock options management.

Payroll can be tied to the ERP system and the time and attendance data entered on the shop floor can be fed into the system for determining number of hours worked and type of job performed. Payroll modules track, monitor, and report on both hourly and salaried employees. Most provide the ability to print checks, calculate monies owed for taxes at all levels, and even garnishee wages for such things as child support.

The training management modules are typically able to track employee enrollment in courses, maintain written course descriptions, define course prerequisites, monitor course availability, review course evaluations, track training expenses, and set up and maintain the training budget.

Training management modules can even be linked into e-learning systems to deliver training to the employee's desktop when it is needed, record how the employee performed during the training, and record the scores into the HR module for later review by a supervisor. Some e-learning programs even print out a completion certificate when the student is done with the course.

Performance review tracking is used to manage the process of assigning review dates, keeping a history of performance reviews, keeping an on-line record of agreed-upon objectives to meet before the next review, and for determining how many employees have reached a certain level within the organization.

Recruitment, retention, and succession planning modules keep track of submitted resumes, ads placed, college visits conducted, and available part-time and temporary workers. It also can be linked to the training module to determine what training employees have received, the jobs employees are qualified to perform, and any certifications or licenses held by the employees. These systems contain information on training programs and tie that information to job types.

The succession planning aspect of these modules helps organizations to designate employees for certain higher-level positions and indicate the training those employees need to move to the next level. Succession planning modules help with the process of identifying and ranking all potential successors to a particular position.

Compensation management involves targeting top performers and aligning compensation and retention initiatives to the strategic objectives of the organization. These packages assess workforce retention risks, replacement costs of key employees, and the likelihood of finding an internal successor.

Time and attendance modules help an organization plan for vacations, coordinate schedules, track sick leave, and are tied to payroll to ensure employees are paid fairly for the work they performed. Many of these systems are tied to employee badges with a built-in bar code reader so employees are not spending a lot of time recording what they are doing. These bar code readers can even be tied into work cells on the shop floor so employees can record movement from one job to another.

Employee stock options management modules allow an organization to implement a stock option plan for employees as a form of additional compensation. These modules can tailor different plans to different levels of employees and even use simulations to determine the impact of different plans and percentages on the organization's cash flow.

## e-Commerce Modules

ERP systems are quickly become part of the e-supply chain. The use of the Internet provides users of ERP systems with platform independence, meaning they can use any operating system or multiple operating systems within the organization and still have everyone connected to the same information via a simple web browser.

This connectedness extends to vendors who are being linked to customers and to customers who are being linked to manufacturers. The web provides organizations with the ability to provide around-the-clock, around-the-calendar business and service hours.[10] The web provides the ability for instant access to inventory levels, work in process reports, and customer order status. The server-side architecture of web applications allows for a solid level of security, easy administration by the information technology staff, and a low cost of maintenance.

e-Commerce opens up new distribution channels with online catalogs and associated shopping carts; customers can order service parts or primary parts directly from the manufacturers without going through distribution channels.

In addition, new methods such as online auctions are opening up for manufactures to provide products to customers who are willing to work with someone they may have never even met before. Many ERP systems integrate with e-mail systems, cell phones, and Personal Digital Assistants (PDAs) to provide alerts and messages from the ERP system to managers and employees, regardless of their proximity to their desk or own computer.

## Summary of ERP Components

ERP systems consist of a variety of modules and softwares. The integrated nature of these systems makes it very important that employees within the organization understand the ramification of their actions. A simple mistake made at the receiving dock can have serious implications in inventory, accounting, capacity planning, and other areas of the organization.

The employees of the organization need to learn about the types of errors common during ERP implementations and daily functionality and be taught how to eliminate those errors. A first step in that direction is to understand the components of the ERP system and how they are integrated with each other. Two valuable resources for learning more about the various modules of an ERP system are *ERP: Tools Techniques, and Applications for Integrating the Supply Chain*[11] and *Enterprise Resources Planning and Beyond: Integrating Your Entire Organization,*[12] both available from the APICS resource catalog or online at http://www.apics.org.

The second step in eliminating data errors within an ERP system is to understand the nature and type of errors that occur within the integrated data residing in the system. The integrated nature of an ERP system requires that all users treat the data carefully and with respect. Understanding the type of errors that could occur helps users identify when they are making an error and helps to reduce the frequency of the errors.

## ERP System Errors

There is a well-known expression in the software business called GIGO, meaning garbage in, garbage out. While it is easy to understand that inputting incorrect data will cause the reports from the system to be erroneous, it understates the degree of importance of the issue. There are actually four levels of "garbage" data. The deeper the level, the more potentially damaging the errors (garbage) in data can be. Figure 2.6 illustrates the relative visibility and degree of problems these errors can impose on the organization. These levels require different remedies and preventive measures.

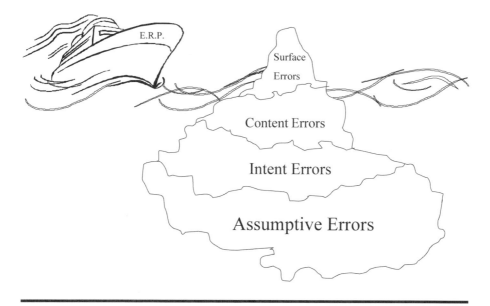

**Figure 2.6    The Four Levels of Errors in ERP Systems.**

The **surface level** of data problems is the day-to-day errors of entry, transposition, and timeliness. These items are generally relatively easy to mitigate with good work instructions and edits. These errors are also not usually catastrophic because they occur singly and are easily caught. System users usually catch these errors either before they are finished entering the information or when a downstream user identifies the mistake.

Errors that occur over and over again because of poor understanding are **content errors.** In this case, the users have been trained to use the system (know what buttons to push or items to click) but are not educated on the underlying functions of the screens they use. These errors of content will consistently be input with the belief that it is being done correctly. Users at this level may be doing the job diligently but are not be able to tell if the input is really consistent with the content expectations of the system.

**Intent errors** arise when the user knows some, but not all, of the system uses of the data. The users believe they are entering data correctly and can substantiate that relative to the portions of the system they use. This may be fine for them but could be creating many problems elsewhere. An example might be a warehouse person who inputs adjustments to the inventory on-hand balances because he thinks the system count is wrong. This corrects their local reports but also introduces many financial adjustments and causes nervous MRP behavior. The intent of the person is to provide accurate information; the result is unreliable reports for the other users of the system.

The deepest level of error usually originates during the implementation. These **assumptive errors** exist because of incorrect assumptions or incorrect paradigms about how the system functions. These errors are often so deeply embedded into the software that it is difficult to even discern them. An example might be an assumption about how the Available to Promise or Capable to Promise function calculates. The result is that one or many of the business processes is calculating results incorrectly. Reports have summaries of incorrect data and people use these reports to make business decisions every day. These types of errors can seem intimidating when beginning the process of implementing an ERP system. However, there is a solution that helps reduce errors.

## Learning Requirements Planning: Linking ERP and People

The good news is that a well-executed Learning Requirements Plan (LRP) uncovers and prevents most of these problems. LRP provides the education and training methodology needed to avoid the most critical system errors. It also helps employees to understand the impact that a totally integrated system covering almost every aspect of the organization will have on their jobs. ERP systems follow a systematic data flow from one module to another with many data dependencies and prerequisite. The LRP process follows the same logic and, therefore, is effective in helping employees within an organization not only survive an ERP implementation but thrive in the new ERP-enabled organization.

## References

1. APICS Dictionary, 9<sup>th</sup> ed., *APICS — The Educational Society for Resource Management*, Alexandria, VA, 1998.
2. Vollman, T. E., Berry, W. L., Whybark, D. C., and Clay, D., Advanced Concepts in Material Requirements Planning, in *Manufacturing Planning and Control Systems*, 4<sup>th</sup> ed., McGraw-Hill, New York, 1997.
3. Orlicky, J., *Material Requirements Planning*, New York, McGraw-Hill, 1975.
4. Hall, R. W., *Zero Inventories*, Dow Jones-Irwin, Chicago, 1983.
5. Goddard, W. and Brooks, R. B., Strategic production planning. In *Production and Inventory Handbook*, 2nd ed., Greene, J. H., Ed., McGraw-Hill, New York, 1987, chap. 7.
6. Wallace, T., *Sales & Operations Planning: The How-To Handbook*, T.F. Wallace & Co., Cincinnati, OH, 1999, chap. 1.

7. Knoch, L., Tight integration critical to CRM, *APICS~The Performance Advantage*, 10(7), 39, 2000.
8. Kapp, K. M., *The USA Principle: A Philosophy for Implementing Your ERP System On Time and On Budget*, e-book, Lionheart Publishing, Inc., Atlanta, GA, 1999.
9. Beecy, R. E., Drive nails with hammers: properly integrating ERP, APS, and SCM tools, in *APICS 1999 Int. Conf. Proc.*, APICS, Alexandria, VA, 1999, pp. 1–3.
10. Westerland, T., Get Digital: an e-business guide for midsize manufacturers, *APICS~The Performance Advantage*, 10(8), 50, 2000.
11. Ptak, C. with Schragenheim, E., *ERP: Tools, Techniques, and Applications for Integrating the Supply Chain*, CRC Press, Boca Raton, FL, 2000.
12. Langenwalter, G. A., *Enterprise Resources Planning and Beyond: Integrating Your Entire Organization*, CRC Press, Boca Raton, FL, 2000.

# 3 Overview of the LRP Model

## Introduction

Learning Requirements Planning (LRP) is a formal, enterprisewide ERP implementation process that is time-phased to meet the long- and short-term learning objectives of an organization. LRP uses the concepts of "explosions," Bills of Learning, Master Learning Schedules, and Gross-to-Net Logic. The six steps of the model consist of Analysis, Diagnosis, Design, Implementation, Evaluation, and Continuation. The LRP logic is simple and the results are dramatic.

Providing a model upon which to base an ERP implementation is an important element to ERP success often overlooked in the literature. The majority of ERP literature focuses upon a "task list" orientation to implemen tation success. The concept seems to be that if an ERP implementation team can list every single item or task required for the implementation and then simply follow the list, the implementation will be a success.

Unfortunately, a task list approach fails on a number of levels. First, the tasks may not directly feed into one another. It is difficult to visualize how one task relates to another by simply viewing a semichronological list. Although many project management software packages have a "roll-up" functionality, the ability to visualize the "big picture" of the implementation is difficult since a "diagram" of the implementation process does not exist.

Secondly, it is nearly impossible to correctly identify each task in the proper order. Inevitably complications arise. These complications are typically not listed on the task list and then a reorganization of the task list becomes necessary. Also, certain resources may become available before a task is to be performed. If the learning and ERP training is not in line with the tasks to be performed, complications arise.

Third, the task list approach makes it difficult to see priorities. In an ERP implementation, a number of tasks are more important than others. Without a clear prioritization methodology, less-important tasks may receive higher priority and more resources than critical tasks.

The fourth problem is that the task lists are rarely revisited once they are established. This means that any new task or item creeping into the implementation process can replace existing tasks in importance, but never be recorded or officially scheduled. This causes problems because the implementation team is not working from an updated task list or, in a worst-case scenario, different team members are using different task lists.

The fifth, and perhaps the most critical problem, is that the learning needs of the organization are not clearly defined with a task list. It becomes extremely difficult to tie the learning needs of the employees within the organization to the long list of tasks. Some of the training needs overlap, others are not obvious, and some are simply not even listed. The ability of an organization to learn during the ERP implementation is critical to the organization's success. A task list of items to accomplish will not identify learning priorities or establish learning criteria for the organization.

In sharp contrast, the LRP process provides a model for ERP implementations that naturally identifies priorities and establishes criteria by which individuals involved with the implementation project can measure their actions and available resources. The LRP process has built-in feedback mechanisms to ensure that employee learning is constantly evaluated and updated.

An implementation model is an important tool for moving the current ERP implementation philosophy from a "task list" focus to an integrated enterprisewide learning focus. To be effective, an implementation model must be both flexible and adaptable. No two organizations will approach an ERP implementation in exactly the same way. The LRP model has been developed using a modular approach in which each element of the model can be approached separately and then combined for maximum effectiveness, as well as being adaptable to various situations. The model is most effective when viewed as a holistic, integrated approach to an ERP implementation.

An ERP system is an integrated set of procedures for running an organization which itself is a highly integrated set of process and procedures. An integrated system must be implemented to maximize the integrated nature of the organization it supports. Application of the LRP model strengthens the integrated nature of the organization.

LRP provides the integrated approach demanded by today's sophisticated ERP software packages and by the integrated nature of business in the global economy. Approaching the implementation based on a model of Learning

Requirements Planning provides a large probability that the ERP system implementation will achieve success.

The model-based approach to ERP implementations provides a visualization and prioritization methodology that simply does not exist with a task list approach. The elements of education, evaluation, and continuous improvement that are emphasized in the LRP model are not necessarily new. However, the learning-focused approach of LRP is new. LRP will revolutionize ERP implementations.

## Understanding the LRP Model

Learning Requirements Planning blends ERP-developed formulas and techniques with a macro level version of the basic instructional design model. LRP is an explosion of corporate strategic goals into discrete, measurable ERP training and implementation objectives combined with proven feedback methods and systematic performance analysis.

With LRP, the ERP implementation initiatives within a company are tied directly to corporate strategic direction, articulated throughout the organization, delivered efficiently, and evaluated for constant improvement. Figure 3.1 shows the LRP model and all of its inter-related functions.

### *Analysis*

The first step in the LRP model is a careful analysis and development of strategic learning objectives based upon the strategic objectives of the organization. Once the strategic objectives of the organization are identified, learning objectives are developed to support the implementation of the ERP system.

Unfortunately, many manufacturing organizations do not attempt to understand the actual business needs driving their ERP implementation. In too many cases, an ERP system is purchased to achieve vague and somewhat idealistic goals that cannot possibly be accurately measured. An example of this type of goal is "reduce inventory."

What exactly does that phrase mean? Reduce what inventory? Purchased parts? Work-in-process? Finished goods? All inventory? After you identify what inventory you are going to reduce, by how much are you going to reduce it? Why? What is the anticipated return on investment (ROI)? Is it possible to reduce inventory without the expense of the ERP system? If so, by how

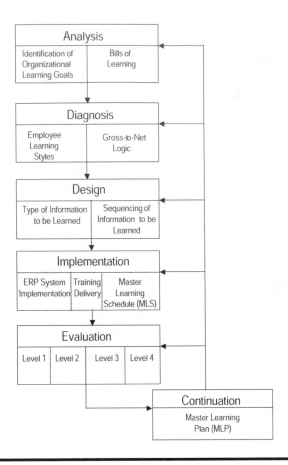

**Figure 3.1    Diagram of LRP Model for ERP Implementation.**

much? And how much more can you reduce inventory with the ERP system in place?

The analysis step of LRP starts with viewing the organization as an inter-related system. This examination provides insights into the integrated nature of the organization and clearly illustrates that "quick fixes" in the area of process improvement do not work.

Several techniques are available to help the organization examine its business processes. Some of the techniques include developing a systems loop diagram, questioning the organization, human resources analysis, and benchmarking the organization against both direct and indirect competitors.

Once the business needs driving the purchase of the ERP system are established, the process of defining learning objectives begins with a meeting of representatives from the major functional groups within the organization.

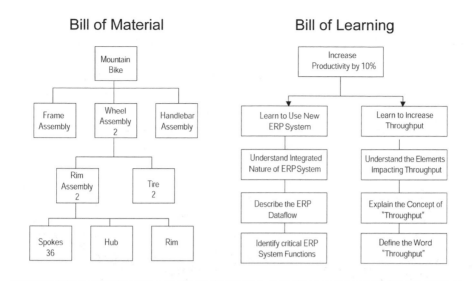

Figure 3.2   Diagram Comparing a Standard Bill of Material (BOM) with a Bill of Learning (BOL).

The sales department, finance department, production department, and others must all be involved. This group defines broad learning objectives for the implementation. This group must analyze the strategic objectives of the organization and develop learning objectives to support the strategy. The learning objectives are broad areas of competencies that the organization must capitalize on or new competencies that the organization must develop.

Next, the learning objectives are "exploded" into Bills of Learning (BOL). Basically, a BOL is a breakdown of corporate strategic objectives into discrete, measurable learning objectives for specific skill sets. The explosion process ensures that the educational initiatives within a company are tied directly to the strategic direction of the company. The explosion process breaks corporate ERP implementation goals into divisional learning goals, then into departmental learning goals, then into individual learning goals. The explosion process is a like a Work Breakdown analysis done for a particular job, but it is done at the organizational level.

A BOL is a hierarchy of learning objectives. The lowest level of the hierarchy contains learning objectives supporting the objectives on the next level that, in turn, support the objectives on the next higher level of the hierarchy. This logic continues until the hierarchy terminates at the strategic organizational goal. A visual comparison of a BOL and a BOM is shown in the Figure 3.2.

The BOL concept is similar to a Bill of Material (BOM). In manufacturing organizations, the BOM lists all of the required material necessary to manufacture a particular item. For example, a BOM for a mountain bike may include, at the top level, the finished bicycle. The next level down may contain the frame assembly, two wheel assemblies, and a handlebar assembly. The next level down for the wheel assemblies may contain a rim assembly and a tire. The next level down from the rim assembly may include 36 spokes, a hub, and a rim.

The BOL provides a visual representation of what is required to reach the strategic and ERP implementation goals of the organization. The BOL also indicates which learning can be obtained internally and which can be acquired externally. The BOL is one of the first elements needed when implementing LRP. A BOL needs to be developed for each strategic objective articulated by an organization. The BOL helps to ensure that learning initiatives within the organization are obtained because the learning needs are clearly stated through the use of the BOL. The BOL allows objectives to obtain organizational visibility.

The BOL concept allows for LRP software packages to have a "drill down" capability. This means that an ERP project manager looking at an upper-level strategic objective can see all of the enabling objectives supporting that upper-level objective. In addition, a "drill up" capability allows the project manager to follow a basic enabling objective through the hierarchy, level by level, until he reaches the final learning objective and, ultimately, the desired strategic objective.

## Diagnosis

The diagnosis step involves the gross-to-net logic of determining what skills and competencies the organization already possesses and what is needed to effectively implement the ERP system. Gross-to-net logic is a concept of comparing the existing skills and competencies within an organization with the skills and competencies required to obtain the stated strategic and ERP implementation goals of the organization. This process compares the BOLs with existing skills and competencies identified within the organization. Use of gross-to-net logic identifies the gaps existing between the ERP-related training needs of the company and the actual ERP-related training delivered to the employees of the company. The gross-to-net logic calculation is shown in Figure 3.3.

The result of conducting the gross-to-net calculation is a list of skills and competencies that are needed within an organization to help implement the ERP system that are not currently available within the organization and cannot easily, quickly, or efficiently be purchased or developed.

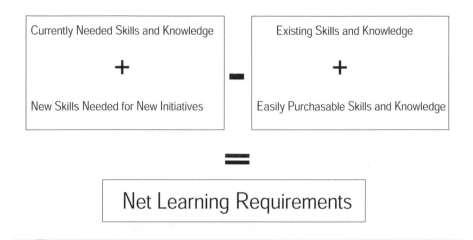

**Figure 3.3 Gross-To-Net Logic Diagram Illustrating Calculation for LRP.**

The purpose of diagnosis is to complete both sides of the gross-to-net logic question. What ERP skills do the employees already possess? What ERP skills can be easily and quickly purchased or outsourced? What skills are currently lacking within the organization? What competencies are needed to succeed in the future but are lacking in our current workforce?

This process yields a strong and visual depiction of the gaps between those competencies and skills the organization already possesses or can easily possess and the skills or competencies it needs to develop in-house. Limited training dollars can then be focused on the skills and competencies most needed for the ERP implementation but not readily obtainable through other means.

In addition, the Diagnosis concept in LRP involves comparing all of the learning goals and BOLs within an organization to identify common learning objectives. Common learning objectives can be grouped together and used to provide a baseline of training within the organization. Pooling learning objectives provides increased efficiency when training employees.

This step identifies the type of learning required to reach each level in the BOL and involves a classification of how employees learn best. It makes no sense to define the objectives needed to be taught unless we understand how to teach the employees.

During the diagnosis process, employees should be taught methods to help them identify their individual learning style. Each employee within an organization approaches learning with a different perspective or style. Some employees need to see the "big picture" before they can dive down into the details while others "stack up" the details of a situation and develop the big

**Figure 3.4    Maslow's Hierarchy of Needs — Each Need in Maslow's Hierarchy Supports the Need Above.**

picture based on their own insights. The Diagnosis step takes the time to allow employees to learn about how they learn. This, in turn, will help employees to more quickly grasp the information that is being taught to them during an ERP implementation.

An organization also needs to conduct a diagnosis of the position of employees based on Abraham Maslow's hierarchy of needs pyramid as shown in Figure 3.4. Understanding Maslow's hierarchy of needs is important when considering any major change in an organization.

The basic assumption in Maslow's hierarchy is that people are motivated by different things based on their position on the hierarchy of needs pyramid.[1] If a lower level is not satisfied, then reinforcement at a higher level will be fruitless. Likewise, once a lower level is satisfied it will cease to be a motivator.

The most important factor to consider when introducing change is the reaction that occurs in people. For most people, work provides the means to provide food, shelter, and security for their family. When a major change is introduced in an organization, the initial reaction of many people is concern over whether those base level needs (food, shelter, and security) are in jeopardy. If an employee's basic needs are not being addressed, he will have a difficult time concentrating on learning how the ERP system functions. Organizations should take the time to diagnosis the employee's skills and level of satisfaction on Maslow's needs hierarchy to receive maximum benefit from employee training.

## Design

The next step in the process is the design of the instruction. This process involves determining the best method of delivering the instruction in terms of sequencing the information, presentation of the information, and distributing the information to the learners.

An organization must develop a series of training classes and events to address the needs of employees. These classes and events should include basic manufacturing classes, ERP integration classes, planning meetings, soft skills training, basic computer literacy education, ERP setup training, a conference room pilot, and functionality training for the end users.

Each training class or learning event needs to utilize different teaching strategies and tactics. Strategies range from developing a simple job-aid containing an abbreviated list of information to a full-blown classroom experience complete with role-play exercises.

The process of developing an effective training design begins with the development of effective learning objectives. If the objectives are developed correctly, they provide a solid foundation for effective instruction. The next step is to categorize the type of learning that needs to take place to reach each learning objective.

Categorizing the types of learning prevents costly and unnecessary training expenses. In many cases information can be transferred to employees quickly and inexpensively without the cost of traditional methods. Following are some methods for designing the appropriate training technique based on the different types of learning that need to occur during an ERP implementation.

**Memorization of names, jargon, facts and acronyms** — Factual information can be transferred to learners through simple job-aids, word associations, and mnemonic devices. When implementing an ERP system, an organization encounters an "alphabet soup" of acronyms. The meanings of all the new acronyms need to be conveyed to the end users of the system and throughout an organization. However, seating employees in a classroom and drilling acronyms into their heads is not an appropriate means of instruction. Employees should be taught the jargon and acronyms as part of ERP overview training and through exposure to the acronyms in classes concentrating on software and ERP concepts. Also, students should be exposed to the terms in settings outside of a formal classroom. This can be done through company newsletters, posters, planning meetings, and informal lunchtime meetings. In some cases, teaching employees how and where to look up information rather than expecting them to memorize is more valuable than teaching the actual information. As Albert Einstein has been rumored to say "… don't memorize anything you can look up."

**Conceptual learning** — One of the best methods for explaining complicated concepts is to use the mentoring or apprenticeship approach. This allows a novice learner to gain insight into concepts and ideas under the watchful eye of an experienced individual. The learner simply asks questions or is told information by the mentor until the learner becomes proficient in understanding the concept. A variation of this method is to have an experienced consultant come into an organization and help a team work through ERP concepts and concerns. For example, an experienced ERP implementer can work with the cross-functional implementation team to determine the level of preparedness of the organization for the ERP implementation. Often, basic concepts are most easily understood with the use of analogies. One author of this book regularly uses the example of planning a dinner or cookout to explain the concept of MRP. Bills of material, lead time, lot size, and projected available inventory is easily understood using this analogy. For concept learning, technology can be utilized by placing reference materials onto an internal computer network or an Intranet. Look for these types of options when selecting an ERP system. Many new ERP systems have help screens linked directly to fields in the screens so users can simply press a function key to clarify a relevant concept. Even a computer-based "chat room" can be an effective method of sharing conceptual information within a company spread across geographical regions. If technology isn't available, a simple reference book or handbook can be effective for some learning styles in conveying conceptual information.

**Problem solving** — This method of learning can be facilitated by a simple checklist of items or issues to consider when addressing a particular problem, such as determining why inventory is rising after an ERP system has been implemented. A database of problems and resolutions can also be an effective tool for helping people learn to solve problems by providing them access to previously solved problems and solutions. Experience is also a good teacher of these particular skills. Adults tend to draw upon previous knowledge when confronted with a new problem. Reading or hearing about other companies who have implemented an ERP system successfully is helpful in this area.

**Soft skills** — These skills deal with the development of communication, leadership, and team building. The teaching of these types of skills involves four steps. The steps model the desired behavior, encourage the learner to develop a mental checklist of the desired behavior, provide numerous examples of the skills, and give learners an opportunity to practice the skill in a nonthreatening environment.

**Physically manipulating objects or psychomotor skills** — Any skill that involves moving various body parts requires practice. This even includes keyboarding skills and teaching employees how to use a computer mouse. An employee can read and study all they want about using a computer mouse, but until he actually touches the mouse the employee has no idea how it really "works."

**Attitudinal learning** — This type of learning is the most difficult to teach because people have different motivations for their attitudes. This area is not one in which classroom training is effective. The best way to teach attitude is by example. If upper management has an attitude of enthusiasm and a sense of urgency about the ERP implementation, the employees will also have that type of attitude. If upper management has a poor attitude toward the software, the ERP process, and improving the manufacturing process, employees will as well. Environmental conditions impact attitudinal learning. It is important that the conditions under which people work reflect the desired attitude. It is also important to set the proper expectations of the implementation prior to starting the process. If the employees do not know what to expect from the implementation and are uncertain what their future roles will be, the attitude will suffer. Upper management must convey information to the implementation team and to the rest of the organization in a timely and effective manner. This approach minimizes rumors, innuendoes, and declining morale due to the implementation of the ERP system. In addition, it is important to understand what motivates the employees within the organization to attend and participate in the instructional process. A systematic method for designing motivational instruction needs to be followed to ensure that the employees are paying attention to the instruction and utilizing the instructional time appropriately.

## Implementation

Once the training is properly designed and sequenced for delivery within the organization, the next step of the LRP process is "Implementation." Implementation involves utilizing the LRP process to effectively implement the ERP system. The proper implementation of an ERP system is a difficult task. An ERP system is a set of rules and procedures for operating a business. When implementing an ERP system, a company replaces its existing set of rules and procedures with ERP-based rules and procedures. Unfortunately, many decision makers do not comprehend the data flow of the ERP system or how the various modules function with one another, nor do they understand that existing business processes will likely need to change to fit the ERP software's design standard.

To make matters worse, organizations do not spend the initial time or effort to prepare existing business processes for automation. In a manual system, many "workarounds" and compromises can be utilized to circumvent bad or inefficient processes. However, when processes are automated, circumvention becomes difficult and tiny mistakes are magnified. Automating complex or nonvalue-added processes with an ERP system will not increase production or improve performance.

Several steps can be taken to avoid implementation failures. The first is to conduct a proper analysis to determine the strategic and learning objectives of the organization. Next, the diagnosis process provides employees with insights into how they can best learn the new information about the ERP system. The design step of LRP ensures that the training delivered to the employees is effective. The next step is to help employees accept the ERP technology into their daily routine.

This means that the ERP system must exhibit certain characteristics to be accepted:

1. The system must offer a relative advantage over the previous method of conducting business,
2. The system must be compatible with the current missions and goals of the company,
3. The system must not be perceived as being too complex,
4. The users must be able to test drive the ERP system before going live, and
5. The users must be given the opportunity to observe how the system works before they will agree to be held accountable for its proper functioning.

Another critical element for successful ERP implementation is to have a well-trained implementation team. For the implementation team to be effective, it must have the following characteristics:

- Clear purpose
- Defined roles
- Established processes
- Effective communication
- Universal involvement

- Empowerment
- Commitment
- Accountability
- Trust
- Exit plan

The actual ERP implementation itself can occur using one of four methods. These methods are (1) parallel, (2) phased, (3) big bang, and (4) pilot. The "parallel" method involves running both the old system and the new ...n concurrently. This is usually preceded by some level of training. This ...sophy is usually driven by people in the accounting or finance depart-... as a way to build their confidence that both systems will provide the same financial results. The reality is that the systems will not give the exact same financial results for two primary reasons: (1) the users will be so severely overworked that they will not accurately enter the same information in both systems, and (2) the two systems will likely have somewhat different inherent business processes that will cause some data to be calculated differently. Indeed, if the new system does not provide better, more accurate data, why change the system in the first place. The parallel approach has fallen out of favor with most professional implementers.

The "phased" implementation method gradually introduces the new system into the organization, one module or discipline at a time. An example would be to implement all the Sales and Accounts Receivable functions completely, then implement the Purchasing and Accounts Payable functions, then move on to manufacturing and inventory, etc. This method is often required in a very large organization or one that is extremely resource constrained during the implementation. The benefit of this approach is to limit the amount of resource commitment and disruption to the organization. The drawbacks are twofold. First, the length of time that the implementation takes is prolonged and people often must support portions of both the old and new systems. Second, this method sets in place the practice of working around the official system because not all the necessary information is available until it is completely implemented. This builds the habit of not using the system correctly — a difficult habit to break.

The "big bang" implementation method describes the practice of defining a cutover date and on that date turning the old system off and the new system on. This method also has benefits and drawbacks. The benefit is that people must learn the new system. They will not have the old system to fall back on (this is called backsliding and is a potential drawback of most of the slower implementation methods). The drawback is that if people have not learned in advance how to perform their function proficiently with the new system, it can bring the organization to a halt.

The "pilot" approach to implementation is becoming the preferred method used by most implementers. In the pilot approach, users are trained in their functions and then, rather than processing all of the business on two systems as in the parallel method, they select a pilot group of items to process on the new system. Normal business proceeds on the old system and only the pilot items are transacted on the new system. This allows users to become very comfortable with the new system yet still be able to handle the added workload without drastically impacting their overall time effectiveness. Once a pilot is successfully completed, the decision is made to "go live" with the new system. The pilot method is often combined with either the phased or big bang methods. Each of these methods has its advantages and disadvantages and each requires a great deal of management intervention and coordinating of schedules.

Managing, scheduling, and coordinating the enterprisewide Learning Requirements Planning process is not an easy task. A Chief Learning Officer (CLO) needs to be appointed to ensure that the learning needs of the organization are implemented in a manner consistent with the ERP implementation. The job of the CLO is to monitor internal training practices, position training to support the ERP implementation, participate in planning the education of the organization's workforce, and champion organizational learning and employee growth and development during the ERP implementation process.

Another critical element the CLO performs is the establishment of a process for evaluating the training that occurs during the implementation. It is poor practice to conduct training for an implementation and not have any measurable results of the effectiveness of the training.

## Evaluation

LRP cannot function without an evaluation of the training and learning that occurs in relationship to the ERP implementation. The organization must perform both formative and summative evaluations during the development process. Formative evaluations are used during the Analysis and Design phases to aid in understanding the learning requirements and designing training to meet those needs.

The LRP process provides for four levels of summative evaluation. These four levels are based on the levels developed in 1959 by Donald L. Kirkpatrick, then a professor at the University of Wisconsin.[2] The four-level classification serves as a framework for evaluating ERP training.

*Level 1* evaluations are conducted by handing out questionnaires at the end of the training session. Was the presenter knowledgeable? Did the presenter carry himself well? Were the ERP concepts explained adequately? Were the MRP formulas easy to understand? At this level of evaluation, initial customer satisfaction is being measured. This is often referred to as measuring the reaction to the training. This measurement is important, especially when you are trying to obtain buy-in from the employees who will be using the system on a daily basis.

A *Level 2* evaluation tests participant learning. At this level, the evaluation includes measurable feedback indicating what was learned and what was not learned. The idea is to see if the participant can pass a test or a demonstration of what he or she learned. For example, students would be tested to see if they could enter a customer order into the ERP system or properly create a Bill of Material for a particular item on the ERP system. This information is then used to help provide remediation to learners and to determine areas in which the training needs to be strengthened.

It is important to realize that a "lack of learning" can occur because the design of the training is poor. More often than not, employees are not able to operate new ERP software because the training is inadequate and not because the employees can't "understand" the new system.

*Level 3* evaluation checks to see if the skills taught in the training are actually being used on the job. Level 3 evaluates the transfer of learning from the learning experience to the job. Many times, employees will attend ERP training and then not utilize the training for months. This is particularly prevalent in large company implementations where thousands of users must be trained. This type of evaluation checks to see if an employee's behavior has changed as a result of the learning experience.

Observing the employee and asking an employee's supervisor or customers to see if they noticed a difference are two methods used for conducting a Level 3 evaluation. This level of evaluation can also check to see if the entire ERP implementation is functioning effectively. If people are being trained far in advance of having to operate the ERP software, then the training is not in synchronization with the educational needs. The LRP process identifies these types of disjointed occurrences quickly and enables the implementation project leader to make adjustments.

*Level 4* evaluation attempts to measure the bottom line result of the training. Did the training positively impact the ERP implementation? Is the implementation faster and more effective because of the type of training supplied to the employees? What aspects of the ERP implementation training were more effective than others? This level of evaluation is difficult to obtain, but must be measured to ensure that the company is not wasting its training dollars.

These four levels of evaluation ensure that the LRP process is effective and yielding the desired results. Training, as with any other unit within an organization, must be held accountable for getting results. The four levels of evaluation within the LRP process ensure that the LRP process is effective for the ERP implementation and held accountable.

## *Continuation*

LRP is not a one-time event. It is a continuous process. Organizations cannot implement an ERP system as they would a spreadsheet or word processing package — install it then instantly use it and gain return on investment. ERP systems provide a ROI over the long term. The purpose of an ERP system is to apply a consistent set of standards throughout an organization. The consistent set of standards allows for easy data sharing, effective communications, and streamlined decision-making. It positions a company to compete in the long term.

ERP systems are only as effective as the ladies and gentlemen utilizing them. A mechanism must be built into the organization to continually develop employee skills as they relate to the ERP system. An absence of continuous training or a constant reexamination of processes and procedures related to the ERP system causes stagnation and an inability to compete.

The LRP process should be undertaken continuously to ensure the maximum effectiveness of the ERP system in both the short and long term. In addition, the LRP process, once perfected within an organization for ERP implementation, can be transferred to other enterprisewide initiatives. The techniques and concepts contained within the LRP framework do not need to be limited to ERP implementations. Many companies are applying these same techniques to other e-technology initiatives like e-commerce, e-supply chain, and e-customer management. Any initiative that requires tying corporate strategic goals to individual employee action and learning can benefit from LRP.

Understanding how to develop a systematic method for continuation of the LRP process and how to transfer the process to other areas helps an organization achieve a strategic advantage.

## Why the LRP Approach to ERP?

What LRP allows an organization to do is to transform from a manufacturing, distribution, or service organization into a learning organization through the catalyst of the ERP implementation. Some experts believe the only competitive advantage left to an organization is its ability to learn faster than its competitors. Unfortunately, few manufacturing organizations emphasize knowledge, innovation, or learning at an enterprise level.

A learning organization is a group of people who have woven a continuous, enhanced capacity to learn into the corporate culture — an organization in which learning processes are analyzed, monitored, developed, and aligned with competitive goals. A learning organization generates knowledge and learning faster than its competitors and turns that learning into a strategic advantage to outmarket, outmanage, and outsell competition.[3] Many of these strategic advantages are the reasons management decided to implement the ERP system in the first place. A focus on enterprisewide learning achieves dramatic results.

An organization that focuses on learning moves beyond simple employee training into organizational problem solving, innovation, and creativity. For instance, in a learning organization, when a product is bad, instead of just scrapping it the employees find the cause of the problem and develop solutions to prevent it from happening again.

The concept of a learning organization is articulated in the best-selling book, *The Fifth Discipline: The Art and Practice of the Learning Organization.*[4] The book was written by Peter Senge, the Director of the Center for Organizational Learning at MIT's Sloan School of Management. *The Fifth Discipline* outlines five areas, or disciplines, necessary for an organization to be classified as a learning organization. The five disciplines are Personal Mastery, Mental Models, Shared Vision, Team Learning, and Systems Thinking. Each of the five disciplines is briefly described below.

**Personal mastery** — This discipline involves an individual's ability to know what he or she wants and to work toward that goal. In a learning organization, creating an environment in which members can develop themselves toward the goals and purposes they and the organization choose (like an ERP implementation) encourages personal mastery.

**Mental models** — Mental models are an organization's and an individual's internal picture of the world — a paradigm. Paradigms must be constantly evaluated, analyzed, and clarified to ensure they are as accurate as possible. A manufacturing organization can easily get caught in an old paradigm and have difficulty reacting to change. Old paradigms are frequently uncovered during ERP implementations. Once discovered, old ineffective paradigms should be shattered and new ones put into place.

**Shared vision** — This discipline embodies the idea of an organization building a sense of common commitment by developing shared visions of the future. This includes developing the principles and guiding practices used to reach the goal. During an ERP implementation, the mission or vision statement is often a tangible symbol of the shared vision of the future.

**Team learning** — Skills learned through teamwork and team involvement enable employees to reliably develop intelligence and abilities greater than the sum of the individual members' talents. Team learning is geared toward developing collective thinking skills. It also involves learning from previously learned concepts and ideas.

**Systems thinking** — This discipline is most critical in terms of helping an organization to successfully achieve ERP implementation success. Systems thinking is a way of thinking about and understanding the forces and inter-relationships that exist between all of the different functional areas within the manufacturing organization. This discipline helps manufacturers to see how to change the systems more effectively and to act more in tune with the larger processes of the economic and industrial world.

While the five disciplines are vital, they do not in themselves provide much guidance on how to begin the journey of building a learning organization. In order to implement these five disciplines, an organization must commit resources to learning, appoint a corporate learning officer, and establish a learning infrastructure.

An organization can transform itself into a learning organization by understanding the tremendous competitive advantage it can achieve by focusing on learning. The transformation to a learning organization can be achieved through the application of the steps of Learning Requirements Planning.

## Application of an e-Learning Approach to LRP

An e-learning approach to training implies the use of a corporate LAN or intranet for the delivery of training to employees. Many large ERP vendors including SAP and PeopleSoft are using e-learning to delivery training both internally to their own employees and externally to clients implementing their systems. The enterprisewide approach of LRP, complete with built-in evaluations and the classification of the type of information to be learned, lends itself to the application of automated training. LRP software is needed in the manufacturing and training industries. Many powerful tools are available to help trainers, performance technologists, and knowledge managers in virtually every aspect of training management and delivery.

The advent of intranets, universal databases, and drill-down capabilities in software make it possible to automate the LRP process. This automation process will bring together different elements of training within an organization. The learner can enter into the learning opportunity within the company through a learning portal.

A learning portal is a "one-stop-shop" on a corporation's intranet that allows individual employees to gain access to all of the training opportunities within their organization. The portal can be programmed to recognize an individual's "profile" and provide him or her with exactly the type of training needed. The "profile" consists of the employee's job title, required skills for the current position, and any skills required to move up within the organization. The information within the profile can be matched to corporate training offerings and the individual can receive a customized listing of the courses he or she should take to qualify for promotion within the organization.

In addition, the portal can provide information on what courses the employee has already taken, alert the employee to additional training opportunities within the company, help the employee to remain current on the latest trends within the organization, and even provide training via the computer to the employee.

In many cases, the learning goals of the organization and individual can be satisfied with intranet-based training so the employee can go directly from the learning portal to a virtual "class." Intranet-based training provides a number of advantages over traditional stand-up, lecture-based training. The first is that individuals taking intranet training can proceed with the training at their own pace. In a classroom, the instructor can only move the class forward at an average pace. During the class, some employees will be ahead of the lecture and some will be behind. With intranet-delivered training, the employees taking the training can proceed at the pace that suits them. The automated training proceeds only when the employee is ready to continue since the employee controls the pace of the instruction.

The next advantage is that an employee can take the training whenever it is most convenient for the employee. This works especially well when dealing with employees on various shifts. An employee can log into the training and receive customized feedback as to his or her performance and take the training during off-peak production times and not at the convenience of the instructor.

Another advantage is that the training is delivered consistently to all employees taking the training. Each employee will receive the same quality of instruction and the same objectives will be taught within the course. It is not dependent upon the trainer.

Intranet training is also cost effective because it can be updated so easily. With the training housed on a central server, any changes that need to be incorporated into the training can be done once and are immediately available to all potential students.

Finally, intranet training can easily track student performance. The system can be established in such a manner that individual scores on tests can be tracked and easily monitored to determine the effectiveness of the instruction and how quickly an individual is able to learn the information necessary for the ERP implementation. A properly programmed intranet-based training system can provide all manner of reports for monitoring student progress and achievement.

The ability to tie all corporate training needs together in one place alongside the individual training needs of employees provides a powerful tool for helping to implement an ERP system within an organization. It is possible to program all of the ERP learning goals into a corporate learning portal and then allow the employees direct access to the training that specifically meets the needs of their role before, during, and after the ERP implementation. This "just-in-time" approach to ERP training provides a tremendous advantage to an organization in terms of the effectiveness, timeliness, and relevance of the training received by employees.

In addition, a properly programmed LRP system allows a corporate manager to "drill down" on corporate learning goals and determine how close the organization is to being trained in the areas critical to the corporation's strategic goals. The visibility of the learning goals within the company also helps to focus the organization on learning.

## Summary

LRP is a systems approach to the ERP implementation process and it can be pivotal to the successful implementation of an ERP system. The application of LRP to a manufacturing organization transforms the manufacturing organization into a learning organization through an effective ERP implementation. Conducting the LRP steps of Analysis, Diagnosis, Implementation, Evaluation, and Continuation is the type of strategic planning process that enables an organization to capitalize on its most valuable asset — human resources — to effectively implement an ERP system that provides the right information for the employees to make well-informed, insightful decisions.

Effectively implementing LRP will provide an effective ERP implementation — one that will be completed on time and within the stated budget. LRP is not an easy process and usually results in significant organizational change. Most organizations claim to value human resources but spend little money or effort adding credibility to their claim. Implementing LRP to help with ERP provides tangible evidence of an organization's commitment to human resources.

## References

1. Goble, F., *The Third Force — The Psychology of Abraham Maslow,* Grossman Publishers, New York, 1970, pp. 36–51.

2. Kirkpatrick, D., Techniques for Evaluating Training Programs, *Training & Development*, January 1996, p. 54.
3. Kapp, K. M., Transforming your manufacturing organization into a learning organization, in *APICS 1997 Int. Conf. Proc.*, APICS, Falls Church, VA 1997, p. 288.
4. Senge, P. M., *The Fifth Discipline: The Art and Practice of the Learning Organization*, Currency Doubleday, New York, 1990.

# 4 Analysis

## Introduction

Learning faster than competitors is a company's only sustainable competitive advantage. Organizations that continually reflect upon themselves grow, mature and stay competitive; those that don't disappear. The successful implementation of an ERP system requires an understanding of the organization into which the ERP system is being implemented. As Figure 4.1 illustrates, analysis is the first step in a successful LRP implementation. A failure to properly understand the subtle interactions between and among departments causes delays, inadequate ROI, and, potentially, implementation failure.

Throughout the LRP process, the emphasis is on learning. An organization needs to learn about its market, employees, competitors, internal processes, and mission. Systematic organizational learning begins with a structured analysis. The LPR process provides tools, ideas, and techniques for organizations to learn about themselves while achieving ERP implementation success.

Unfortunately, few organizations take the time to analyze how they are functioning prior to implementing an ERP system. Organizations tend to focus on the automation aspects of ERP and not on learning. Ignoring the analysis step of the LRP process robs an organization of its greatest opportunity to make order-of-magnitude improvements.

## Overview of the Analysis Process

Organizational analysis starts with viewing the organization as a system. This examination yields insights the manufacturer can use to plot its course through the implementation of the ERP system. The next step is to bench-

**69**

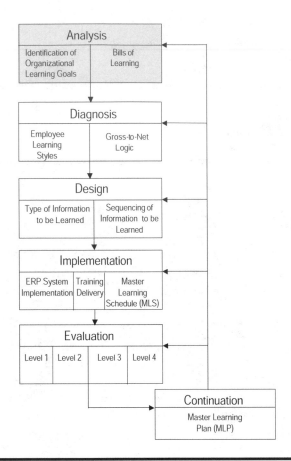

**Figure 4.1 LRP with Analysis Highlighted. Analysis is the first step in the LRP process.**

mark against direct competitors, indirect competitors, and best-in-class organizations.

Once the internal and external analysis is completed, the organization must develop explicit and well-communicated strategic goals to guide the ERP implementation. Once strategic goals are determined, analysis must be conducted at the learning level. Learning analysis, overlooked in many ERP implementation plans, is the critical glue that holds strategies established by upper management to the processes workers perform daily.

Process-level analysis determines if the individual processes within an organization are aligned with the strategic goals of the organization. Many opportunities exist within an organization for process-level improvements. If process problems are left unexposed, they will severely hamper the implementation.

The final step in the analysis process includes an "explosion" of the initial learning goals into discreet, measurable learning objectives. This explosion process ensures that training is maximized throughout the ERP implementation and that organizational processes and strategic goals are aligned.

The analysis step serves as a catalyst for organizations that allocate the necessary time to conduct this step in the LRP process. The single largest opportunity within an organization implementing ERP is the ability to obtain results not previously achievable because of the limitations of the existing manual or automated (legacy) systems.

## Need for Analysis

If an organization implements ERP merely to increase the efficiency of its existing processes, it will not receive the desired ROI. Increasing the speed at which ineffective and inefficient processes operate does not improve operations. In fact, it can destroy a company. Here is an actual example from the Heating, Ventilation, Air-conditioning, and Cooling (HVAC) industry in which one company conducted a careful analysis and their competitor did not.

Manufacturer ABC was selling an item as a loss leader to attract customers. The item was difficult to manufacture and sold at a low price across the industry. Many companies in the HVAC industry were selling this item inexpensively with the belief that it was a loss leader. Manufacturer ABC decided to conduct an internal analysis of the manufacturing process and an external analysis of what customers really wanted. As a result of the analysis, ABC determined that the item was a major financial loser and that subsequent purchases by customers who bought the loss leader were not profitable purchases. ABC determined they were losing a lot more money on this item than they had assumed all these years. The loss-leader item was dropped almost immediately.

While dropping the loss-leader item made financial sense to ABC, the sales department wanted to be able to refer their customers to another source for this item. A decision was made to enter into a relationship with a competitor who was manufacturing the item. ABC would recommend the competitor as the source for the low-priced item that ABC was no longer carrying.

The competitor, XYZ Corporation, was thrilled with all of the new orders they anticipated but neglected to conduct an external or internal analysis of the item and never really knew how much money they were losing on this loss leader.

XYZ did receive a large number of orders for the item that ABC no longer carried. Within six months, XYZ filed for bankruptcy. The increased volume of the loss-leader item destroyed corporate profitability since no analysis was ever done. It took XYZ too long to determine where they were losing all their money in spite of the fact that sales volumes had never been higher.

This example illustrates the importance of conducting a careful analysis prior to making a business decision. The implementation of an ERP system is a major business decision costing an organization anywhere from $250,000 to over $2 million in terms of software, consulting, overtime, and human resources. The analysis step of LRP minimizes the costs associated with implementations.

In another example of the failure to conduct analysis, a trainer from an ERP vendor was conducting a training class at a large Fortune 500 equipment manufacturer. During the class, the employees, who would be using the system on daily basis, noticed that the system did not requisition material in the same manner as their current procedures.

Students asked the instructor what internal process they should follow when requisitioning material. The instructor from the ERP vendor did not know the answer to the question since he was not familiar with the existing process and he was not authorized to establish a corporate procedure for material requisitioning. Immediately the students became upset. They were uncertain of how this critical process would occur once the system was implemented the following Monday. The students were not comfortable with what they should be doing. Consequently, they did not feel ready to "go-live" the following Monday.

Since none of the employees in the purchasing department had ever seen the entire ERP system function together, no provisions were made to determine how to deal with the new method of requisitioning material in the system. It wasn't even on the priority list of the implementation team. The ERP implementation was delayed for two weeks while a procedure was developed to deal with the new requisitioning structure.

In this case, an analysis would have averted the problem. If the implementation team had conducted an analysis of the current requisitioning process, they would have known that it did not match the functionality of the ERP system. In fact, the purchasing employees should have been involved in the meeting to determine the new requisitioning procedure. Springing an entirely new requisitioning system on employees one week prior to going live does not lead to ERP success stories.

Careful analysis does. A pipe-fitting company in Western Pennsylvania conducted a detailed three-month analysis of all their strategic, process, and learning needs. The results of the analysis were shared with every employee in the company through a series of corporate meetings, small group sessions, and well-written newsletters. The result was that the company implemented their ERP system and had it fully operational and returning value to the company within six months. Many of the changes instituted were put into place prior to the ERP system being fully functional. The improvements within the manufacturing plant, the streamlined customer service, and the increased productivity paid for the system within a year.

Conducting an organizational analysis focusing on strategic learning and process needs is not easy. It can take many months to gather and interpret the data. It takes valuable human resources to make the proper inquires. It takes research and persistence to find the "root" of many of the organizational assumptions. The amount of resources and the potential for delay causes many executives to unwisely forgo the analysis portion of the implementation process and forge ahead with the automation effort.

While this solution seems to make sense in the short term, the long-term impact can be disastrous. According to Dick Kuiper, vice president of Expert Buying Systems, an American company specializing in helping manufacturing organizations choose ERP systems, 25 to 50% of all ERP/MRP II projects experience significant failure during implementation.[1] In addition, 75% of all new systems implemented are considered poor implementations because they fall short of customer expectations. An astounding 90% of all major system projects are significantly over budget, either in money, time, or both. Many of these failed implementation share the same sad story: no time to conduct an analysis, simply forge ahead with system automation and worry about problems as they arise. Sound business decisions demand careful analysis.

Since an ERP system is fully integrated, each functional area within the organization must understand how information entered into their ERP screen reacts and impacts upon the information entered by others. Employees and upper management must understand that both the organization and the ERP system are fully integrated systems that must function smoothly together to maximize the potential of both.

An investment in analysis is returned to the organization over and over again in terms of faster rate of system acceptance, streamlined processes, and increased morale. One of the most valuable by-products of implementing an ERP system is that it forces an organization to take a critical look at itself on all levels. This in-depth examination provides an opportunity for organizational learning critical for long-term success.

According to a study released by the Washington, D.C.-based Brookings Institute, 60% of an organization's competitive advantage is derived from internal advancements in knowledge, innovation, and learning.[2] Organizations can buy and implement an ERP system and receive a small competitive advantage; however, if they take the time to learn about their organization during the process, they can receive a large competitive advantage. Failure to conduct a careful analysis prior to the ERP implementation is a squandered opportunity.

## The Manufacturing Organization as a System

A manufacturing organization is not simply a collection of independently operated functional areas. For every action within a manufacturing organization, there is an opposite and equal reaction.[3] Each area within the organization is intimately tied to all of the other areas within the organization. Unfortunately, traditional business analysis techniques look at each area separately.

Focusing exclusively on the individual parts of an organization and not the whole causes problems. A change in one part of a manufacturing organization, like increasing sales quotas, ripples into other functions such as increased paperwork in payroll and added workload in shipping.

An excellent way to begin the task of analyzing a manufacturing organization is to focus on the organization as a system. The concept of viewing an organization as a system received increased acceptance in the early 1980s. During that time, different disciplines began to develop models, theories, and practices to examine the synergy between and among various parts of an organization. This focus on the whole, as opposed to the parts, is known as "systems thinking."

Systems thinking is a way of thinking about and understanding the forces and interrelationships existing between the different functional areas within a manufacturing organization. Systems thinking helps manufacturers see how to change their organizations to act more in tune with the larger processes of the economic environment in which they function. Several disciplines developed the concept of systems thinking independently. A brief examination of each of the areas illustrates the value of systems thinking in a variety of functional areas.

In the manufacturing arena, Eliyahu Goldratt developed his Theory of Constraints and stated that an organization was a like a chain and was only as strong as its weakest link. Goldratt believed that an organization should not focus on improving each individual link in the chain but, rather, focus on improving its weakest link or constraint within the system. The model developed by Goldratt recognizes that constraints determine the overall performance of a manufacturing system. A constraint is defined as anything that limits performance relative to the goals of making money now and in the future. Constraints can be physical, such as a material shortage, or they can be managerial such as a procedure or policy.

In the area of finance, the concept of Activity-Based Costing (ABC) gained popularity. ABC uses the concept of identifying overhead costs associated with specific activities ("cost drivers") within an organization. Traditionally, costs are associated with a department or an area within an organization. With ABC, costs are assigned to business processes regardless of whether they cross department boundaries or not. The cost of an item is determined not by which department it falls under, but upon the processes utilized to make the item salable. This includes production processes as well as order entry, accounting, and other business processes.

In the area of quality, W. Edwards Deming promoted the concept of avoiding suboptimization. Deming urged those who would listen, to view their entire organization as a whole rather than allow one functional area to improve at the expense of others. For example, a situation might exist where the purchasing department buys a specific item in bulk to save money even though production rarely uses the item and the inventory department doesn't have the space to store the excess. In many organizations the purchasing department would be rewarded for saving money while the inventory department would be chastised for excessive inventory. In this case, the purchasing department is achieving suboptimization at the expense of the inventory department and the entire organization.

In the field of learning, Peter Senge, founder and director of the Center for Organizational Learning at MIT's Sloan School of Management, brought the concept of "systems thinking" to the forefront of the human resource (HR) departments. Senge named systems thinking as the most critical of his five disciplines required to create a learning organization. Senge writes that systems thinking is a way of thinking about and understanding the forces and interrelationships that exist between all of the different functional areas within an organization.[4] Systems thinking helps organizations change and improve internal process and to act more in tune with the larger processes of their marketplace.

All of the applications of systems thinking illustrate the value of using this approach to analyze an organization from a systems perspective. A manufacturing organization works as a system with many conflicting and sometimes diametrically opposed goals and objectives. Prior to developing a learning focus for an ERP implementation, a clear picture of the interrelated systems within the company needs to be developed.

The following case study of Marshall Manufacturing is designed to high-light the various problems encountered due to the integrated nature of a manufacturing organization. Marshall Manufacturing manufactures a wide range of metal products. Some are sold directly to retailers and some are sold to other manufactures for inclusion in their products. The case study of Marshall illustrates how a manufacturing organization is a system and how it reacts when one part of the system "suboptimizes" at the expense of others. Understanding how a manufacturing system functions is essential to success-fully implementing ERP. Viewing symptoms of nonsystems thinking at fic-tional Marshall Manufacturing illustrates how different goals and objectives impact one another.

## Marshall Manufacturing

Recently, production employees of Marshall noticed an increase in the amount of inventory on hand. Raw material seems to be arriving earlier than it is needed and in many cases Marshall has plenty of material that production doesn't need, and can't seem to get critical components that are needed. The purchasing manager has been heard saying, "I only purchase what we need … unfortunately, no one knows what we need!"

Even though there are shortages, raw materials inventory keeps getting higher and higher because safety stock is being raised to avoid all of the stock-outs. More than an entire year's supply of packaging material is sitting in the warehouse.

WIP inventory is getting higher as well. The shipping department is constantly taking apart subassemblies to get parts required for urgent orders. The lead time for items in the major product line is increasing even though a team of expeditors is roaming the floor hurrying material and operations along. Also, the production department can't find WIP material when it is needed and setup times are getting longer and longer. The manufacturing manager has been heard saying, "I can only track white-hot orders on the floor, other orders aren't tracked until they are white hot."

Walking on the shop floor is like maneuvering though an obstacle course. Employees are forced to dodge both good-quality inventory and scrap mate-rials placed wherever a vacant space is available. In fact, there has just been a workman's compensation claim because someone broke a toe on a die left in the middle of an aisle. The inventory manager has begun a cycle-counting program but is having trouble keeping up with the material because hurried employees do not store it in the proper location or make the associated transactions.

One shining area in this company is the sales department. It is going to exceed its monthly quota. Sales just landed a huge sale of one of Marshall's normally low-selling items. The customer wants 350 units. The maximum ever kept on hand for this item is 50 units. The entire shop floor is now dedicated to this order. Sales people are becoming very upset because the regular customers can't get their orders. Customers are placing orders early so they can ensure delivery of product in time for their own production schedules. They are also starting to complain that the quality of Marshall's products is slipping.

In many cases, the shipping department is not shipping on time because they have to break apart already packaged inventory and then repackage it. This is due to the fact that items previously manufactured were boxed in customer "A's" custom packaging in anticipation of demand based on the sales forecast. If demand for the same part comes from a different customer and none is in stock, shipping unpacks the customer "A's" items and repacks them in the new customer's required packaging.

The vendors are not able to support the schedules either. The supply of raw material is intermittent, causing purchasing to order ahead and in larger quantities than needed. This strategy is employed in hopes that the needed materials will be received in time for the actual need date. This is not happening. The vendors are not able to keep up with the demand and are becoming more and more resistant to the last-minute changes Marshall keeps making to the orders.

The accounting department is extremely upset because they cannot get a proper reconciliation of the actual inventory in stock and profits are trending downward at an alarming rate. The accounting manager is demanding more detailed tracking of labor and materials against work orders but is not making any progress. The employees on the shop floor are too busy getting orders out the door to stop and record labor and material use. The entire company is dreading the complete physical inventory scheduled for the following weekend.

However, more than the physical inventory, the upper-level managers are dreading the task of implementing the ERP system just purchased by the president to "turn the company around in 9 months."

## A Systems View of Marshall

The problems encountered at Marshall can all be viewed in isolation. They can be listed on a sheet in priority order and individually attacked and possibly solved. However, problems within a manufacturing organization are tied to each other. Marshall's poor-quality products are due to a combination of poor-quality material purchased from a vendor and quantity-focused performance metrics.

Attempting to solve problems in isolation is impossible in a complex manufacturing organization. In addition, if the problems are worked around in the short term, the underlying dynamics of the organization cause the problems to reappear. A priority list approach to Marshall's problems takes a long time to implement and doesn't result in long-term improvements in the underlying system dynamics.

A more effective approach is to analyze Marshall from a systems perspective. This approach can reach the underlying dynamics. When analyzed from a systems perspective, it becomes clear that each attempt within Marshall to remedy the situation in isolation causes an undesirable reaction or backlash within the entire system. The purpose of a systems perspective is to step back from the daily functions of the organization and determine which action causes which reaction. Simply "trying harder" does not solve the deeply rooted problems at Marshall. In fact, trying harder worsens the problems.

As an example, customers are canceling orders placed at Marshall because the delivery dates of Marshall's products were slipping. What was originally quoted as a five-week delivery time frame has been averaging closer to eight weeks. The canceling of customer orders caused great concern at Marshall. Therefore, the Vice President of Sales decided to provide an incentive to his sales force to sell more products by offering a trip to Bermuda. Whoever sold the highest quantity of any product would win a free trip for two to Bermuda. In addition, the president of the company decided to give large discounts to customers who purchase in quantities above 300 units even though the discount resulted in profit margins that were extremely thin.

Subsequently, Joe, one of the newest salespeople, landed an order for 350 units, the largest order in the history of the company. Not only was it the largest order, it was for an item that was not normally sold or kept on hand in quantities greater than 50. This meant that the entire production department had to stop work on other orders and concentrate on producing enough of this product to satisfy the large order.

While the large order was being filled, smaller, more profitable orders could not be filled because all the capacity was dedicated to the order of 350 units. As a result the lead time for customer orders increased from the already elongated time of 8 weeks to an even longer 12 weeks. As a result of the longer lead time, more customers canceled their orders.

The continual cancellation of smaller orders only helped to reinforce the VP of Sales position that fewer, larger orders were better for the company. Therefore, more incentives were created to obtain larger and larger orders.

**Figure 4.2   Linear Thinking. An illustration of the linear thinking that can occur in different departments within a manufacturing organization.**

The downward spiral will continue until someone examines the entire business system at Marshall.

The underlying problem is that two functional areas within the organization see the same elements of the problem from two different directions. The sales department sees the solution as encouraging larger orders. These large orders are expected to provide an influx of cash into the organization. The VP of Sales believes that receiving a large order is beneficial and continues to work harder and harder to encourage large sales.

From the perspective of the accounting department, large sales orders are not more profitable since the incentive for a customer to purchase a large order is a discount on price. So while large orders are beginning to arrive, the smaller, more profitable ones are being canceled.

The production department views the large orders as a problem because they must continually change schedules and tear down and set up machines in an attempt to accommodate both the existing smaller orders and the newer, higher-priority larger orders. This, in turn, upsets the accounting department because of all the labor and overhead associated with setups and teardowns.

Figure 4.2 illustrates the linear thinking of two of the departments. Commonly, the different perspectives regarding the large orders are only seen from one side by a department. In isolation, the decision to encourage sales to sell larger orders seems to make sense to the sales department, but when viewed from a systems perspective, it doesn't.

## *System Analysis Tools*

Fortunately, over the last 10 years a number of effective tools and techniques have been developed to help organizations focus on Systems Thinking. The tools include a Systems Loop Diagram, Organizational Questioning, and HR Analysis. All of these tools can be used during the analysis phase of

| Too many wrong parts | Not enough right parts |
|---|---|
| Delivery lead times are increasing | Vendors are not cooperating |
| Trouble tracking labor hours | Breaking apart packaged goods and repackaging |
| No one knows what to purchase | Sales are down |
| Receipt of large customer order | Profits are down |

**Figure 4.3  Marshall's List of Symptoms.**

LRP to help an organization understand itself and to prepare for the ERP implementation.

## Systems Loop Diagram

A systems loop diagram provides a visualization of the cause and effect of interrelated problems within a manufacturing organization. The steps outlined below for creating the systems loop diagram are based upon the work of Senge and others in the book *The Fifth Discipline Field Book*.[5]

The first step in analyzing an organization as a system is to list all of the individual events that are symptoms of the problem. Figure 4.3 lists a number of symptoms from Marshall.

The second step is to look for actions and reactions that relate the seemingly independent events to each other. For example, when the large orders are received at Marshall, delivery times increase for smaller, more profitable orders. When delivery times get longer, customers cancel existing orders. Once actions and reactions are identified, map them into a chart to view the relationship between the two as shown in Figure 4.4.

The third step, shown in Figure 4.5, is to map the items onto a circular systems loop to which they belong. The loop should indicate the number one problem of the system. In this case it is "Profits are Declining." The loop should then identify the cycle that is directly impacting the number one problem. It is possible to have multiple loops, all contributing to the same problem. In that case, the loops should be shown on either side of the number one problem.

This approach provides a "picture" of the problems within the organization and clearly identifies the interrelationships of the various departments. The management team can then determine which items in the loop need to be broken to stop the unproductive cycle. For this loop, eliminating incentives for larger orders and focusing on eliminating long delivery times would help

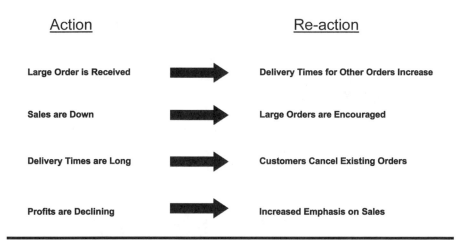

## Action                           Re-action

| Action | | Re-action |
|---|---|---|
| Large Order is Received | → | Delivery Times for Other Orders Increase |
| Sales are Down | → | Large Orders are Encouraged |
| Delivery Times are Long | → | Customers Cancel Existing Orders |
| Profits are Declining | → | Increased Emphasis on Sales |

**Figure 4.4    Identifying Actions and Reactions at Marshall.**

solve the problem. Often, a single answer will not solve a systems problem; it needs to be a multifaceted approach to be truly effective.

## Question the Organization

Another technique available for examining the organization as an integrated system is a series of thought-provoking questions. Answering the questions

**Figure 4.5    Mapping Problem Items at Marshall onto a Circular Systems Loop.**

forces the organization to consider its current and future situation relative to implementing an ERP system.

This technique begins by assembling key managers from the various functional areas within the organization: sales, production, inventory control, accounting, quality, human resources, information technology, and purchasing. The questions are then posed to the group. Each member of the group first answers a question individually and then the group attempts to reach consensus on an answer. Once an answer is determined, the group decides if action should be taken as a result of the insights gained from the discussion of the answer.

Interesting and unintended results can occur from using this technique. At one company, the group of managers gathered to answer the questions realized that this was the first time this group of managers had gotten together to discuss organizational issues in the history of the company. The managers decided, before ever answering the first question, the priority in the company should be to schedule a similar meeting every month to discuss high-level strategic issues. They realized that many organization problems stemmed from the fact that they never met together as a group to discuss the relationships and interactions among and between the various departments.

The following questions should be asked to determine if effective business strategies exist prior to an ERP implementation.[6]

1. **Does the company have too many active projects with constantly shifting priorities?** This symptom can be especially damaging to an organization attempting to implement an ERP system because the ERP system will be the top priority at the beginning of the week and then go begging when a new improvement concept is introduced at the end of the week.

2. **Does the company determine whether to pursue opportunities solely on the basis of anticipated monetary gain or on projected Return on Investment?** ERP systems provide many benefits beyond simple ROI. In fact, many organizations consider the implementation of an ERP system to be a corporate infrastructure issue and not a competitive advantage. As such, many ERP systems are implemented without the traditional ROI analysis being conducted. As an example, an organization cannot be a viable partner in a supply chain without having the ability to share information automatically with both customers and vendors. The information that needs to be shared is the information contained in ERP system.

3. **Does the company allocate resources based on previous budgets and/or statistics?** A company does need to do some resource allocations based on the past. However, a far greater emphasis should be placed on looking toward the future and on investing in projects that move the company into a competitive position, not merely maintenance of an existing advantage. An ERP system can provide that advantage if implemented properly.

4. **Does the company make decisions that move different areas of the company in different directions?** Often organizations without an overarching strategy will have subdivisions within the company fighting for resources. This infighting leads to conflicting signals being sent to employees and sometimes even to customers.

5. **Does the company take a short-term view when it comes to making a business decision; doing everything it can to avert risk?** A risk aversion strategy does not lead to large leaps in innovations or competitive advantage. Good strategies will lead a company into the future without an unduly high risk.

6. **Is the company's vision implicit or unknown?** The strategic goals as well as the learning goals of the company must be known throughout the company. When a goal is openly discussed and targeted, employees work both consciously and unconsciously toward achieving the goal.

7. **Does the company attempt to compete against all competitors in the business?** There are several forms of competitive advantage and competitive strategy. A company must choose one or two of those areas on which to focus. Companies must work on their core competencies and not spend too much time concerned with far-off competitors.

Answering, "yes" to any of the above questions means that the organization needs to develop a working strategy that is effective and articulated throughout the organization. A successful ERP implementation relies on a sound company operating the system. If effective strategies do not exist within the organization, steps must be taken to develop those strategies. The first place to start to develop effective strategies for an ERP implementation is to undertake an analysis of the company's human resources.

## Human Resources Analysis (HRA)

Once the technical issues have been addressed in terms of examining the processes and systems within the organization, a careful analysis should be undertaken of the issues surrounding human resources. In a manufacturing organization, human resources have the potential to be the only appreciating asset an organization has. People are capable of increasing in value through education and careful training. An organization that analyzes its training potential and makes learning an organizational priority will have a distinct and irreproducible competitive advantage.

First analyze the organization with a few key questions. Does anyone in the organization have the word "learning" in his or her job description? Is "learning" in the corporate mission statement? Does every recruiting effort, new hire, succession plan, incentive dollar, and promotion involve recognition and appreciation of learning? Are learning, education, and training a focus of the current improvement or implementations efforts occurring within the company?

In addition to the review of the internal focus on learning, the analysis needs to consist of a review of:

■ *Job descriptions.* A review of job descriptions can help to determine if employee expectations are well defined or vague. Are employees tied lockstep into a position or do they have freedom of movement within the position?

■ *Productivity records.* Is employee productivity trending upwards or downwards? It is important to establish a benchmark to determine how the ERP implementation is going to impact the organization. Benchmark data provide necessary leverage for additional funding if needed, especially when previous funding has resulted in outstanding returns.

■ *Employee interviews.* This level of analysis is usually not effective unless conducted by an outside agent. Typically, employees do not reveal actual feelings, impressions, problems, or beliefs when providing information to a person acting in an "official" capacity. However, this information is good to know in terms of the general attitude toward change within the organization and toward the ERP implementation project. One good research source in this area may be a local university willing to conduct the interviews and report the findings to upper management.

■ *Observation of how people are performing.* Much can be learned simply by observing employees on the job. Are they idle for long periods of time waiting for setups or inventory items. Do they seem to be running all day? Are desks overflowing with paperwork? Are people stepping over each other to accomplish the desired tasks? These types of observations can reveal trouble areas within the organization.

■ *Focus groups.* A focus group is a gathering of several individuals within the organization who are brought together in a group and asked to respond to a group of questions asked by the facilitator. The advantages are that, with many people in the same room, ideas can be exchanged and built upon. One person's idea will typically spark the idea of another and help lead to a new, better idea. One disadvantage is that if one person is particularly negative about the implementation and is vocal, he or she could sway the general consensus of the focus group (this phenomenon is called "group-think"). The group may end up representing an opinion that is not necessarily shared by the entire group.

The information collected from the internal analysis is used to determine who does what, who knows what, who needs to learn, and what constraints and resources affect learning. Because of the concern for potential misuse of this information, this step usually meets with some resistance from the workforce.

A good strategy for helping to prevent mistrust and uncertainty among the production workforce is to appoint one or two senior production members to the committee to reassure production employees of the fact that the analysis process is designed to improve corporate learning. Management must make it clear that internal analysis is not part of an overall scheme to downsize or eliminate less productive workers or areas.

## ERP Software as a System

Just as a manufacturing organization must be understood and analyzed as a system, so too must the ERP software be understood as a system. ERP software is a system of integrated procedures, rules, and algorithms designed to function consistently time and time again. ERP software can only function effectively if the programmed rules are understood and utilized properly within an organization. Because these rules allow for tight integration between modules, employees need to understand how their interactions with the ERP software impact other areas of the organization.

For example, data entered on the shop floor concerning the number of labor hours applied to a work order, or the amount of inert material used in a chemical recipe, can have immediate impact on the General Ledger due to the real-time processing power of many of today's systems.

While this level of data availability is extremely powerful, it can possibly be misleading and dangerous. Information entered on the shop floor can be immediately used to make bad decisions without careful examination of the integrity of the data. Everyone in the organization responsible for implementing the ERP software must understand the rules and algorithms contained within the software.

Many of today's packages include flags and switches allowing a general, all-purpose ERP system to be "customized" to a particular company's unique operations without the underlying code being modified. The philosophy of creating options and switches allows the same ERP package to run successfully in different types of manufacturing environments. This allows for easy updates of the software and minimizes the opportunity for a customer to customize the ERP software so much that it can't be properly updated without even more customization.

ERP software provides a set of tools that allow the support and integration of various manufacturing philosophies under a single piece of application software. One of the main differentiators between ERP software and the previous generation of MRP II software is the inclusion of a variety of manufacturing processes within ERP. Modern software contains the ability to handle both discrete work orders and flow orders, JIT and MRP, EDI, and hand-entered orders. These powerful features are turned on or off by using flags or switches contained in control files.

While this is effective for easy updates, it means that few people (including customers and even software vendors) are able to understand the ramifications of every possible combination of flags in the various control files. When users encounter "strange" or unexpected results from the software, they should examine the various control files to see if their particular combination of flags is causing the unexpected results or if any of the flags have been changed recently.

For example, at one multinational organization, this lack of control file understanding resulted in many inadvertent errors with rippling effects that went unchecked for a substantial period of time. The large number of data errors resulted in serious business problems. Ultimately, the entire ERP implementation was placed on hold and implementation support personal were fired. These scenarios can be avoided when the system algorithms and formulas are understood.

ERP software functions effectively because of the well-studied and proven algorithms and formulas included in the software, but employees who use the system daily are the key to its success. If the people do not understand the scrap calculation the system performs, or the MRP logic behind the generation of a purchase order, or the automated appearance of a lot size of 100 when only 1 unit is needed, then the system will not be trusted or utilized properly by the workforce. People working on the ERP system must understand how the integrated ERP system functions and how data entered on the shop floor impacts many areas including financial reports printed from the General Ledger.

This level of understanding can be gained through education and training of the employees. It can be aided through the display of system flow diagrams. Many systems have detailed diagrams that can be posted on the walls of a conference room and referred to when necessary. These diagrams typically show the interdependencies of the various modules. Visually depicting the relationships between modules reinforces the concept that the ERP software is an integrated system that is more than the simple sum of its parts.

Implementers who understand that they have control over functionality of the software are more comfortable working with it and are willing to experiment in setting up control files because they know they are not permanent. During the analysis phase of LRP, do not forget to spend time analyzing and documenting the functionality and setup of the ERP control files and system flags.

# Benchmarking[7]

The futurist Daniel Burrus stated at the 1996 APICS Conference that no consumer ever asked for a self-cleaning oven, Why? Do people like to clean ovens? No. It's because they didn't know it was possible.[8] Organizations can't expect employees to remain competitive, cut costs, and improve productivity if the employees don't know what's possible. The reason benchmarking is so important is because it provides organizations and people with a "taste" of what is possible. When developing strategic goals, learning goals, and process improvement goals, organizations need to be exposed to what is possible prior to developing a future direction.

If an organization only examines its own opportunities for improvement, it may not be able to visualize a strategic goal or advantage because it is viewing the world from its own limited perspective. Organizations focusing only on themselves cannot grow and mature into market leaders even if they do implement an ERP system.

Benchmarking is a systematic process of comparing a company's products, services, costs, processes, and procedures against those of competitors. Benchmarking can also involve comparing an organization's processes to those considered best-in-class regardless of industry.

For example, if Marshall Manufacturing wanted to focus on reducing its delivery times, it could benchmark against Federal Express's overnight delivery process. Marshall could determine what practices, policies, procedures, and processes Federal Express used to guarantee the overnight delivery of a package. While Marshall may never achieve overnight delivery of its products, it might gain enough insight and ideas to streamline its existing processes and reduce its current elongated delivery time frame.

In terms of benchmarking for the ERP implementation, organizations can study how some companies have successfully implemented an ERP system in nine months or how an ERP system has helped an organization save thousands of dollars in late shipment penalties.

Benchmarking can also be undertaken to determine what strategic direction an organization should take to become competitive in the marketplace. A firm looking to become more innovative could borrow 3M's idea of "Genesis Grants" which support internal entrepreneurship and the testing of new ideas through the awarding of up to $50,000 per project.[9] These grants foster innovation and provide seed money for the development of working prototypes.

Typically, two types of benchmarking are utilized by manufacturing organizations. The first is performance or competitive benchmarking and the other is process benchmarking. Each of these practices has an application during the analysis phase of LRP. An organization that knows what its competitors are doing and knows what processes constitute best-in-class in terms of delivery, cost, quality, and customer service can achieve a competitive advantage that is hard to beat.

## Performance Benchmarking

Performance benchmarking involves tracking and monitoring measurable product characteristics. For example, Marshall may keep track of its top competitor's best selling brand. Marshall would track the product's cost, durability, reliability, number of defects, product life and the fit and finish of the product.

Performance benchmarking may also involve performance under some very specific circumstances, such as, "Our chairs can withstand a 500 lb weight being dropped on them from a height of 6 ft." These data are readily available for most products. Two excellent sources for consumer related products are J.D. Power and Associates reports and the reports published by *Consumer Reports*. Many companies purchase a competitor's product and test or "reverse engineer" it. Sometimes, companies in regulated industries are required to publish data on the performance of their products

Performance benchmarking is helpful in telling an organization what product or service standards need to be met. For instance, the cancelled orders at Marshall are an indication that the delivery time frame of 8 to 12 weeks is not acceptable by their customers. The cancellation also signals the availability of a competitive product and an alternate supplier: both might be benchmarking targets.

While knowing performance standards within the industry is critical, simply knowing the standards does not help in understanding how to achieve those standards or in determining what strategic direction the company should take to beat competitors. Learning the process, procedures, and practices used by a company to achieve best-in-industry or best-in-class results is called process benchmarking.

## Process Benchmarking

Process benchmarking goes outside of an industry to look at true best practices. For example, Merck may be viewed as a company that has best practices in the area of Research and Development. Amazon.com may be studied to learn about best practices in the area of corporate branding. The goal of process benchmarking is to look at processes unrelated to the company's specific industry, but that represent the best possible processes and achieve the highest possible results.

For example, a small furniture manufacturing company wanted to improve its customer service. Their competition was a large, multinational company with call centers all over the world. This small company could not duplicate its competitor's setup but it studied a major catalog company that provides superior customer service via its vast network of call centers. The small furniture company discovered that this other company was able to maintain a high level of customer service by recruiting retired individuals to help out during peak seasons and high absentee periods.

The company trained these individuals and equipped them with phone lines and home computers so they could be "patched in" quickly. The result was that customers were always able to reach a customer service representative. The furniture company benchmarked this process and successfully implemented it. Their customers were then given the same level of customer service as the catalog company's customers, without much added expense to the company.

When benchmarking ERP implementation success, it is important to measure overall implementation time, rate of acceptance of the new system by employees, amount of interruption to the organization's customers or

| Publications | Agencies | Personnel | Web Information |
|---|---|---|---|
| Annual Report | Local Chamber of Commerce | Employees | Corporate Web Site |
| Magazine Articles | Government Statistics | Vendor Representatives | Industry Web Site |
| Product Sheets | Professional Organizations | Customers | Results from Search Engines |

**Figure 4.6   Benchmarking Sources.**

vendors, amount of ROI anticipated vs. actually achieved, and other measurements the organization wishes to track.

When benchmarking strategic direction or strategy it is important to determine how long a strategy has been in place, how successful the strategy was initially, how receptive customers and vendors were to the strategy, the amount of time it took for a tangible return to be generated from the strategy, and other information that may be specific to the strategy the organization is benchmarking against.

Both performance and process benchmarking data can come from a variety of sources. A few of the sources are listed in Figure 4.6.

Benchmarking enables an organization to understand what is possible. This is especially critical when implementing an ERP system in an environment in which the employees never had experience with ERP or MRP systems. Benchmarking allows an organization to see what other companies are doing and to reach its goals. Once an organization understands where it stands in terms of performance among industry or world leaders in ERP potential or success, it can set enterprise goals.

## Establishing Strategic Goals

The first step toward establishing strategic goals is to develop a vision for the company. According to the authors *of Built To Last*, a landmark publication outlining the successful traits of visionary companies based on a six-year research project, a corporate vision consists of two parts.[10] The first is a core ideology and the second is an envisioned future. Peter Senge calls the envisioned future a "shared vision." A good vision encompasses the belief in certain principles that are unbending within the organization as well as the ability of the organization to pursue a variety of activities as long as they are anchored to those unbending principles. An example would be 3M. 3M has a core ideology of constant innovation, yet has a vision that allows it to pursue product development in a variety of industries.

A vision of a company is not developed as much as it is discovered. The discovery process must involve upper management in a discussion of what drives the organization. For example, the vision of a hospital may be to provide high-quality medical services. The vision of a furniture manufacturer may be to provide innovatively designed pieces of art or it may be to provide functional, practical everyday furnishings.

For an organization to move toward a successful ERP implementation with LRP, top management must provide direction, leadership, and vision. The intent is to create a reason for people to change their attitudes. This is especially important where there is no visible crisis compelling an organization's employees to move in this new direction. Top management must adopt a vision of what the company is and will become. Everyone in the organization at all levels should understand this vision. It is more important to communicate the vision often than it is to ensure the quality or degree of refinement of the vision. Development of the vision is a two-way street. Once the process is started, input can come from anywhere within the organization.

One way to start developing a vision for the company is to form a vision team to brainstorm ideas. As the vision team considers possible directions, it can use a tool called a "visonweb." Creating a visionweb begins by recording, in the center of a chalkboard, flipchart, or piece of paper, a central point or idea that represents the ultimate vision and then drawing lines that extend from the center. Each line contains an area of focus for the company in the future. From each line, other lines can be drawn to show extensions of thought on various ideas. In addition, dotted lines can be drawn to illustrate the interrelatedness of various items to each other. The visionweb provides a visual representation of all the items contributing to the corporate vision. The visionweb can then be transformed into a written vision statement. Figure 4.7 illustrates the general format of a visionweb.

The best way to articulate the vision of the company is to develop a carefully worded mission statement. A mission statement is a company's statement of purpose. It declares to all stakeholders the vision and mission of the company. A mission statement should answer the questions: "Who are we and what is our reason for being?"

A well thought out mission statement is important because it controls the scope of the business of the firm. A mission statement that is too specific can be confining. For example, if a furniture company were to pick for its mission statement, "We are in the chair manufacturing business," it would

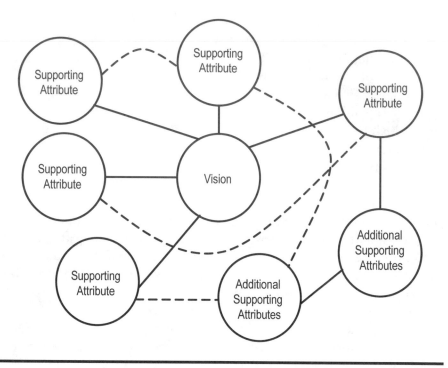

**Figure 4.7 Visionweb. Illustration of a template for a visionweb used for determining an organization's future vision and mission.**

limit its business to just making chairs. A broader statement such as, "We are in the office furniture business," would allow the inclusion of all sorts of other products (e.g., lamps, desks).

On the other hand, a mission statement that is too broad tends to lose its focus on the main business of the company. For example, a mission statement such as, "We are in the consumer products business" would allow entry into everything from furniture to clothes to action figures to cars and might divert the company's attention from its primary goal or business, where it can best leverage its resources to gain a strategic advantage.

A mission statement should have the following characteristics:[11]

■ Not too broad
■ Not too narrow
■ Fewer than 100 words
■ Able to convey a feeling of pride in the company
■ Provide a learning-focused approach to the organization

A possible mission statement for Marshall Manufacturing might be as follows:

*Marshall Manufacturing is dedicated to creating efficient, effective, high-quality metal products to the consumer and OEM industries.*

*Our experienced and professional staff provides each customer with personal attention because our staff is highly trained and always learning the latest in manufacturing and customer service techniques.*

*We strive to be a strong member company in our industry, our region, and our community through a high work ethic and an empowered workforce.*

Once a mission is established, the organization develops one or two strategic goals upon which to focus. The goals should revolve around the organization's strengths and enable it to counter competitors. Typically, in any market niche, an organization has several main dimensions on which it can compete: quality, cost, flexibility, image, and delivery time. A company cannot be the best in all these dimensions at the same time.

At this point, the organization determines at what level, and in what markets, it wants to compete. One method of identifying and deciding what markets to enter and how, is to conduct a SWOT analysis. SWOT stands for Strengths, Weaknesses, Opportunities, and Threats. The SWOT analysis begins with the drawing of a square divided into four sections. In each section of the square are spaces for writing down each of the four elements of the SWOT analysis, as shown in Figure 4.8.

Internal strengths are the areas in which the organization excels. It could be a superior customer service ethic, innovative products, special patents, talents, or knowledge. These are the areas of the organization that provide a competitive advantage against other organizations. For example, the strength of Merck Pharmaceuticals is its research and development efforts. Merck spends tremendous amounts of money each year to ensure that it provides

| Internal Strengths | Internal Weaknesses |
|---|---|
| 1. | 1. |
| 2. | 2. |
| 3. | 3. |
| 4. | 4. |
| 5 | 5. |
| **External Opportunities** | **External Threats** |
| 1. | 1. |
| 2. | 2. |
| 3. | 3. |
| 4. | 4. |
| 5. | 5. |

**Figure 4.8   SWOT Analysis Chart.**

the most state of the art pharmaceuticals in the world. This effort allows Merck to stay at the forefront of new medicines.

Weaknesses are areas in which the company may not be performing as well as it could or where a competitor has an advantage. Perhaps delivery of product is weak or competitors are introducing product variations more quickly. Weaknesses may not always need to be addressed. For example, a weakness of the Ferrari car line is that the overall number of eligible buyers for ultrahigh-performance cars is not as large as that for mid-priced cars. However, since Ferrari has configured their business toward low-volume production with relatively high profit margins, this is not a weakness after all. For a start-up competitor in that market, the small size of the market will be a weakness to consider. A typical weakness of large organizations is that they are not as responsive to customer needs as smaller, more entrepreneurially focused companies.

Opportunities are areas of the business that the company can find a new competitive advantage in a particular industry. For example, in the mid and early 1990s the World Wide Web was an untapped market for selling books. However, that opportunity is not as large at this writing due to the on-line presence of Barnes & Noble (www.bn.com) and Amazon.com. Finding an untapped market need can be accomplished by asking customers what they desire to have as features of a particular product, looking to markets with similar customers, developing strategic relationships with other companies, and designing unique and new product applications.

Threats are any competitor, government agency, economic, or social situation that negatively impacts an organization's likelihood of success. An example from the 1980s would be the government's decision to deregulate the airline industry. This decision dramatically impacted the profitability of many airlines. Microsoft encountered a similar governmental threat with a court ruling regarding its market protection practices in the late 1990s and early 2000s.

Threats should be ranked from most likely to least likely. They should also be classified as most damaging to least damaging. The most damaging, most likely threats should be countered either by taking action to eliminate the threat or by developing effective contingency plans.

The information from the SWOT analysis is used to help develop the strategic goals of the organization in terms of the ERP implementation. The strategic goals must be set for both the organization and the ERP implementation.

A possible mission statement for the ERP implementation at Marshall might be as follows:

*Successfully implement the ERP package into Marshall Manufacturing within a 12-month time frame with little overtime, undue delays, or disruption to our customers or vendors. The task will be accomplished effectively and used as an opportunity to learn about our company, its processes, and ourselves.*

## Developing Strategic Learning Goals

A strategic learning goal is a high-level objective that states the types of learning that must occur within the organization for it to successfully compete within its chosen industry. Strategic learning goals are necessary to help an organization effectively implement an ERP system because they provide the anchors and the system keystones upon which other systems and subsystems are built.

An ERP system should be implemented to address specific business needs. The adult learners within the organization need to be aware of the vast areas of improvement that can be achieved from ERP implementations.

The establishment of goals (both business and learning) prior to implementing an ERP system is of extreme importance. In too many cases, an ERP system is purchased to achieve vague and somewhat idealistic goals that cannot be accurately measured. An example of this type of goal is "reduce inventory." What exactly does that phrase mean? Reduce what inventory? Purchased parts? Work-in-process? Finished goods? All inventory? At what point in time are you measuring the level of inventory?

After identifying what inventory to reduce, by how much will it be reduced? Why? What is the anticipated ROI? Is it possible to reduce inventory without the expense of the ERP system? If so, by how much? And how much more can you reduce inventory with the ERP system in place? Measurable goals must be established that represents the needs of the entire organization.

To develop a strategic learning goal, companies must determine how they are currently competing within their industries and how they would like to compete in the future. The competitive options include price, quality, innovation, delivery, and/or reputation. The choices relevant to this decision should be easily identified from the "strengths" portion of the SWOT analysis. For example, some companies like Wal-Mart and Amazon.com compete on price while others like 3M and CISCO SYSTEMS compete on innovation. Of course, highly successful companies compete using a blend of strategies. Lucent Technologies for example, has a reputation for high-quality, innovative products.

Learning goals are statements about what an organization needs to learn to be competitive in the existing and future marketplace. For example, one manufacturing company determined that innovation was a necessary competency in their particular high-tech market. Therefore, it developed the goal of fostering out-of-the-box thinking. For another company, fast delivery was a competitive issue. The company developed a learning goal of understanding the concept of just-in-time delivery based on the corporate strategic goal of on-time customer delivery.[12]

These learning goals clearly support the strategic goals and directions of the company. A similar process can be used when determining the strategic and subsequent learning goals that support an ERP implementation.

## Analysis of Key Processes

Once strategic goals are established and learning goals developed, the next step of analysis is to examine existing processes within the organization to see if they are congruent with the strategic and learning goals. There are a number of methods for examining processes within an organization. Each of the methods can be used individually, but are far more effective when used in combination.

### Process Diagramming

A technique used to analyze a manufacturing process is called simply "Process Diagramming." Process diagramming is an excellent tool for understanding internal processes. The first step is to determine what symbols to use for representing the different parts of the process. A common set of symbols may include a square to represent an operation such as entering a customer order into the ERP system, a diamond may represent a decision, a triangle may represent filing or storing an item or information, a five-sided symbol could be used to represent wait or queue time, and finally, an arrow can represent move time. More symbols could be used for specialized areas within a process. However, it is best to keep the number at a minimum to avoid diagrams that are too confusing and hard to read. A sample set of symbols is shown in Figure 4.9.

Once a set of symbols has been chosen, the action is to gather all employees who have a role in the process into the same room. Then, have them each draw their understanding of the process using the predetermined symbols. When finished, ask the employees to compare and contrast their separate drawings of the same process. This will typically yield fascinating, and sometimes frightening, results.

| Symbol | ■ | ▲ | ◆ | ⬡ | ➡ |
|---|---|---|---|---|---|
| Represents | Task | File or Store | Decision | Wait Time | Move Time |
| Production Example | Cut Metal | Place cut metal in bin. | Does cut metal pass inspection? | Cut metal sits in front of workcell. | Move cut metal from inspection to workcell. |
| Office Example | Complete required form | Place form in drawer | Are signatures required? | Form sits on desk | Form taken to accounting for review |

**Figure 4.9   Sample Set of Process Diagramming Symbols.**

Next, ask the group to reach consensus on the actual process. This may take some time. When the group reaches consensus, have that process diagrammed and posted in an area as close to the actual process as possible. During the comparison stage, take notes on the areas of difference among process participants. These differences are usually areas in which trouble occurs during the ERP implementation. These differences need to be addressed prior to the ERP system being implemented.

Once the group agrees upon the process diagram, label each step using the following codes:[13]

- V — This step adds value to the process and must be kept.
- R — This is a rework step and needs to be eliminated.
- U — This is an unnecessary move or wait step.
- P — This step is important but problematic.

These codes will help the group determine the true value-added steps and separate those steps from steps that do not add any value. The goal is to simplify the entire process so only the value-added steps remain, eliminating nonvalue-added steps and problems. Simplified processes make the ERP system implementation smoother since they are easier to teach and perform

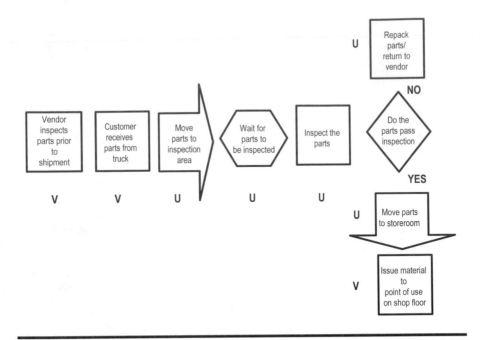

**Figure 4.10  Diagram of an Inefficient Process at Marshall Manufacturing.**

consistently. ERP software companies tend to have developed simple but effective methods of handling the processes that are common to most companies in their target markets.

Figures 4.10 and 4.11 illustrate a process before and after it went through analysis by the ERP implementation team at Marshall. The team first diagrammed the process, then labeled each step in the process, and finally eliminated steps in the process that did not add value to Marshall's customers.

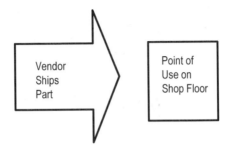

**Figure 4.11  Diagram of the New Streamlined Marshall Process after the Nonvalue-Added Steps Have Been Removed.**

## Walk the Process

A second powerful process analysis technique is to simply "walk the process." For example, a work order is walked from order entry then from operation to operation until the item is completely manufactured, shipped, and paid for. Carrying a customer order, work order, or purchase order through the entire organization from start to finish provides many unique insights into organizational processes. While walking the process, it is important to look for unnecessary wait, move, or queue time. In addition, identify any search and retrieval tasks, extra handling of material, extremely long delays, reentry of data from one system to another, and other nonvalue-added work.

While walking the process, ask the following questions of each and every step within the process:[14]

- What are the value-added steps?
- What is the purpose?
- Who are the internal and external customers?
- What value is added during the process?
- What is the ideal desired output?
- Is the ideal ever obtained? How, or why not?

This technique is simple, easy to use, and highly effective. It is not unusual to encounter many opportunities for improvement while actively walking through a particular process. The advantage of this technique is that the team or individual walking the process has an opportunity to engage the participants in the process while they are actively involved in the process. Often, observers see actions that employees are not even consciously aware they are performing since they are caught up in their activities. The combination of Process Diagramming and Walk the Process is referred to as "Value Stream Analysis" by proponents of the Lean Manufacturing movement.

## Fishbone Analysis

Often, problems can be easily identified in a process but the root causes of the problems can be very difficult to determine. One effective method for looking at all of the possible causes of a particular problem is to use the fishbone diagram technique. This technique starts with a particular problem and divides all the possible causes of the problem into four major categories. Under each category, specific items that may be the root cause of the problem

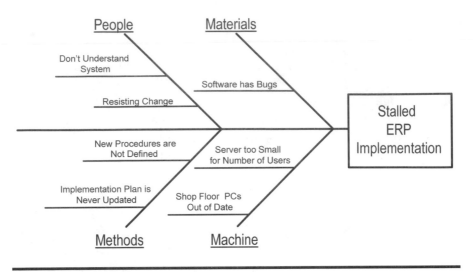

**Figure 4.12   Fishbone Diagram for Identifying the Causes of a Stalled ERP Implementation.**

are identified. The technique is called a fishbone diagram because the completed diagram resembles a fish skeleton.

Five types of causes are relevant in most situations — people, materials, machines, methods, and measures. Fishboning is a technique to promote brainstorming of process inputs, then classifying those inputs by category. The purpose of each major category is to help focus the team on the possible root causes of a problem. The fishbone diagram does not need to be limited to five major categories.

The fishbone diagram technique is a good when the root cause of a problem is not easily identified. It is also effective when a team has attempted to solve a particular problem with little success. Often fishboning a problem will reveal several additional possible causes of a problem. The group may want to attempt to solve the problem by remedying several of the causes listed on the diagram. When analyzing processes for an ERP implementation, do not forget such categories as administrative procedures or processes, reward structures, peer influence, processing rules, working environment, and other potential causes of problems. Figure 4.12 illustrates the use of a fishbone diagram to determine the reasons for a stalled ERP implementation.

## Velocity Analysis

Another key area to examine within an organization is the velocity of a product from order entry to the plant floor to final arrival at a customer site. Velocity is the total elapsed time consumed by a process divided by the actual value-added time contributed by the same process. Value-added is the actual increase in worth of raw material as it is transformed into a finished product. Only work done that increases the value of the material can be considered value-added. Work like inspection or movement of material is nonvalue-added.

Velocity of a process would be determined as follows. If the lead time or typical total elapsed time for an assembly process, including all paperwork, material movement, and inspection, is 5 days at 8 hours a day, and the actual value-added time is 4 hours, the velocity is 40/4, which is 10. For most industries, world-class velocity is less than 2.[15] The velocity number should be posted on the bottom of the diagrammed process and revised as the velocity of the process improves during the implementation. The "before" and "after" velocity number can then be used as benchmarks.

## Summary of the Analysis of Key Processes

A careful analysis of the key processes within the organization provides a firm knowledge base for the Diagnosis and Design stages of the LRP process. The techniques mentioned in this section will allow an ERP implementation team to examine its organization and to make informed, accurate decisions regarding areas of strength and weakness. Once identified, the areas of strength can be leveraged for further competitive advantage and the areas of weakness can be addressed.

# Bills of Learning

Once the analysis has resulted in the development of learning goals and the processes of the organization have been examined, learning goals are exploded into Bills of Learning (BOL). Basically, a BOL is a breakdown of corporate strategic objectives into discrete, measurable learning objectives for specific skill sets. The explosion process ensures that the education initiatives within a company are tied directly to the strategic direction of the company. The explosion process breaks corporate goals into divisional learning goals, then into departmental learning goals, then into individual learning goals. The explosion process is like a Work Break-Down analysis done in the field of project management, but it is done at the organization level. From an instructional design standpoint, it is like a hierarchal task analysis. An example of this process and its result is shown in Figure 4.13.

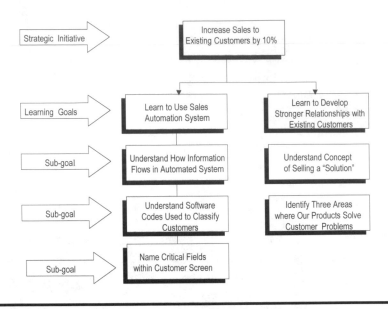

**Figure 4.13 Bill of Learning.**

A BOL is a hierarchy of enabling learning objectives required by an organization to support a strategic goal. The lowest level of the hierarchy contains learning objectives that support the objectives on the next level which, in turn, support the objectives on the next higher level of the hierarchy. This logic continues until the hierarchy terminates at the strategic organizational goal.

The BOL concept is similar to a Bill of Material (BOM) in a manufacturing environment, or recipe in a processing company. In manufacturing organizations, the BOM lists all of the required material necessary to manufacture a particular item. For example, a BOM for a bicycle would include, at the top level, the finished bicycle. The next level down may contain the frame, two wheel assemblies, and handlebars. The next level down for the wheel assemblies would include spokes, a hub, a rim, a tire, and an inner tube. Other legs of the BOM define all the other parts of the bicycle.

The Bill of Learning (BOL) provides a visual representation of what is required to reach the strategic goals of the organization. The BOL also indicates which objectives can be obtained internally and which can be acquired externally. The BOL is one of the first elements needed to implement LRP. Develop a BOL for each strategic objective listed by the organization. The BOL helps to ensure that learning initiatives within the organization are obtained because the learning needs are clearly stated. The BOL provides visibility of learning objectives because of the organization of the objectives into a logical hierarchy.

The BOL concept allows for a "drill down" capability. This means that, with the proper software, a user can click on the upper-level strategic objective and see all of the enabling objectives supporting the upper-level strategic objective. In addition, a "drill up" (pegging) capability allows the user to search from a basic enabling objective and move through the hierarchy, level by level, until the final learning objective and ultimately the strategic objective is identified.

## Practicality of Analysis

Although it seems impractical to spend time conducting an analysis of a moving target like an ever-evolving organization, many of the tactics explained in this chapter can be achieved with relatively little time commitment and the results are long-ranging and dramatic for organizations that take the time to learn about themselves. Of course, the best time to conduct a detailed LRP analysis of the organization is prior to the purchase and implementation of an ERP system. If the analysis was not conducted prior to the installation of the ERP software, problems can arise. However, it is possible to undertake the analysis process when an implementation is failing.

The following is an actual case study of conducting an analysis after the ERP system was installed.

### Case Study: Conducting an LRP Analysis When Implementation is Failing

A Japanese-owned drivetrain manufacturing plant had purchased an ERP system from a small ERP software vendor and had tried unsuccessfully for six months to integrate the software into the daily operations of the plant.

The plant was a model of manufacturing efficiency and state of the art manufacturing equipment. The raw metal was cut, pressed, stamped, shaped, molded, heat-treated, and assembled all under one roof. The floor was so clean you could eat from it.

The implementation was in trouble from the start. First of all, no analysis was undertaken of the organization's needs, and secondly the organization had no clear strategic or learning goals. Due to the urgency of the matter, the LRP analysis was conducted within a two-day period through a series of interviews with all of the key managers. The third day was used to convey the findings to the management team.

The interviews were conducted one-on-one with the researcher and the individual managers. Since the implementation was going poorly, it was felt that the managers would be more open with a researcher in a one-on-one. All answers were kept confidential and names were not used in any report to the executive team at the plant.

The purpose of the one-on-one interviews was to determine the root cause or causes of the implementation delays and apparent failure. The interviewer primarily used a list of pre-established questions to determine the current state of the company, the depth of understanding of the ERP system that was purchased, and the level of commitment of the organization to the system.

The questions focused on the velocity of manufacturing, which was quite high, the number of inventory turns, the adherence to procedures, the level of communication between the various divisions, and the informal systems that had developed to make sure production goals were met.

The implementation was examined in terms of a SWOT Analysis. The strengths of the ERP system and its weaknesses were cataloged, as well as threats to the usefulness of the system and opportunities that would be developed because of the system.

An interesting finding was that the project leader from accounting was still running her books using the old PC-based accounting package and not the new ERP system. This meant that she was attempting to manage two separate accounting systems. The old system was actually identified as a threat to the new system since she did not want to switch to the new system because she didn't "trust" the data entered by the manufacturing and receiving departments.

Her fears were not unfounded. A weakness identified during this process was that the receiving department was one to two days late in entering receipts into the ERP system. This was because no input terminal was available on the receiving dock. The receiving clerk and his helper spent the majority of their time on the dock and not in the receiving office. Therefore, the receipts were entered intermittently whenever one of the receiving personnel had time.

The analysis also revealed that the project leader was not well respected. This was not because of the job she was doing or her level of competence, which was quite high. It was because she was in a position of power in a southern state of the U.S. working for a Japanese organization. At that time, in the late 1980s, neither the southern state nor the Japanese culture supported women in roles of leadership.

The final level of difficulty encountered during the implementation was the language barrier. The president of the U.S. company spoke little English, as was the case with many of the upper-level Japanese managers. The American employees spoke little Japanese. Effective communication was difficult for the entire implementation team.

The LRP analysis resulted in a number of recommended solutions. The first was to reassign the project manager to the lead accounting position and appoint a dual Japanese/American project management team. The second recommendation was to eliminate the dual bookkeeping in accounting. The third was to establish specific, measurable strategic goals for the organization. The fourth was to place a terminal on the receiving dock. The final recommendation was to develop learning goals targeted to support the strategic goals.

The recommendations were taken, and within 12 months the plant had successfully implemented 90% of the software and was well on its way to implementing the rest.

### Lessons Learned

One of the most critical lessons learned from the above case study is that it is never too late to conduct a LRP analysis of the organization during an ERP implementation. Although it is best if it is applied early, the LRP process can be utilized at any stage of an organization's ERP process.

Another lesson is that the results of an analysis are not always pretty. It is important to understand that analysis results may lead to issues and problems that upper management or other employees do not want to hear. The analysis team must be willing to confront problems as they arise and be willing to stand firm when the data indicate the need for unpopular actions.

## Summary

A critical step in conducting the LRP analysis and developing the subsequent BOLs is to tie the analysis information together and then to link the results of the analysis to strategic goals for the creation of learning goals. If learning goals are developed, based upon careful analysis of the organization and from the learning process undertaken by the organization, then the learning goals will be effective in helping the organization to achieve implementation success.

## LRP Analysis Checklist

| Analysis Task | Completed Yes | No | Date |
|---|---|---|---|
| **General Tasks** | | | |
| 1. Explained the need for careful analysis of the organization to top managers. | ___ | ___ | ___ |
| 2. Conveyed importance of the analysis step to all employees. | ___ | ___ | ___ |
| **Systems Thinking** | | | |
| 3. Taught concept of Systems Thinking to management. | ___ | ___ | ___ |
| 4. Developed a systems loop to address problems within the manufacturing organization. | ___ | ___ | ___ |
| 5. Examined the organization as an integrated system through a series of thought-provoking questions. | ___ | ___ | ___ |
| 6. Conducted a Human Resources Analysis. | ___ | ___ | ___ |
| 7. Conveyed the concept, through effective education, to managers and employees that ERP software is a system and should be treated as such. | ___ | ___ | ___ |
| **Benchmarking** | | | |
| 8. Conducted performance benchmarking. | ___ | ___ | ___ |
| 9. Conducted process benchmarking. | ___ | ___ | ___ |
| 10. Developed strategic goals for the organization. | ___ | ___ | ___ |
| 11. Developed strategic goals for the ERP implementation. | ___ | ___ | ___ |
| 12. Conducted a SWOT analysis. | ___ | ___ | ___ |
| 13. Developed strategic learning goals based on the strategic goals of the organization. | ___ | ___ | ___ |
| **Analysis of Key Processes** | | | |
| 14. Chose symbols for process diagramming | ___ | ___ | ___ |
| 15. Diagrammed key processes. | ___ | ___ | ___ |
| 16. Reach consensus on desired process. | ___ | ___ | ___ |
| 17. Walked key processes. | ___ | ___ | ___ |
| 18. Used Fishbone analysis for difficult-to-solve problems or difficult-to-understand process problems. | ___ | ___ | ___ |
| **Bills of Learning** | | | |
| 19. Created a Bill of Learning for key learning objectives. | ___ | ___ | ___ |
| 20. Compared learning objectives across the various bills of learning. | ___ | ___ | ___ |

# References

1. Kupier, D., Taking the mystery out of software selection, in *APICS 1998 Int. Conf. Proc.*, APICS, Falls Church, VA, 1998, p. 205.
2. Carvenale, A. P. Learning: The Critical Technology, *Training Dev.*, 46(2), 2, 1992.
3. Apologies to Sir Isaac Newton.
4. Senge, P. M., *The Fifth Discipline*, Currency Doubleday, New York, 1990, chap. 8.
5. Senge, P. M. et al., *The Fifth Discipline Field Book*, Doubleday, New York, 1994, chap. 13.
6. Weiss, M. S., Does your company have a business strategy, in *APICS 1995 Int. Conf. Proc.*, APICS, Falls Church, VA, 1995, p. 219.
7. Kapp, K. M., *Just-In-Time Certification Review Course: Instructor Guide*, Rev. 2, APICS, Alexandria, VA, 1998, pp. 2-22 to 2-25.
8. Kapp, K. M., Transforming your manufacturing organization into a learning organization, in *APICS 1997 Int. Conf. Proc.*, APICS, Falls Church, VA, 1997, p. 288.
9. Masters of Innovation, *Business Week*, 10 April, 1989, p. 58.
10. Collins, J. C. and Porras, J. L., *Built to Last*, HarperBusiness, New York, 1994, chap. 11.
11. Kapp, K. M., *Just-In-Time Certification Review Course: Instructor Guide*, Rev. 2, APICS, Alexandria, VA, 1998, pp. 8–13.
12. Kapp, K, M., Moving training to the strategic level with learning requirements planning, *Natl. Productivity Rev.*, 18(2), 15, 1999.
13. Kapp, K. M., The USA principle — implementing ERP on time and under budget, in *APICS 1999 Int. Conf. Proc.*, APICS, Alexandria, VA, 1999, p. 456.
14. Kapp, K. M., The USA principle: the key to ERP implementation success, *APICS~The Performance Advantage*, 7(6), 62, 1997.
15. Langenwalter, G. A., *Enterprise Resource Planning and Beyond: Integrating Your Entire Organization*, CRC Press, Boca Raton, FL, 2000, p. 46.

# 5  Diagnosis

## Introduction

Each year thousands upon thousands of training dollars are wasted by organizations on misguided training on the wrong topics at the wrong time delivered to the wrong people. Many ERP training programs consist of nothing more than a list of courses provided by the vendor. Employees attend the classes because management told them to "be there." Such programs are a waste of time, money, and effort, undermining the ERP implementation.

Organizations cannot blindly apply training without first determining what type of training is needed and how employees can learn from the training. Organizations spend thousands of dollars to have an ergonomically correct chair fitted to a person but will fail to spend any money on diagnostics to determine how that person learns best. Within any organization, employees have various levels of interest and knowledge concerning their jobs. Some employees are enthusiastic about coming to work. Others are tolerant of the work environment. Some employees are eager to learn new information while others seem to be motivated only by the impending end of the shift.

Every organization has unique educational needs that are not addressed with traditional implementation techniques. Prior to the full-scale implementation of an ERP system, the organization needs to take some time to diagnose the learning needs of the employees and of the organization. Figure 5.1 illustrates the location of Diagnosis within the LRP process.

Not all employees learn at the same rate or using the same techniques. For example, Robert in sales learns best by interacting with others and listening to what they have to say about a topic. In the production department, Helen learns by watching someone else do the job first and then she tries. In

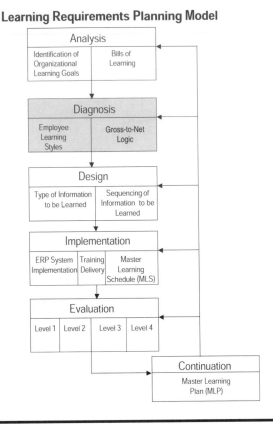

**Figure 5.1    LRP with Diagnosis Highlighted. Diagnosis Is the Second Step in the LRP Process.**

engineering, Fred methodically reads every manual and researches in detail a topic on the Internet before he really learns the information. A different approach must be taken toward educating each of these individuals about the ERP system because they each have a different learning style. Unfortunately, many traditional implementation and training plans include the one-size-fits-all approach to training. This approach is not effective and completely ignores the natural differences in learning preferences among individuals.

In addition to understanding individual learning styles, learning goals of the organization must be compared to the present level of knowledge and competencies of its people. The gap between what employees already know and what they need to know must be identified so training can be delivered effectively.

Finally, the organization must look at and determine the needs of individual employees and make sure that their basic and advanced needs are addressed. If employees are struggling with basic physiological and psychological needs, it becomes difficult for them to concentrate on the ERP implementation.

The Diagnosis step of LRP, as highlighted in Figure 5.1, serves a key role in the implementation process. Diagnosis utilizes the information developed during the Analysis step to determine the best method of reaching the learning and strategic goals of the implementation. This is of critical importance.

Often organizations set strategic goals but fail to turn the goals into actions. This can lead to implementation failures and disappointments. LRP prevents that from happening because each step of the model moves to action. As an organization utilizes the LRP model, it will gain momentum toward implementation success. The output of one element of the model feeds the other, systematically allowing the organization to build one success upon another.

Diagnosis defines what it will take for employees to learn the material related to the ERP system and what types of training should be conducted to provide the most benefit to the organization and individual employees. Once those two items are determined through the Diagnosis step, the information is fed into the Design step. The design step establishes the types of training to be created and the sequence in which the information should be presented to the learners.

Diagnosis serves as the catalyst for future training development. It ties the high-end analysis of strategic and learning goals to the actual needs of the individual employees. This level of connectedness ensures that top management goals are translated into actions that can be accomplished by frontline employees without undue levels of difficulty.

## Overview

The first step in the Diagnosis step of the LRP model is to determine what training is actually needed. This is accomplished by comparing existing skills of employees with skills that will be required in the future. Most organizations do not conduct this type of diagnosis because they have difficulty knowing what skills they will need in the future. The LRP process identifies needed skills through the establishment of Learning Objectives during the Analysis phase of LRP.

Once the future skill needs are determined, the Diagnosis step consists of reviewing existing skills within the organization and determining the level of those skills. This can be accomplished using a variety of methods.

Once the existing and future skills are examined, a simple comparison of the needed and required skills is conducted. This gap analysis highlights the greatest areas of need within the organization in terms of ERP education. This targeted approach prevents unnecessary training classes and allows the limited training time available for the ERP implementation to be optimized. This training optimization saves the organization implementation time as well as training dollars.

The process of determining the training needed for successfully implementing the ERP system is called gross-to-net logic. This process is similar to the gross-to-net logic used in MRP calculations. The end result, Net Learning Requirements, is the learning that must take place within the organization to achieve implementation success. This prevents too much or too little training for the ERP implementation because the calculation determines just the right topics and amount of training for success.

In addition, the process is iterative so when training needs within the organization shift or learning objectives change, the training program can be adapted to the new needs of the organization. This method is a far cry from many corporate universities that simply create a catalog of training classes and hope that employees enroll in the right classes and learn what they are supposed to learn to improve their own productivity.

The second, equally important, phase of the Diagnostic process is to determine how each employee or group of employees learns most effectively. Too often, training is presented as a one-time event and is delivered in one particular style. This method is not efficient.

In order to increase the velocity of the ERP training throughout the organization, several different versions of the same material must be presented multiple times to the employees, using different presentation styles. It usually takes more than a mere mention of an idea or concept in a training class to convert the "learned" information into action.

Advertisers have known for years that they cannot simply tell a message once and then assume that consumers will act on that single message. Instead, advertisers present the same piece of information over and over again knowing that repetition breeds action. Advertisers also know that one method of getting a message across is not enough. Ads are placed in magazines, delivered over the radio, television, Internet, and by telemarketers. People do not all learn from the same type of presentation and so the advertisers repackage the same information in different formats to reach a broad audience. Figure 5.2 illustrates presenting the concept of inventory reduction through various educational channels.

During an ERP implementation, training must be repackaged again and again to meet the needs of all the employees. This does not mean that the same lecture-based Introduction to ERP class must be taught ten times to

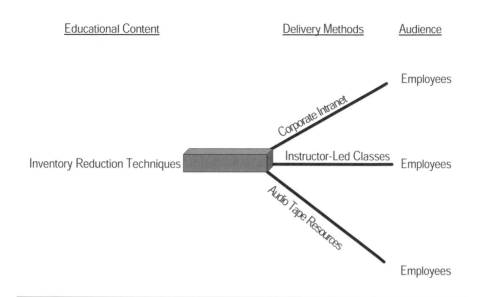

Educational Content        Delivery Methods    Audience

Employees

Corporate Intranet

Inventory Reduction Techniques

Instructor-Led Classes    Employees

Audio Tape Resources

Employees

**Figure 5.2    Multiple Channels — Presenting a Concept through Various Educational Channels within an Organization.**

the same employees. It means that the basic concepts of the class must be presented by several methods, such as meetings, videos, audiotapes, and through the corporate intranet. The goal of the organization should be to present the message in a manner that is congruent with a variety of employee learning styles.

A learning style is a preferred method people use to process new information. If new information is presented in a manner not congruent with an employee's learning style, it will take the employee longer to understand and utilize that information. During an ERP implementation, the best method for increasing the velocity of training is to increase the number of learning styles addressed by the training.

Increasing the targeted number of learning styles will allow a larger number of employees to learn the ERP information faster and more effectively. This increase in learning will help to avoid mistakes during the implementation process and help the ERP system to run more effectively when the entire system is implemented.

Organizations need to diagnosis the learning styles of employees and use that information to help the employees become efficient, effective learners. Not only will the ERP implementation benefit, but the employees will benefit as well because they will know how to most effectively learn information in the future.

The final phase of the Diagnosis process is to ensure that basic and advanced employee needs are addressed. These can include feelings of insecurity about their job, feelings of uncertainty about their new roles and responsibilities as related to the implementation, and concern about their status within the organization. All of these concerns can negatively impact the employees and jeopardize the success of the implementation. If time is not taken to ensure that the basic physiological and psychological needs are addressed, employees will not be focused on the implementation. Understanding the basic hierarchy of needs will help managers, executives, members of the implementation team, and employees adjust to the new system. A discussion of Abraham Maslow's hierarchy of needs is included later in the chapter.

## Gross-to-Net Logic

The Diagnosis step involves determining what skills and competencies the organization already possesses and what is needed to educate the workforce on the issues related to ERP implementation. Gross-to-net logic is a concept of comparing the existing skills and competencies within an organization to the skills and competencies required for obtaining the stated strategic goals of the organization.

This process compares the Bills of Learning developed during the analysis step with existing skills and competencies identified within the organization. Use of gross-to-net logic identifies the gaps existing between the training needs of the company and the actual training delivered to the employees of the company.

Once learning needs are defined, the organization then subtracts the skills and knowledge already possessed and determines those that can be easily purchased. The result is a list of skills and knowledge needed that cannot easily, quickly, or efficiently be purchased or developed. The resultant needs are called the "net learning requirements."

During the Diagnosis process, similar learning goals can be identified and maximized. The advantage is that if certain objectives are evident in many BOL structures, grouping training for those objectives can be coordinated to optimize training time. The purpose is to complete both sides of the gross-to-net logic question. What skills do the employees already possess? What skills can be easily and quickly purchased (outsourced)? What skills are currently lacking within the organization? What competencies are needed to succeed in the future but are lacking in our current workforce?

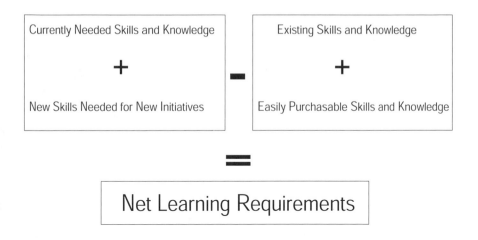

**Figure 5.3 Gross-To-Net Logic. Formula for Determining the Net Learning Requirements in an Organization.**

This process yields a strong and visual depiction of the gaps between the competencies and skills the organization already possesses or can easily possess and the skills or competencies it needs to develop. Limited training dollars can then be focused on the skills and competencies most desired by the organization but not easily obtainable through any other means.

The first phase of the Diagnosis step is to determine the net learning requirements of the organization. This is accomplished through a four-step process. The use of the process ensures that the training will be targeted to the needs of the organization and avoids a "shotgun" approach where training is delivered to every employee whether they need it or not. Figure 5.3 illustrates the gross-to-net learning equation that is used to determine the net learning requirements of the organization.

## *Variable One*

The first step of Diagnosis is actually the first variable in the gross-to-net equation — *Currently Needed Skills and Knowledge.* In this step, the implementation team examines the current situation and determines what training is needed to meet the currently desired levels of productivity. The team looks for gaps in performance, comparing current capabilities or possibilities with current reality.

In some organizations, it is simple to determine what skills or knowledge are needed. Employees have clearly defined job descriptions, internal processes are clearly defined, and each person knows what is required to perform a specific task. In these cases the employees can indicate what they need to know to do their current job more effectively. Some organizations even have a computer-based system for tracking employee skills and skill gaps. A look into the system can indicate what skills are currently needed within the organization.

For example, a utility company in northeastern Pennsylvania has a mainframe system listing employee name, job description, list of competencies required to perform a particular job, training classes supporting each competency, and competencies that support each job. The system even provides the ability to see what competencies are underrepresented in the workforce.

Prior to the ERP implementation, an organization needs to know the current training needs of employees. If the current needs are not known, time and money may be spent training employees for future roles when they are not even properly trained for their current roles. When this occurs, employees resist training and implementation efforts because they believe they will end up in the same situation they are in currently — strict job expectations with no training to support their efforts.

The Diagnosis step of LRP in organizations without clear records consists of the development of job descriptions for each position within the organization. This can be accomplished by asking the employees in the position to write down the tasks they perform. Alternatively, it can be determined through interviewing various people working in the same position to determine what similar tasks they perform.

Another technique is to provide employees with a list of various competencies, skills, or tasks and ask them to circle each of the items that match the requirements of their job. A cross-correlation of multiple lists can identify the most critical elements of a specific position.

A third technique is to review productivity records and ask the top performers in each job class to explain how they perform their job and what skills they need to know to perform effectively. This technique can be useful for determining the "ideal" skills set for a particular position.

In addition, the Occupational Outlook Handbook published every 2 years by the U.S. Department of Labor has 19 occupational clusters describing over 200 jobs. Each job description tells about the nature of the work, working conditions, as well as required training and other qualifications. This information can be used to compare jobs within the organization to "standardized" job descriptions and training requirements. While the descriptions will not exactly match the jobs performed within the organization, they can be an excellent jumping off point for the identification of currently needed skills.

The information collected from the diagnosis of currently needed skills and knowledge is used to determine who needs to know what and why they need to know. Because of the potential misuse of this type of information, this step may meet with some resistance from the workforce.

An effective strategy for helping to prevent mistrust and uncertainty among the production workforce is to appoint one or two senior production members to help in the diagnosis process. Management must make it clear that the information collected is not part of an overall scheme to downsize employees, but rather is a method of determining the skills and competencies the organization currently needs to maintain productivity levels. If the employees do not trust the diagnosis process, they will not participate appropriately.

## *Variable Two*

The next variable in the calculation of the gross-to-net learning requirements equation is *New Skills Needed for New Initiatives*. This variable can be relatively easy to determine because the Analysis step of the LRP process identified learning goals required to reach the strategic goals of the organization. Those goals were then exploded into BOLs that contain all the objectives necessary to support the learning and strategic objectives of the organization. Any of the strategic goals that are new to the organization require examination because they may require new types of training.

The successful implementation of the ERP system is an excellent example of a new initiative. While employees may possess some of the skills and competencies required to operate the ERP system such as keyboarding or creating work orders, many new skills like "pegging demand" and defining configurator variables must be learned to optimize the performance of the ERP system and to integrate it into the daily operation of the organization.

Identifying these new skills is critically important. Often in an ERP implementation, the attitude is one of "doing the same thing as before — only better." If this type of attitude exists, new training programs will not be developed. Employees will receive the same type of training they have always received. Not exposing employees to new ideas or new concepts cripples an organization's attempts to be progressive in spite of any upper management edict. Organizations can't expect employees to remain competitive, cut costs, and improve productivity if they don't have the proper training in new techniques, ideas, and operations methodology. The reason training for new initiatives is so important is that employees are provided a "taste" of the possible.[1]

Once employees are exposed, through training, to new ideas and concepts, they can begin to consider and eventually implement those ideas. Identification of the skills and competencies employees need to turn concepts into actions is critical. Employees quickly become frustrated when they learn about a new concept or idea but do not have the skills required to implement that idea. The training of new skills must be closely coordinated within the organization.

However, not all new initiatives require skills that are completely new to the organization. In many cases, the skills already possessed by the workforce simply need to be redirected toward the new initiative. An examination of the Bills of Learning developed from the strategic and learning objectives of the organization will reveal many items that are similar. These should be grouped together. In addition a comparison of BOLs between existing and new objectives will reveal areas of redundancy. In some cases, those areas will require refresher training. In other cases, those areas will not require any new training efforts at all.

For example, an organization may have a new goal of "increasing inventory accuracy to 99%." This goal may require the skill of cycle counting and the use of a new bar-coding inventory control system. Employees may already have started cycle counting inventory items and, therefore, no cycle counting training is needed. Cycle counting skills are placed on the "currently existing" side of the net learning requirements equation.

However, employees may not be familiar with the process of bar-coding inventory. To make the bar-coding process work effectively, employees may require training. The training could consist of teaching production employees how to properly scan an item's bar code, teaching storeroom clerks how to create the proper labels for the items, and teaching employees in receiving how to compare the Bill of Lading bar code information with received containers. This information is then placed under the category of the equation variable New Skills Needed for New Initiatives.

Identifying the new skills needed for new initiatives, although not a common practice, is critical to the success of an ERP implementation. Employees must be given the proper skills to maximize any new productivity improvement effort. Identifying the needed skills helps to focus the training specifically in the areas that most require new information.

Together, the *Currently Needed Skills and Knowledge* and the *New Skills Needed for New Initiatives* are the gross learning requirements of an organization. These are the learning needs of the organization before the netting of the current and easily purchasable skills.

## Variable Three

The third variable in the equation is *Existing Skills and Knowledge.* Information for this variable is available using the same techniques and resources as determining the *Currently Needed Skills and Knowledge:* reviewing existing records and the Occupational Outlook Handbook, observing employees, asking employees to identify what they already know how to do, and asking them what tasks they perform daily.

Unfortunately, many organizations do not know what skills or competencies their workforce currently needs to continue to support their existing levels of productivity. Often, the only complete training records an organization will have are those they are required to have by the government agency responsible for the health and safety of employees, the Occupational Safety and Health Administration (OSHA). While OSHA safety training records are important, they should not be the only training records an organization processes.

Good training records help supervisors assess existing employees, move an employee from one assignment to another, identify areas of need within the company, and formulate succession plans. All of these types of records help to indicate the skills the employees already possess and can indicate what areas require additional training.

Organizations that do not have good records, job descriptions, internal processes, or an automated record-keeping system may have difficulty determining what skills currently exist within the organization.

An important part of the LRP process is to develop a system for tracking employee skill sets and to continually monitor those skills. The monitoring of the skills helps to determine what skills are needed now and in the future. Once skills are analyzed across the organization, training decisions can be made with a higher degree of accuracy.

If an automated system is available, supervisors can simply query the system to determine what skills currently exist. Many current ERP systems, like PeopleSoft, have the capability of tracking employee training, competencies, and skill sets, and even highlight what skills are needed to reach the next desired level. This information is important to collect because it helps upper management make critical human resources decisions.

## Variable Four

The final variable in the equation is *Easily Purchasable Skills and Knowledge.* Too often in an organization, a lack of skills or knowledge automatically leads to the conclusion that training is needed. While training can have a profound impact on the organization, often simpler, more cost-effective methods of addressing a perceived training problem can be utilized.

An example of this is a New York manufacturer of cement mixers. The company made a motor subassembly with more than 60 parts, each from a different vendor. The kitting of the parts and the associated paperwork swamped the small manufacturer, not to mention the need to train assemblers to sort and bag the kits.[2] The assemblers, mostly women, had a high rate of turnover because the job did not pay well and the work was tedious.

The organization decided that rather than continue to train assemblers to sort and kit the material, it would outsource the kitting to a preferred vendor and use the assemblers in other parts of the process. The results of the outsourcing were dramatic. Not only was turnover reduced, but an added benefit was that the outsourcing of the kitting process eliminated 59 purchase orders, 59 invoices, and 59 receipts. This was a substantial reduction in paperwork for the small company.[2]

A more common example is the payroll function within a mid-size manufacturing organization. It takes an enormous amount of effort to keep current with the latest state, local, and federal tax laws concerning payroll deductions, wage garnishing, 401(k) regulations, and other items impacting payroll. In many cases it is far more cost effective to "purchase" the payroll skills necessary than it is to continually train a person internally to stay current in that area.

In another instance, a manufacturing organization was having a high reject rate because productions workers were having problems reading and interpreting a series of gages to regulate heat, air volume, and vibrations during a manufacturing process. The initial solution called for the development of a two-week training course to teach all the workers on that machine how to properly interpret the series of gages.

A consultant was brought into the plant to begin to design the instruction. Rather than beginning to develop training right away, the consultant first conducted a mini-needs analysis to determine the nature of the problem and how it could best be solved.

Based on the findings of the needs assessment, the consultant decided to recommend to the upper managers that training should not be conducted to teach employees how to read the complicated series of gages. Instead, he recommended that a simple, color-coded LED display screen replace all the gages. The display screen would indicate what actions needed to be taken and when to maintain the equipment. The consultant realized that even after two weeks of training, employees would eventually slip back into their old habits because of the complex nature of the process and because new employees frequently cycled into the work cell as part of an ongoing cross-training program within the organization.

The development and implementation of the solution actually cost slightly less than the budget for the development of the customized two-week training course once losses of productivity figures were calculated into the equation. Often, nontraining solutions are available for less expense and trouble than training-based solutions. The secret is to have enough creativity to develop a simple, effective solution that does not involve hours and hours of training. These types of solutions and the ability to hire an outside group quickly and easily to perform a specific task is what is meant by *Easily Purchasable Skills and Competencies.*

Purchasing off-the-shelf training solves many training problems. Often the initial upfront investment in the training is returned over and over again to the organization. One example is of a company that provides off-the-shelf training for many organizations is Eduneering, a New Jersey-based company specializing in supplying safety and compliance training. The service offered by Eduneering is one of supplying OSHA and other types of regulated training via self-paced instruction delivered over the web for a fee per employee. The advantage for a manufacturing organization is that they do not have to conduct mandatory yearly training by having someone from the training department come to the plant for all three shifts and teach two or three employees the same regulated training they taught the employees 12 months ago. Instead, an employee simply logs onto the Eduneering website and spends an hour or less reviewing the training information and then takes a test to verify that they have learned, or still know, the information. The system tracks employee performance and scores and keeps that information for the future. The service offered by Eduneering and similar companies frees training department personnel to develop training that adds value to the bottom line and not simply maintains compliance with governmental regulations.

Prior to developing any training program, personnel within the organization need to look outside of the organization to determine if already-prepared, high-quality training materials exist to support internal efforts. Several sources of already-prepared training exist for manufacturing organizations.

One such organization is APICS~The Educational Society for Resource Management. APICS is a not-for-profit international educational organization that is dedicated to using education to help businesses improve their bottom line. APICS offers a series of classes which can be attended by personnel in manufacturing and service organizations who are interested in increasing their knowledge of basic business fundamentals, as well as basic manufacturing processes and procedures.

APICS offers two certification programs, each providing a slightly different focus. The first is the Certified in Production and Inventory Management

(CPIM) program. The CPIM course of studies offers education in the principles and techniques involved in business operations with a focus on the production and inventory management environments. The studies are designed to enhance the ability of professionals to effectively function in a manufacturing or service based business environment. Employees who finish this program have a solid understanding of the various elements within an organization from manufacturing to business operations.

The second program is the Certified in Integrated Resource Management (CIRM) course of studies. The integrated resource management education course presents a complete and solid understanding of the many business functions within an organization and how they interact with each other. This is a managerially focused program that presents information to new and seasoned managers to help them understand how decisions and actions impact all of the functions within the organization.

Another source of purchasable training is academic institutions (universities and community colleges). Many manufacturing organizations have specific needs that can be addressed by university faculty through collaborative efforts. For example, Booz·Allen & Hamilton has established a relationship with some universities in the Washington, D.C. area in which faculty members actually teach at the Booze.Allen site. The relationship is mutually beneficial since the university is able to reach an audience that is not normally accessible, employees get training delivered to their workplace, and the organization gains highly trained employees.

Another source of purchasable training is a learning portal. A learning portal is a location on the Internet where individuals and corporations can purchase and attend on-line training classes as well as sign up for instructor-led classes, purchase training videos, and other training-related materials on a wide variety of topics. A learning portal is a "one-stop-shop" for training programs and information.

Large and small organizations can benefit from adding a link to a learning portal from their own internal intranet. In addition, many learning portals will customize the interface to the portal. This customization allows the employees to feel as if they are still within the confines of the organization although the content they are accessing is stored outside the organization. Learning portals also provide forums for discussions of various issues and topics related to training, ERP, or any other topic that is placed on the portal.

One of the largest learning portals is www.click2learn.com. This portal provides users with the ability to not only take courses and sign up for instructor-led training, but also offers advice from learning industry experts on various training topics. It also provides the ability for members of an organization to create training classes and host them on the click2learn portal.

Other sources of purchasable training include independent consultants, books, tapes, and companies that provide industry-specific training. This is especially true of the ERP market that has many different resources to help a company through the difficult task of ERP implementation. The creative organization actively seeks training solutions that do not require internal development of materials. Internal development is costly and difficult to keep current.

## Net Learning Requirements

Once all of the variables in the equation are determined, the gross training requirements should be subtracted from the available training to determine the net learning requirements. The net learning requirements are the identified training needs that should be addressed during the ERP implementation.

Once the net learning requirements are identified, the organization should prioritize each of the requirements to determine which to address first, second, etc. The learning requirements can be prioritized on the basis of economic value (e.g., cost value to the organization), impact (number of people affected), ranking scale, or ease of access and timeliness (e.g., through a learning portal available on the Internet today).[3]

Since the design of the training for the ERP system relies on the results of the gross-to-net learning equation, the process of determining the net learning requirements must be done carefully and methodically. Sloppy or haphazard diagnosis leads to inadequate identification of needs, under-trained employees, misguided training programs, and if left unchecked, ERP implementation failure. The learning equation is effective but it must be conducted with care. The proper use of this equation ensures that the training delivered to support the ERP implementation provides the greatest positive impact on the organization.

Once the net learning requirements are identified and prioritized, the next step is the effective design of the instruction. The Design step is discussed in detail in the Design chapter (Chapter 6) of this book.

Not only can the gross-to-net learning equation be used for the entire organization to determine learning requirements for ERP, the equation can be used by individual divisions and departments to determine their learning requirements for ERP and other technology implementations and/or organization initiatives. Even individuals can use the equation to determine what training they need to reach career or personnel goals.

## Learning Styles

Once the net learning requirements are determined and prioritized, the next step in the Diagnosis process is to determine how each employee within the organization learns. Just as organizations spend thousands of dollars on process improvements like Statistical Process Control (SPC) and Single Minute Exchange of Die (SMED), an investment should be made in the only appreciating assets in the factory, the employees. Improving an employee's learning velocity and educational throughput positively impacts the timeliness of the ERP implementation and builds a knowledge advantage in the company.

It makes no sense to define the learning objectives needed to successfully implement the ERP system unless the organization understands how to effectively teach the employees. Tools, techniques, and insights are available to objectively examine the learning styles and preferences of individuals. Once learning styles and preference are identified and designed into the ERP instruction, employees can learn the most amount of information in the shortest period possible.

## *What is a Learning Style?*

A learning style is simply the preferred method a person uses to learn information. If an individual has a certain learning style, it does not mean that the individual learns all things using that particular style. It does mean that the learner prefers to use that style for most of his or her learning. When a person knows and understands his learning style, it helps him to learn more effectively. People approach a new situation with a preferred style of learning and attempt to assimilate that new information into their own personal body of knowledge using techniques that are most comfortable for them.

Perhaps the most valuable reason for addressing the subject of learning styles with employees is that often employees do not even realize that they have a specific methodology they use to learn new information. Helping an employee become aware of his or her learning style provides a tool that person can utilize to improve productivity in learning, living, and work. Effectively applying a learning style strategy to a specific body of new information dramatically reduces the overall learning time for that individual and, consequently, for the organization.

Not only do learning styles dictate learning preferences, but an individual's learning style also influences how he or she deals with ideas, solves problems, sets goals, manages others, and approaches new situations. Tailoring training toward individual learning styles is an untapped resource in many organizations. Gaining an understanding into the different ways people approach learning helps organizations maximize employee effectiveness.

## Learning Style Classification Schemes

Many different methods have been developed to classify learners into different learning styles. Some of the methods include only two opposite learning styles while others involve up to eight different approaches to learning. Organizations will want to choose a method of evaluating employee learning styles based on the feasibility of administering the evaluation tool and the types of work conducted within the organization. Most of the instruments used to help determine learning style are called "self-report" instruments. This means that the employee completes a questionnaire indicating certain likes and dislikes. The results are then analyzed and calculated to determine which style the employee prefers.

One advantage of modern technology is that many of the learning style assessment instruments have now been placed online. This means that employees can take a few minutes to answer some questions on an intranet or Internet page and then receive detailed feedback concerning their individual preferred learning styles.

In this section five different learning style classifications will be examined. A few of the styles have self-reporting instruments that help to determine learning styles of employees. The styles are

- Deductive vs. Inductive
- Visual, Auditory, and Tactile/Kinesthetic
- Myers-Briggs Type Indicator
- Gardner's Multiple Intelligences
- Kolb's Learning Style Inventory

### Deductive vs. Inductive

This classification scheme simply divides learners into one of two categories based on how the learner prefers to organize information. Learners either approach the learning of new material from a deductive or inductive viewpoint. Inductive learners like to go from "specifics" to the "whole."[4] On the other hand, deductive learners would first like to see the "big picture" and then learn about the details.

An example might be the concept of "Just-In-Time." The inductive learner might first concentrate on what causes excessive inventory even though that may only be a small part of the JIT philosophy. The inductive learner may generate several examples of causes of excess inventory such as inaccurate BOMs, mislabeled parts, parts placed in wrong bins, or untrained personnel. Once the learner understood the "inventory" elements of JIT, he or she would then move to the "quality" elements and then eventually construct his or her own idea of the overall JIT philosophy. The learner would learn the concept of JIT from the small pieces of "evidence" presented during instruction. The inductive learner uses facts and observations to infer a principle.[3]

Conversely, the deductive learner firsts want to understand the overall philosophy of JIT. Providing the details to deductive leaners at first only confuses the learners. They want to know what general JIT characteristics exist. They want the instructor to "sum up JIT in 25 words or less." Once they understand the overall concept, they will then look at the various elements in terms of that concept. Once the deductive learner understands that JIT is about "continuous improvement," he or she will look at inventory reduction as a part of the continuous improvement effort. The deductive learner works from a principle to deduce applications and consequences.

The implication for instruction of deductive and inductive learners is that the instruction needs to provide two separate approaches to the information a top-down approach and a bottom-up approach. One method of accommodating both of these learning styles in a classroom is to have learners divide into two groups based on their stated learning style (simply ask at the beginning of class if they want the big picture or the details). Once the learners are divided, provide information to each group based on their preference. Another technique is to schedule the same class twice and indicate on the schedule that one class will start with a big picture approach and one will start with the details.

If the instruction is online, it can be programmed to branch in different directions based on the stated learning preference of the user. The software can have various links to either detailed explanations, or to more globally focused information working down to the details.

## Visual, Auditory, and Tactile/Kinesthetic

Another method of classifying learning styles is to examine how learners perceive new information. There are three primary methods of perceiving new information. They are seeing, hearing, and interacting. Each of these methods is used to classify learners as either visual, auditory, or tactile/kinesthetic.

The visual learner prefers information to be presented in the form of pictures, charts, diagrams, tables, illustrations, and videos. The visual learner likes to sit near the front of the classroom to see the body language and facial expressions of the instructor as well as gain a clear view of any visual materials presented. The visual learner will tend to draw pictures of concepts and may seem to be doodling in a notebook.

If the visual learner does not understand a concept he or she will say, "I don't see it," or, "I can't picture what you are saying." When they understand they will say, "I see what you are saying," or, "Now I see." Color-coding is an effective tool for visual learners as well as providing graphically focused online training sessions or videos. This is the type of learner who wants to see a graphical display of the entire ERP system so she can see how all the pieces fit.

The auditory learner learns best when information is presented in the form of a lecture, class discussion, conversation with a classmate, or through an audio tape. The auditory learner tends to speak a lot in class, carry on side conversations about the class topic, and seek verbal clarification of what they are learning: "if I hear you correctly, you are saying that JIT is actually … ."

Auditory learners prefer to have charts and diagrams explained verbally rather than decipher them from visual cues. They benefit from online training that has an accompanying audio track or music. Auditory learners like to study with the radio on. One method that works well for auditory learners when studying technical jargon is to tape record the words and definitions and then play them back over and over again.

Tactile/kinesthetic learners prefer to be moving around and touching working models when learning new concepts or ideas. Educational games that simulate the manufacturing environment are effective for these types of learners. They enjoy hands-on exercises and find it hard to remain still for long periods of time. Occasionally a tactile/kinesthetic learner will get up and pace in the back of the classroom while listening to the instruction. The movement and pacing helps them to concentrate.

In a manufacturing environment, many of the employees are tactile/kinesthetic learners who need to be actively involved in the learning. Teaching inventory reduction techniques or explaining the material requirements planning logic with models or out on the factory floor is an effective method for teaching these individuals. Taking apart an inventory item to learn about how a BOM is structured is an effective teaching technique for tactile/kinesthetic learners.

The implication for instruction is that the classroom environment must allow each of the different learning perception styles to be accommodated. The instructor must include some hands-on exercises for the tactile/kinesthetic learner, some lectures for the auditory learner, and plenty of charts and graphs for the visual learner. Also, if the instructor understands that some learners need to walk around during class or talk to themselves a little while learning, he or she should not become annoyed thinking that they are not paying attention or are not interested in the material.

## Myers-Briggs Type Indicator[5]

An instrument that can help to measure employees' learning styles is the Myers-Briggs Type Indicator available from Consulting Psychologists Press.[5] The self-report instrument is designed to provide information about personality types and how they prefer to interact with their surroundings and information. When a person learns about his type, he can then better understand his personal learning styles and preferences. There are four different categories of personality type. Each of them has two dimensions.

The first type is Extraversion/Introversion. Extraversion represents people who focus on the outer world of people and things while Introversion is a focus on the inner world of ideas and impressions.

The second is Sensing/Intuition. The Sensing type tends to focus on the present and on concrete impressions gained from their senses. The Intuition type tends to focus on the future with an eye toward patterns and possibilities.

Next is Thinking/Feeling. The Thinking types base their decisions on logic and objective analysis of cause and effect. The Feeling types base decisions primarily on values, on subjective valuation, and person-centered concerns.

Finally, Judgment/Perception. The Judgment types like a planned and organized approach to life and like to have things settled. The Perception types like a flexible and spontaneous approach to life and prefer to keep many irons in the fire.

Each of the types can be combined with other types to form 16 possible combinations. The combination of the types indicates an individual's overall type and provides insight into how the person most likes to learn. The implication is that once a personality type has been identified, instruction can be tailored to meet the needs of the personality type identified by the Myers-Briggs Indicator.

## Multiple Intelligences[6]

Another classification method is Howard Gardner's concept of multiple intelligences. Gardner had done work with brain-damaged individuals and was interested in the various skills that were either retained or lost depending upon the area of damage to the brain. He took that interest and developed what he called "Multiple Intelligences." He believes that people can be intelligent in many different ways. His list includes:

- Verbal/Spatial Intelligence
- Verbal/Linguistic Intelligence
- Logical/Mathematical Intelligence
- Bodily/Kinesthetic Intelligence
- Musical/Rhythmic Intelligence
- Interpersonal Intelligence
- Intrapersonal Intelligence

While a few of these types of intelligences have no apparent bearing on an ERP implementation, a number of them should be of concern when developing instruction for delivery to employees of an organization.

*Verbal/Spatial Intelligence* — These individuals think in terms of pictures and need to create vivid mental images to retain information. These are typically the people who can look at a blueprint and "see" how it will look when completed. Often, people with verbal/spatial intelligence will be employed in the engineering or drafting departments of an organization.

*Verbal/Linguistic Intelligence* — These individuals think in terms of words rather than pictures. They have well-developed listening skills and are generally elegant, effective speakers. These are typically the people who can quickly write a memo or edit another's memo into clear and concise language with little effort. Often, people with verbal/linguistic intelligence will be employed as a legal council, contract writer, proposal writer, secretary, or trainer.

*Logical/Mathematical Intelligence* — These individuals are logical, methodical, and are good with numbers. They can see patterns and make connections between various pieces of information. They are typically curious and like to see how various parts of the organization can work together. Often, people with logical/mathematical intelligence are buyer/planners and accountants.

*Bodily/Kinesthetic Intelligence* — These individuals enjoy physically handling objects and express themselves through movement. They have a good sense of balance, hand-eye coordination, and physical dexterity. They frequently use their hands to create or build things. They need to "touch and feel" objects to learn about them. Typically, these individuals work in the inventory or production departments of an organization.

*Musical/Rhythmic Intelligence* — These individuals are musical and are able to think in terms of keys, notes, and scores. They are appreciative of music and like to listen to music while they study or work. Typically these types of individuals do not play prominent roles within manufacturing organizations, they are more likely to be musicians, disc jockeys, or singers. However, if a person within the organization leans toward this intelligence, he or she may prefer training to be accompanied by music or be more vocal. This may be helpful to know when purchasing or producing multimedia-based on-line learning.

*Interpersonal Intelligence* — These individuals are able to relate well with others. They understand how people relate to one another and are able to talk comfortably with many different types of people. They use both verbal and nonverbal skills (reading body language) to interact with people and to learn new information. People with interpersonal intelligence tend to be in the sales department of an organization or a department manager.

*Intrapersonal Intelligence* — These individuals are highly internally focused and tend to be very self-reflective. They think about how they "think." These people tend to be in the research departments of organizations.

The implication is that different employees will learn different types of information more or less effectively depending upon the type of intelligence they possess. While it is difficult to develop training that addresses all of the various types of multiple intelligences in every educational situation, organizations should help to make their employees aware of their particular strengths. Once employees identify their strengths, they can obtain coaching to help them learn more effectively by prompting the instructor to provide information that works to their strength.

## Kolb's Learning Style Inventory[7]

One of the best-known learning style categorizations comes from David Kolb, who developed the idea of four different types of learning preferences and then combined those learning preferences into four different learning styles. Kolb then developed an assessment instrument to determine an individual's learning style. To understand Kolb's learning styles, first it is important to understand his definition of the four different learning preferences.

The first preference described by Kolb is learning by watching others. Information is learned by observing a situation or by listening carefully to instructions or directions. The second learning preference is feeling. In this case, learning develops from relating to people, being sensitive to others, and from specific emotional events. The third learning preference is thinking. Many times a person will logically analyze ideas and learn by acting on an intellectual understanding of a particular situation. The fourth learning preference is doing. Learning by doing involves hands-on experiences. In this case, the learning is from actually being involved in the situation.

The four types of learning identified by Kolb can be described as Reflective Observation (watching), Concrete Experience (feeling), Abstract Conceptualization (thinking), and Active Experimentation (doing). Some of these learning methods are actually polar opposites of one another.

For example, Concrete Experience is actually quite different from Abstract Conceptualization. Individuals oriented to learn through Concrete Experience perceive through their senses by immersing themselves in the here-and-now and relying heavily on their intuition to learn, while individuals who prefer Abstract Conceptualization like to step back from a situation and think of the underlying theory or concept that can help them learn the new information. These learners want to know the "why" behind everything they are learning.

Reflective Observation is very different from Active Experimentation. These two learning preferences deal with how employees process or transform information and experiences into knowledge. When processing new experiences, some learners jump right in and try their hand, while others would choose to carefully watch others who are involved in the experience and reflect on what happens. The doers favor Active Experimentation, while the watchers favor Reflective Observation.

Each of the four methods of learning can be summarized as follows:

- *Concrete Experience* — This learning method emphasizes personal involvement with people in everyday situations. When using this method, a learner tends to rely more on feelings than on a systematic approach to problems, situations, and new information.
- *Reflective Observation* — This approach involves an attempt to understand ideas and situations from different points of view. The approach relies on patience, objectivity, observation, and careful judgment prior to taking any action or synthesizing any new information.
- *Abstract Conceptualization* — This involves using logic and ideas rather than feelings to understand problems, situations, and new learning opportunities. Typically, this type of learning involves relying on systematic planning and the development of theories to solve problems.
- *Active Experimentation* — Learning with this approach involves an action in the form of experimenting with variables within the new learning environment. This is a practical approach concerned with what really works as opposed to simply watching a situation or reading a case study. This approach helps learning by allowing people to see the results of their influence directly upon the situation.[8,9]

Since some of the different learning approaches described above can actually be opposites, each person's learning style is a combination of these four basic approaches to learning.

## Kolb's Definition of Learning Styles

Kolb identified the unique way in which an individual combines the four approaches to learning as "Learning Styles." According to Kolb, research indicates that individuals combine the four different approaches to learning into four different learning styles. The learning styles are Converger, Diverger, Assimilator, and Accommodator. Following is a description of each style:

*Converger* — Combines the learning approaches of Abstract Conceptualization and Active Experimentation. Employees with this learning style are best at finding practical uses for ideas and theories. A preference for this learning style indicates an ability to solve problems and make decisions based on finding solutions to questions or problems. These individuals would rather deal with technical tasks and problems than with social and interpersonal issues. This learning style is important for effectiveness in specialist and technology careers.

*Diverger* — Combines the learning approaches of Concrete Experience and Reflective Observation. Employees with this learning style are best at viewing concrete situations from many different points of view. A preference for this learning style indicates one in which the individual would be more likely to sit back and observe a new situation than take action. These individuals enjoy situations that call for generating a wide range of ideas, as in brainstorming sessions. They also tend to have broad interests and like to gather information. This learning style is important for effectiveness in arts, entertainment, and service careers.

*Assimilator* — Combines the learning approaches of Abstract Conceptualization and Reflective Observation. Employees with this learning style are best at understanding a wide range of information and putting it into concise, logical form. A preference for this learning style indicates a high interest in abstract ideas and concepts and a lesser focus on people and feelings. These individuals find it more important that a theory have logical soundness than practical value. This learning style is important in science and information-related careers.

*Accommodator* — Combines the learning approaches of Concrete Experience and Active Experimentation. Employees with this learning style have the ability to learn primarily from hands-on experience. A preference for this learning style indicates a willingness to get involved in new and challenging experiences and to carry out already developed plans. These individuals tend to act on "gut" feelings rather than on logical analysis. In solving problems, they may rely more heavily on people for information then on technical analysis. This learning style is important for effectiveness in action-oriented careers such as direct production positions or sales positions.[8,9]

## What Is the Learning Style Inventory (LSI)?

Based on the four learning styles, Kolb developed a self-assessment instrument called the Learning Style Inventory (LSI). The LSI is a self-descriptive instrument that assesses an individual's preferred method of learning. It describes how a person deals with ideas and situations in which he must learn new information. The LSI is self-administered, self-scored, and self-interpreted. The results allow employees to identify their learning styles. This, in turn, helps employees to understand how they absorb and deal with new information. Once people know how to deal with new information in the most efficient manner possible, they will learn faster and more effectively.

The LSI is a 12-item questionnaire. Each item asks the learners to rank-order four sentences ending in a way that best describe how they prefer to learn. The instrument design is determined by three objectives. The first is that the test is brief and straightforward so that it can be used in discussing the learning process with individuals and providing feedback. The second design objective is that the test be constructed in such a way that individuals respond to it somewhat as they would respond to a learning situation. Third, the instrument predicts behavior in a way consistent with the theory of experiential learning.

The instrument is then tallied and scored to determine an individual's relative emphasis on each of the four learning orientations. The LSI determines which of the four learning styles are most favored by an individual. It also helps an individual to determine which methods he should focus on when learning new information. Most people can complete the LSI within 10 minutes, and complete administration, scoring, interpretation, and discussion can be accomplished in under 2 hours.

## Implications for Instruction

The knowledge of learning styles is important on several levels. The first is that knowledge of learning styles can be used by organizations to design training that meets the needs of all the employees. Second, knowledge of learning styles will help trainers within the organization understand how best to deliver the ERP information to the learners. Third, it makes the employees, management, and trainers aware of the fact that training material should be presented in different ways to different employees based on how they learn.

Trainers tend to deliver and design training in the same style in which they are comfortable learning. This works well when all the students have the same learning style as the instructor. Unfortunately, that is seldom the case.

For example, individuals who tend toward training are Divergers because they like to view problems and situations from many different points of view. These individuals enjoy situations that call for generating a wide range of ideas, as in brainstorming sessions, and they like to focus on the social aspect of situations. Individuals who tend toward engineering careers are typically Convergers. They would rather deal with technical tasks and problems than with social and interpersonal issues. This can cause a problem when the Diverger trainer teaches the Converger engineers in a Diverger style. The answer is for the trainer to adapt his or her style to accommodate the learner.

As another example, a trainer going into the computer-services department to teach an ERP concepts class needs to understand that employees in a computer-oriented career are most likely Assimilators. The trainer must adapt to those types of learners or risk an ineffective presentation of the material.

Knowledge of the types of learning styles present within a certain type of organization provides trainers with a method of tailoring the training to the learning style of the employees. This makes the training more effective for the individuals and the organization.

## Summary of Learning Styles

Understanding learning styles is an excellent method for delivering effective, efficient training. Unfortunately, people don't wear badges identifying their individual learning style. In fact, many people are unaware that they even have a particular style of learning. Trainers, managers, and ERP implementation team members must constantly deliver training using a wide variety of methods to accommodate as many different individual learning styles as possible.

For example, at the beginning of training programs instructors or computer programs could ask learners how they learn best. The material could then be delivered in the preferred learning styles. This method can be extremely effective when designed into an online training delivery program where the user can log in the first time and have his or her learning style assessed and then the software can change the delivery of the material based on the determined preference. This would mean that the material would be stored in a database and configured by the software into the preferred sequence. For example, for a learner who was more visual, an image would appear. For a learner who was more verbal, text would appear that described the image.

While it may seem time-consuming and impractical to spend valuable time and energy determining the learning styles of employees, the payoff can be dramatic. Teams that are constantly fighting or not making progress have benefited by learning how others on the team learn and interact. Training times have been reduced because the training focused on a particular style congruent with the employees' motivation to learn because employees are comfortable with the material and able to "get it." With so much money being spent on training during the ERP implementation process, a small investment in making sure the training is effective is worth the expense. Developing a multifaceted approach to training and course development ensures that employees learn quickly and efficiently. This, in turn, ensures that the organizations can complete the ERP implementation in a timely manner.

## Final Step

The final step in the Diagnosis process is to make sure that employees are prepared to learn and contribute to the ERP system without undue outside concerns. If employees are distracted with physical or psychological matters related or unrelated to the ERP implementation, they will be unable to effectively participate in the implementation or to learn new skills and com petencies for their jobs.

The basic needs of employees must be met prior to attempting to reach higher goals like a totally integrated, effectively functioning ERP system. One of the best-known classification schemes for making sure that basic needs are met is called Maslow's Hierarchy of Needs.

Maslow proposed a sequence consisting of physiological, safety, social, esteem, and self-actualization needs that need to be met in a specific order before the next higher need can be addressed. According to the hierarchy and its theory, a person's behavior is motivated by unsatisfied needs. Once a need is satisfied, its importance to the individual diminishes and the person can then focus on needs at the next higher level of the hierarchy. Therefore, since an organization is simply a collection of individuals, the ERP implementation team must make sure that the lower-level needs of the individuals of the organization are addressed before attempting to obtain higher goals for the entire organization.

This concept is of importance during the diagnosis phase because each manager within the organization implementing the ERP system should be aware of what motivates his or her employees. This becomes especially important when dealing with the large amount of change that will occur during the ERP implementation. If the manager can diagnosis the types of motivators for employees, then he or she can motivate the employee more effectively toward the goals of the organization.

When the goals of the organization and the goals of the employees are congruent, great things are possible. The employees are intrinsically motivated to work to reach a higher and higher level of the hierarchy and the organization reaches new heights of productivity and profitability. Congruent corporate and individual goals are a powerful combination to watch.

However, when the goals are not congruent, the results are disastrous either for the employee, for the company, or both. Managers can help align organizational and individual goals by addressing each level of Maslow's hierarchy for his or her direct reports. The lower-level needs are more focused on the individual and the higher needs are more organizationally focused.

The lowest level of need identified in Maslow's hierarchy is that of physiological needs. These are the most basic needs of people: food, shelter, and clothing. This may not seem to be a major concern for many manufacturing organizations; however, if production employees are living at or below the poverty level, they may not have as many of these needs taken care of as assumed. If workers are hungry or cold, they are not really going to care too much about the ERP implementation. Fortunately, in many factories the employees have satisfied their basic physiological needs. In fact, these basic needs motivated many workers to find employment in the first place.

The second level in Maslow's hierarchy is that of safety needs. People need to feel physically and psychologically secure in their environment. Most companies, due to OSHA standards, governmental regulations, and a healthy appreciation for their workers, maintain high physical safety standards and employees do not feel physically threatened.

However, during an ERP implementation many workers may feel psychologically threatened. If employees feel that their jobs will be taken because of the new ERP system, they will be less than willing to help implement the system. Even if employees do not feel they will lose their jobs, they may feel insecure about their new role or responsibilities. Managers must take measures to ensure employees that they will not lose their jobs and provide enough training to make them comfortable with their new assignments.

Once employees feel safe, the next level in the hierarchy is that of social needs. Social needs are the need to belong, be accepted by others, and to give and receive friendship. This need can be fed during the ERP implementation by forming ERP study groups in which several employees get together informally during lunch or after work and discuss various concepts, ideas, and concerns about the ERP system. This socialization process helps employees to accept their new roles because they understand that every one of them is in a similar situation concerning the implementation.

The next level is esteem need. This is the need for the respect of others and for a sense of accomplishment and achievement. Esteem needs are challenged when a worker feels he or she will lose some "power" when the new system is put into place. The worker may feel that people respected him because of his knowledge or control over certain aspects of the process. When that control is given to the ERP system the person may no longer feel he will have the respect of others.

If a worker has issues with esteem, the implementation team or management should attempt to help the worker understand that he is still a valuable member of the organization. The worker needs to be made to feel important and that he contributes to the success of the company, even if he must relinquish some previously held power or authority.

This can be accomplished by helping the worker understand what the new system will do for him personally. Another strategy is to invite the person to help out with an important piece of the implementation. This will allow that person to shift from a feeling of unimportance to a feeling of importance. Another issue may be that the person doesn't understand how the organization will benefit from this new system. The old way was just fine. Help that person understand the benefits to the company and to the other employees.

Once esteem issues are addressed, the next level is one of self-actualization. This is the highest level and is the most elusive to obtain. This is an individual's need for self-fulfillment. While it is difficult, if not impossible, for a manager or implementation team to help someone reach self-fulfillment through an ERP implementation, it is possible that the implementation opportunity may help others strive toward fulfillment. It can be very satisfying to see "old Joe" finally understand the value of an exception report or to have the production manager excited about a work order prioritization chart. The project leader may have a sense of fulfillment when the system is finally up and running; the inventory manager may have a good feeling when the cycle count reconciles with the actual quantity on hand.

While these small successes are not the grand self-actualization that Maslow envisioned, they are satisfying and can in some way make the monumental effort to implement the ERP system worth it. The implementation team, executives, managers, and employees must celebrate successes — however small — and brush off defeats — however large.

## Conclusion

The Diagnosis process is probably one of the most overlooked steps in any ERP implementation. Few organizations are aware of the inefficient way in which training needs are determined, and even fewer are aware of the ineffective manner in which training is delivered.

Determining the net learning requirements of the organization is the first step to remedying the problem. An accurate identification of required training provides an excellent basis for conducting effective ERP training. The utilization of outside training resources can considerably reduce training costs and provide instant access to high-quality, targeted information.

Making employees aware of their own individual learning styles, the second step of the Diagnosis process, will dramatically improve the velocity of training. When employees understand how they learn best, they will not waste time in training situations that are not geared toward their learning styles. This will maximize the training they receive and minimize time wasted during training classes that are not effective for them.

Finally, an implementation is only as good as the people participating in the process. Managers, executives, and implementation team members must be aware of the basic and advanced needs of the employees. The human needs of the employees must be addressed prior to the higher-level needs of the organization.

When all the areas have undergone the Diagnosis process, the next step is to take that information and design the appropriate ERP instruction for the organization. A careful diagnosis will streamline the design process to make the ERP implementation more effective.

## LRP Diagnosis Checklist

| Diagnosis Task | Completed | | |
| --- | --- | --- | --- |
| | Yes | No | Date |

### Gross-To-Net Learning Requirements

1. Identify currently needed skills and knowledge.
2. Identify new skills needed for new initiatives.
3. Identify existing skills and knowledge.
4. Identify easily purchasable skills and knowledge.
5. Calculate net learning requirements.
6. Prioritize net learning requirements appropriately.

### Employee Learning Styles

7. Introduce topic of learning styles to executives and upper management.
8. Introduce topic to employees.
9. Assess employee learning styles.
10. Educate employees on the implications of their identified learning style.
11. Design instruction to include multiple learning styles.

### Maslow's Hierarchy of Needs

12. Identify if any employees have "physiological" needs.
13. Address the physiological needs.
14. Identify if any employees have "safety" needs.
15. Address the safety needs.
16. Identify any "social" needs.
17. Address any social needs.
18. Identify any "self-esteem" needs.
19. Address any self-esteem needs.
20. Identify any "self-actualization" needs that can possibly be impacted by the implementation. This will require input from employees.
21. Help employees who have identified a self-actualization need associated with the implementation to satisfy their need.

# References

1. Kapp, K. M., Transforming your manufacturing organization into a learning organization, in *APICS 1997 Int. Conf. Proc.*, APICS, Falls Church, VA, 1997, p. 288.
2. Kapp, K. M., The USA principle: a three-step solution to re-engineering, *Manufacturing Systems*, August 1996, pg. 94–96.
3. Kemp, J. E., Morrision, G. R., and Ross, S. M., *Designing Effective Instruction*, 2nd ed., Merrill, Upper Saddle River, NJ, 1998.
4. Hannum, W. and Hansen, H. C., *Instructional Systems Development in Large Organizations*, Educational Technology Publications, Englewod Cliffs, NJ, 1989.
5. Myers, I. B., *Introduction to Type*, 6th ed., Consulting Psychologist Press, Palo Alto, CA, 1998.
6. Gardner, H., *Multiple Intelligences: The Theory into Practice*, Basic Books, New York, 1992.
7. Kapp, K. M. and Latham, W. F., Making your training dollars sizzle — identify employee learning styles for fun and profit, in *APICS 1999 Int. Conf. Proc.*, APICS, Alexandria, VA, 1997, pp. 390.
8. Kolb, D. A., *Learning-Style Inventory Technical Manual*, McBer & Company, Boston, 1978.
9. Kolb, D. A., *Learning Style Inventory*, rev. ed., McBer & Company, Boston, 1985.

# 6 Design

## Introduction

An ERP system can only be successfully implemented if the training for the system is effectively designed. Poorly designed training results in poorly prepared employees, poorly understood procedures, and inadequate use of the ERP system. Too often, the training for an ERP system implementation consists of nothing more than a poor presentation of the information in the help system or user manuals.

Often the level of training provided stops at the base level of need for employees. Rarely is ERP training designed to provide employees with critical problem-solving and decision-making skills that are required to run ERP, not just as a manufacturing management system, but as a strategic tool to reach new competitive heights.

If the employees are to learn about the ERP system in the proper manner, the materials used to teach about the ERP system must carry an instructional message. It is not enough to provide ERP information to the user; effective design provides instruction and education. There is a big difference between *telling* someone about ERP concepts, rules, and procedures and *teaching* someone about ERP concepts, rules and procedures

The previous steps in the LRP process, Analysis and Diagnosis, provided the input into the Design step. Figure 6.1 illustrates the location of Design within the LRP process. The design step is crucial to ERP success because it links the instruction presented to the employees to the strategic goals of the organization. Effective instructional design is the methodology for providing employees with the necessary tools for the organization to achieve its strategic goals.

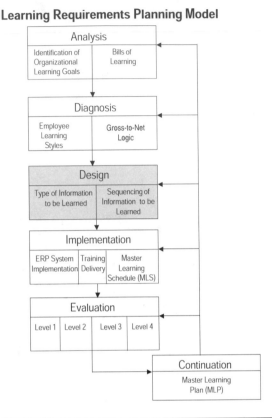

**Learning Requirements Planning Model**

**Figure 6.1 LRP with Design Highlighted. Design Is the Third Step in the LRP Process.**

Unfortunately, few organizations place any emphasis on designing good ERP instruction. Only in rare cases are the instructional packages offered by the ERP vendors based on sound instructional theory. The company implementing the ERP system must take responsibility for the quality and content of the training the employees receive. Taking the time to design effective instruction will return tenfold to the organization in terms of increased morale, more effective use of the tools in the ERP system, and more capable employees able to solve simple and complex problems independently. The design step of LRP ensures that the dollars spent on employee training are not wasted. Often ERP instruction is not effective because it is not designed properly. The information to be learned is treated universally. A detailed plan is not devised for ensuring that the proper classes and learning events are presented to the employees in the proper sequence.

# Overview of the Design Process

Prior to discussing the design of effective instruction, it is important to note that not all learning occurs in a formal classroom setting. Situations like a conference room pilot, a planning meeting, or an informal discussion group can serve as educational events. These events can be more effective in conveying knowledge than a traditional classroom setting. Therefore, when designing an ERP learning program using LRP, do not overlook nontraditional instructional events. These events should be planned and designed using the same rigor as used for designing effective classroom instruction.

The Design of instruction can be approached on three levels. The first level is an examination of the types of classes and learning events that should be taught to prepare an organization for an ERP implementation and to help that organization through the implementation. This would be the design of training at the curriculum level.

At this level of the design process, a sequence of classes and learning events should be laid out and planned for the entire length of the implementation. This level of design involves determining who should attend each class or event and what general types of topics should be covered. At this point, the information gained from the gross-to-net learning requirements process can be used to determine the net learning requirements of the organization. These net requirements are then used to plan the sequence of classes and events to be provided to the employees.

The second level of the design process is more detailed. This level involves the design of the instruction used within those classes and learning events. Regardless of the class or learning event occurring within the organization, the required information must be presented to employees in a manner that is easy for them to comprehend.

During this level of design, three important components are considered. The first is the development of quantifiable learning objectives. The second is the development of effective learning strategies to help employees reach those objectives. The third is the proper sequencing of the instructional content.

The first component of this level of design is the most critical. Measurable objectives must tie directly to the learning objectives developed during the analysis step of LRP; in turn, the learning objectives must tie to strategic objectives. The objectives used during the design process stem from the BOL explosion process.

The second component is the application of the proper learning strategies to the information to be learned. The types of information that are required to be learned during the ERP implementation process are varied and unique.

Employees must learn new jargon, concepts, rules, and how to solve ERP-related problems. Some employees must learn new motor skills like using a mouse, track ball, or bar-code scanner. Most likely, the organization would also like to focus on teaching a good "attitude" toward the new ERP system.

These varied instructional goals require a determination of the type of information to be learned and the best way to present that information to the employees. One-size-fits-all does not work in shirt sizes and it doesn't work for presenting information to learners. Instruction must be tailored to the type of information to be learned during the ERP implementation process and the student's preferred learning style.

The third component is the proper sequencing of the information to be learned. Sequencing is the proper ordering of the content to be learned in a manner that makes it easy and efficient to learn. Some learning during an ERP implementation has an implied order in which it must be learned. An example would be learning to enter a customer order. The order entry clerk must follow a specific sequence when entering the order and the training would most likely follow that sequence.

However, learning the concept of "process reengineering" does not have an explicit order. The designer of the instruction must develop a methodology for presenting employees with the information in the proper order so they can understand the concept as efficiently and effectively as possible.

The final level of the design process is the design of the actual instruction. Each instructional episode, whether it is a lesson or a sublesson, should contain the following four steps. The first is to gain the attention of the learner, second is to present the content to the learner, the third is to allow the learner to interact with the content, and the fourth is to provide feedback and closure for the learner.

Organizations that take the time to focus on designing effective instruction gain the advantage of having a quick and effective ERP implementation with employees who know and understand the advantages, techniques, and procedures involved with ERP.

## Types of Classes and Learning Events

An ERP system is first and foremost a business system developed to help an organization increase productivity, reduce inventory, and cut operating costs. A deliberately designed training program is required to reach those goals on time and on budget. Training classes and learning events must be carefully planned and executed to be effective. The entire ERP training effort should

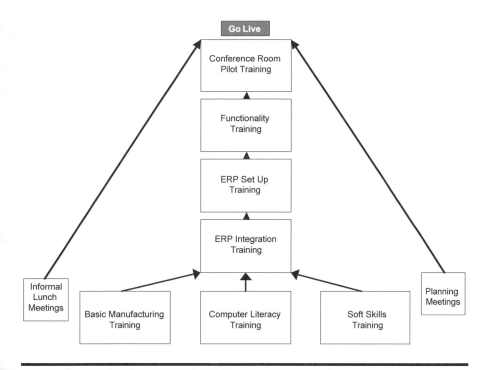

**Figure 6.2 Go-Live Training Pyramid. All the Training Events Needed to Support the ERP Go-Live Date.**

be focused on the "Go Live" date. The "Go Live Training Pyramid" shown in Figure 6.2 represents the concept of having all the training efforts within the organization converge at the proper time to maximize effectiveness of the enterprise wide training effort.

## *Basic Manufacturing Classes*

The first classes that should be taught in an organization prior to implementing an ERP system are basic manufacturing concepts classes. These classes should teach the basic principles of inventory management, production activity control, MRP functionality, and other fundamentals of manufacturing. APICS — The Educational Society for Resource Management has a series of such classes to benefit the organization. Experience shows that when organizations take advantage of manufacturing concepts classes, their implementations proceed at a rapid rate with less delays and problems. Often, organizations receive immediate, tangible benefits just from attending basic manufacturing classes.

The employees in an organization often have never had training on manufacturing fundamentals. They are typically hired for a position, trained by a journeyman employee, and told to produce. Unfortunately, this process can yield less than satisfactory results and can prolong the time period it takes for a worker to become valuable to the organization. While a systematic training program may seem long and counterproductive in terms of producing tangible results quickly and adding value to the organization, well-designed training programs always provide a positive return on the investment.

It is surprising how much value an organization can receive from basic manufacturing training. As an example, in mid1990s a mid-size manufacturer of high-tech refrigeration equipment in Stone Ridge, NY, named **FTS Systems,** faced a challenging business environment with too much inventory, informal systems, long lead times, and consistently late delivery of product. The company underwent a massive training effort in the area of basic manufacturing concepts. Specifically, they used the APICS Body of Knowledge as a basis for educating their employees. As a result of that training and a lot of hard work on the part of the employees, from October 1997 to July 1998 **FTS Systems'** on-time shipments went from 68 to 95%. Delivery time decreased over the same period from 11 weeks to 7.5 weeks. Past due customer orders went from $600,000 to $0–$60,000.[1] Basic manufacturing training needs to be an integral part of the ERP implementation process.

These types of classes can be taught in-house by personnel familiar with manufacturing basics or by a local APICS chapter. These local chapters have a predefined curriculum containing a series of courses highlighting different critical areas within a manufacturing organization.

## ERP Integration Classes

The second set of classes that should be taught within the organization are ERP integration classes. These classes should be designed to provide upper-level managers with a clear picture of the interrelated nature of the ERP system. These classes are high-level overviews of how the various functions of an ERP system can add value to the organization and help it to compete. These classes must also stress that an ERP implementation is no small undertaking and the system cannot be up and running in a week like spreadsheet or word processing software.

One good exercise to conduct in this type of training class is a role-play. In the role-play, the upper-level executives should play positions that do not reflect their daily roles within the organization. The executives are each handed a role and required to "act" as that role describes. For example, one role might be that of the VP of Finance who may have the following description for his or her role:

> *As the company's VP of Finance, you are concerned with saving money and getting a high margin item out the door. You want to produce as much product as inexpensively as possible and sell it at the highest possible prices. You do not think any long-term partnerships with vendors or customers can be profitable to your organization. You are against price breaks for your customers unless they order a lot of product from your company. You are really concerned with the increasing inventory levels within the organization and want to reduce inventory as much as possible. Your motto is "Low inventory equals high profits." You are reluctant to authorize money for the new ERP system because you do not think automation is the answer to the problems within the organization.*

Each major executive should be given a role similar to the example for the VP of Finance. The entire team should then be given an ERP implementation problem. The goal is for each person to negotiate and reason based on the description of the role they have been asked to play. The group must then work together to reach a compromise concerning the solution to the problem.

This exercise helps executives to understand that the ERP implementation is not really about hardware and software but about business processes and determining which process receives attention as well as how all the processes can be brought together to work as a single, effective system. The exercise also provides insights to the executives in terms of thinking outside of their current roles and helps them to see that the issues involved with implementing an ERP system are not black and white.

These types of classes need to be taught by a consultant or seasoned individual who has been involved with a number of implementations. This type of person can provide actual case examples and illustrations of what to avoid and what to capitalize upon when going through an ERP implementation. The experience and insight of a knowledgeable consultant can save an organization literally hundreds of thousands of dollars a year.

## Planning Meetings

A wonderful opportunity for learning occurs whenever the ERP implementation team holds a planning meeting. These meetings consist of determining how to proceed with an implementation, how to solve problems involved with the implementation, and assignment of work tasks. Each of the items on the agenda can be an opportunity for learning. Do not be afraid to schedule time in the meeting for education of the team members. Time can be spent learning about ERP integration issues as well as the needs, responsibilities, processes, and procedures occurring within each department. The other members of the team can learn from the plans made in each department.

It is important to have a written agenda at these meetings and a person taking notes. Many times decisions are made or information is learned in a planning meeting, but because no one recorded the facts, the decision or the information learned is lost. The decision has to be made again and rationale restated because no one can remember what was decided or how it was decided. This not only wastes time in multiple meetings, it can lead to frustration within the team. When frustration levels are high and team members are disillusioned, the planning meetings will cease to be of educational value.

## Soft Skills Training

With most ERP implementations, the training focuses on technical skills (hard skills) such as computer usage or system functionality, but these types of training programs do not provide all of the training necessary for an ERP system to be implemented successfully. According to management maven Tom Peters, 5% of the success of an organization is technology and 95% is psychology and attitude. Information technology, no matter how powerful, is only an enabler. An organization can be wired from the shop floor to the executive conference room, but in the end it's a people game.[2] People must be willing to share knowledge, information, and expertise with each other to make the ERP implementation work.

Soft skills training in problem solving, decision making, needs assessments, or other areas greatly improves the ERP implementation process because ultimately people make or break the implementation. Although this attitude is not shared universally, a MIS director once said, "ERP systems would be easy to use and implement — if it wasn't for the users!" Unfortunately, nay fortunately, the users are the *reason* for the system. No users — no need for a system. Therefore, the users must be trained in skills that make the system work.

Remember, ERP is about integrating across functional units and the key component of integration is communication. In a typical manufacturing organization the implementation team never receives this type of training and the departments don't communicate naturally on their own. Lack of communication is one of the most often-quoted reasons for ERP implementation failures and missteps.

Not only will soft skills training improve and simplify the ERP implementation but, once learned, soft skills are transferable to other corporate projects. Most implementations do not fail because of poor software functionality; they fail because of integration and communication issues. These are issues that can be addressed through soft skills training.

Team building is an important area in which to conduct soft skills training for the implementation team. While the team members work for the same company and may work with each other from time to time, their participation together on the implementation team is typically the first time they are working together to solve a common problem. The team needs to have some guidance and direction on team dynamics and decision making to be successful.

## Basic Computer Literacy Classes

The third set of classes taught should be basic computer literacy classes. These classes should be offered to any individual within the company who feels he or she needs to learn or brush up on using a keyboard, mouse, or the computer operating system. Unfortunately, not many people will volunteer the fact that they do not know a computer mouse from a field mouse.

This type of training is best made mandatory, even if the employee is pretty sure he or she already knows it. Making it mandatory at least lets everyone brush up on his or her skills. A fundamental level of computer literacy is needed for ERP success.

This type of training should not be conducted for prolonged periods of time. An hour is long enough for people to begin to get familiar with the computer but not become too frustrated. Conduct a series of hour-long classes and allow repeat customers until most people feel comfortable just navigating around the computer.

It is important to divorce the computer classes from the ERP classes. Conduct classes that focus on using the Internet, word processing packages, or spreadsheets. This will enable employees to get comfortable with computers in a context other than the ERP system. Then, when the ERP system is ready to be implemented, the company can focus on the ERP functionality training and not on computer training.

## ERP Setup Training

This series of classes needs to be attended by all managers to understand how to set up their ERP system. Some mid-sized systems have over 500 flags/fields that need to be set prior to running the system. Each flag represents a policy decision. Larger ERP systems have even more flags/fields: fields like, "Do you want a credit check at time of order entry? Yes or No?" or, "Do you want net change or regenerative MRP?" or, "Do you want the pricing policy to come from the customer master, item master, or product category code?"

Each of the setup screens in an ERP system has direct impact on the department setting up the screen as well other departments. Often, a flag on a setup screen answers the question "Why is that piece of information printing there?" or, "How come it is planning a lot size of 100 when I entered a demand of 1?" Since each module in an integrated ERP system impacts other modules, managers from all functional areas must attend the setup training for all modules. Figure 6.3 illustrates an Order Entry Control file screen from Lilly Software Associate's repetitive manufacturing system.

## Informal Lunch Meetings

One effective method of conveying information is to discuss the issues with employees in an informal setting. Lunchtime discussion groups are excellent forums for the exchange of ideas between implementation team members and production or office employees. These sessions can be in a question and answer format or in a more structured approach such as a miniworkshop or lesson. The topics can be as varied as reasons for excess inventory, MRP formulas, or improving interplant communications.

Meetings of this type are effective for a number of reasons. First of all, the meetings are informal so there is little pressure for the employees since they know they will not be tested on the information. Secondly, the sessions are short so they are able to hold the attention of the employees. Finally, the lunchtime sessions usually provide more of a two-way dialogue than a traditional classroom setting.

## Conference Room Pilot

An important learning event in the life of any ERP implementation is the conference room pilot. The conference room pilot starts after the implementation team and other employees have set up the ERP system as they think it should function. The team then runs actual orders through the system,

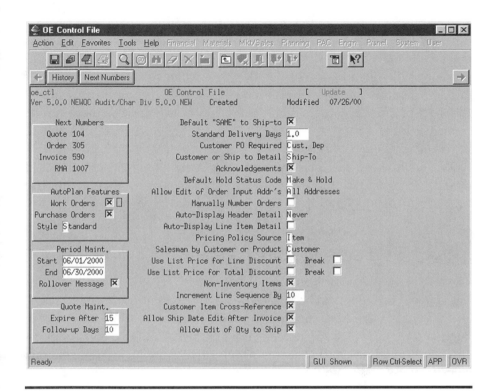

**Figure 6.3  Order Entry Control File Screen of the Lilly Software Associates Repetitive Manufacturing System. (Courtesy Lilly Software Associates, Inc. With permission.)**

testing the functionality of the ERP system, and comparing actual to expected results. The purpose of this event is threefold. First, it is to determine if the setup files are correctly established. Second, it is for the team to gain confidence in the ERP system's ability to function in their environment. Third, it is for the team to learn the overall flow of the ERP system and how the system reacts to exceptions within the order, production, and shipping processes. A great deal is learned from a conference room pilot. It is advisable to conduct multiple pilot training sessions to ensure the incorporation and understanding of all system functions.

## Functionality Training

The final type of classes that need to be taught are the daily functionality classes. These classes teach the employees the daily operations of the ERP system. This training gives employees practice in following the procedures and performing the same functions that they will do on the job. Focused functionality training should be immediately transferable to the business process the individual performs. It should also be coordinated as closely as possible to the "go live" date of the ERP system. Functionality training conducted several months prior to the actual ERP system becoming functional is a waste of time. Employees don't remember the training and they must be trained again.

While certain types of classes are required for an effective ERP implementation, within those classes the information to be taught must be approached in a certain manner in order to be effective. The first step in designing effective ERP training is to appropriately classify the content of each class.

## Managing Classes and Learning Events

The task of making sure all employees are properly trained and prepared for the "go live" ERP date can be challenging. One method of keeping track of all the classes, learning events, and personnel that need to be trained is to develop a training plan. Figure 6.4 shows an ERP training plan to support an implementation. This plan contains information on the type of training, a description of the training, the actions that need to be taken to ensure the training is conducted, the estimated time frame, and the people and resources needed to make the training happen. The plan also contains a brief explanation of the problems that resulted from not having a detailed plan at a sister site. Developing and distributing a detailed training plan will help employees know what is needed to conduct the training and when they should plan on attending training classes and events, or timeliness to complete self study.

## Classifying Information

During an ERP implementation or any large-scale enterprisewide learning event there are different categories of information to be learned. The different categories can be classified into "domains" of learning. There are three domains of learning: cognitive, affective, and psychomotor.

The cognitive domain covers information, knowledge, naming, solving, predicting, and other intellectual aspects of learning.[3] Bloom and associates developed the most well-known classification in the cognitive domain in 1956. The classification is in the form of a taxonomy, with knowledge at the lowest level while the higher mental abilities are classified into five increasingly more intellectual levels. The mental abilities are labeled, *knowledge,*

**Initiative** ERP Software training for implementation, new staff and ongoing new functionality additions.

**Objective** To ensure every user of the ERP Software system has the knowledge required to do their job with efficiency and accuracy.

**Status** Current Initiative

**Current State:**

The ERP Software training approach to date has focused around three areas.

- Many key users in the corporate ERP team and the Kansas City (KC) staff attended OEM training from the ERP Software vendor. This was necessary because of the concurrent efforts at the Beta site of *configuring* the system as the same time as *go-live*. It was expected that these individuals would be able to lead the implementation efforts at KC to ensure high-quality use of the system. Due to the high level of staff turnover in KC, most of those trained at that facility have left the company. There is no training plan in place to replace that knowledge.

- The ERP team has focused on day-to-day "knowledge transfer" with managers and supervisors in Kansas City to filter down to the staff. Each manager and supervisor was deemed responsible for the training of their direct reports. Again due to the high degree of turnover, this training has had limited success. A few departments have created some organized training, most have not.

- The Kansas City training staff has begun to document day-to-day procedures for each department that are intended to be used for training. Many procedures have been drafted, but have not yet been approved. Many more must be developed. Additionally, no coordinated training strategy has been developed utilizing the procedures. The training documents are limited in focus to specific tasks and do not provide any education for understanding the "big picture" of the ERP system or the integrated nature of ERP. This lack of general understanding has resulted in many inadvertent errors with "rippling effects" that went unchecked for a period of time. A large number of data errors have resulted leading to serious business problems.

The ERP team in consultation with a third party consultant has identified the need to develop a comprehensive training strategy that will assist Kansas City in training their current staff and provide support for all future implementations of ERP Software at other sites. In addition, the plan needs to provide ongoing support for new employee training as well as future ERP functionality changes.

There are four types of learning support necessary for users of ERP Software. Each type is appropriate depending upon job function. All four types need to be addressed both during "go live" implementation and for new users in the future.

| Element | Description | Actions | Est. Time | People/Resources |
|---|---|---|---|---|
| Type 1 Training | OBJECTIVE: Provides instruction on basic concepts of Supply Chain Management. The scope, complexity and integration of an ERP system requires many users to understand the "big picture" in order to understand the overall objectives of the system. This broad education does not necessarily explain ERP Software concepts, but integrated *business* concepts to give everyone a common frame of reference for understanding the functionality of the system. An external firm will provide this education in 2–3 days of training. Possible providers include Ollie Wight, APICS. | 1. Select provider for Supply Chain Management. Establish budget and schedule. | 1/2 week | Director of Org. Learning VP IT Training budget |
| | | 2. Work with ERP team and training provider to modify cirriculum, as needed. | 3 weeks | Director of Org. Learning ERP Team |
| | | 3. Establish training records and video-record sessions when taught. | 2 weeks | Training administration Instructional Designer |

**Figure 6.4 ERP Software Training Plan.**

| Element | Description | Actions | Est. Time | People/Resources |
|---|---|---|---|---|
| | PARTICIPANTS: This training will be provided for all managers and supervisors along with many designated employees in each department. | 4. Develop training plan for future new hires. | 1 week | Director of Org. Learning |
| TOTALS: | | | 6.5 weeks | |
| Type 2 Training | OBJECTIVE: Gives a small number of key "super-users" in-depth knowledge of ERP Software functionality of specialized modules. Those trained by ERP Software will serve as in-house "resident experts" for functions learned. A "yellow-pages" directory of experts and their areas of expertise will be made available through an on-line look-up system on the intranet to connect to her users to these highly trained individuals when needed. For chats, etc. PARTICIPANTS: This training will be made available on an "as needed" basis based on job position. | 1. Provide regritration support for OEM ERP Software training, as requested. 2. Develop and maintain "yellow-pages" directory of ERP Software experts. Promote its purpose and availability. | As needed  1 week | Training administration Directory of Org. Learning  Instructional Designer Directory of Org. Learning Training administration |
| TOTALS: | | | 1 week | |
| Type 3 Development | OBJECTIVE: Organizes the "knowledge transfer" process between higher-level users for knowledge areas not addressed in Type 2 training. These higher-level users have responsibility to implement and support the ERP Software processes in their functional areas at their site. This responsibility includes ensuring that departmental staff properly learns and uses the system and also providing a first line of troubleshooting when problems arise with transactions. The development plan will utilize several knowledge-management techniques including; - Knowledge area checklists and "certifications" for each functional area to track the learning and development of each individual. - A "yellow-pages" of employees and contact information for specific topics and issues maintained on the intranet. - Facilitated networks of people ("special interest groups" — SIGS) with similar responsiblities who collaborate on a real-time basis to discuss issues, problems, and questions. - FAQs ("frequently asked questions") created and maintained on the Intranet for various functional issues for easy reference. - A library of ERP Software OEM training manuals. PARTICIPANTS: Includes managers, supervisors and designated senior employees. | 1. Work with ERP team members and functional managers in SJ and PA to establish knowledge area checklists for higher-level users. 2. Expand "yellow-pages" directory to include higher-level users. 3. Establish and facilitate designated functional "Special Interest Groups"; develop support tools to enable efficient functioning of the groups; promote their purpose and availability. 4. Establish and maintain "frequently asked questions" page on intranet. 5. Establish and maintain library of ERP Software training manuals. Promote purpose and availability. | 4 weeks  1/2 week  4 weeks (develop) 2 days per week (ongoing)  2 weeks  3 weeks | Instructional Designers ERP Team members Department managers in SJ and PA  Instructional Designer Training administration  Instructional Designers Director of Org. Learning Training administration  Instructional Designer Training administration Director of Org. Learning Training administration |
| TOTALS: | | | 13 1/2 weeks (and approx. 2 days per week ongoing) | |

| Element | Description | Actions | Est. Time | People/Resources |
|---|---|---|---|---|
| Type 4 Training | OBJECTIVE: Provides the "hands-on" learning every user needs to do their daily jobs. Included with this training will be an orientation to the overall "flow" through the ERP Software system and how each users' individual functions fit in the system. This orientation will give everyone an understanding of the close interaction of all functions and data in the system and the possible ramifications of errors made. The orientation portion of this training will likely be delivered in a classroom setting with a qualified trainer and will be added to the training plans of all new hires who will use the ERP Software system. The task-specific "hands-on" training will be based on detailed procedures (customized for each site, as needed) and certifications. Successful certification on specific training modules will be a prerequisite to a user being granted security access to ERP Software functionality. This training will be provided via computer-based training (CBT) at the user's desktop in a "just-in-time" manner with support from a qualified "mentor." | 1. Conduct needs assessments for manufacturing, finance and distribution. Develop detailed training objectives. | 3 weeks | Instructional Designers ERP Team members |
| | | 2. Review existing training procedures developed in SI. | 1 week | Instructional Designers |
| | | 3. Design and develop ERP Software orientation. Coordinate implementation at all ERP Software sites. | 6 weeks | Instructional Designers Training administration Site Training Staffs |
| | | 4. Design and develop ERP Software "basic navigation" training. Coordinate implementation at all ERP Software sites. | 6 weeks | Instructional Designers Training administration Site Training Staffs |
| | | 5. Design and develop CBT delivery platform. Develop all end-user training modules. Coordinate implementation at all ERP Software sites. | at least 40 weeks (depends on number of modules defined) | Instructional Designers IT Software/hardware |
| TOTALS: | | | 56 weeks (minimum) | |

**Figure 6.4   ERP Software Training Plan (Continued).**

*comprehension, application, analysis, synthesis,* and *evaluation.* Too often during an ERP implementation, the learning is focused on the lowest level — knowledge — and not on the higher levels of synthesis and evaluation.

The second domain of learning is the affective domain. This domain deals with teaching attitudes, values, and respect. This domain is important during an ERP implementation since the organization is trying to encourage the employees to embrace changes and willingly work with the ERP system. Some new users may feel reluctant or hesitant or even act hostile toward the new way of running the organization. Since change can be intimidating, the implementation team should spend time designing instruction to meet the emotional needs of the employees.

The taxonomy for the affective domain within an ERP implementation includes, *Ignoring, Receiving, Responding, Valuing, Organizing,* and *Championing.* This affective taxonomy moves from simply sitting through what is being taught at the *Ignoring* level, all the way to *Championing* the implementation and incorporating the ideas into the employee's basic belief system. Figure 6.5 illustrates the different attitudes on the ERP attitude taxonomy.

It is important to keep the various attitudes in mind when designing and planning instruction during an ERP implementation. Later in this chapter, strategies will be discussed for teaching attitudes.

The third domain is the psychomotor domain. This domain deals with learning physical movements. While it may not seem that there are many physical movements to be learned in relation to an ERP system implementation, keyboarding and mouse manipulation skills may be new for some employees. Ignoring the need to teach employees how to comfortably utilize the computer input devices could cause frustration among the users.

As an example, in one MRP software training program where some computers had a key labeled <Return> and some of the newer computers had a key labeled <Enter>, a class was being taught to a group of production employees. The instructions on the software screen prompted the users to press the <Return> key to continue. One gentleman in the class just sat and stared at the computer keyboard and then stormed out of the room.

When the instructor went after this individual, the man said that the keyboard had no <Return> key, yet he was instructed to press the <Return> key. The student began to wonder what other incorrect or misleading instructions were contained in the software and he decided the manufacturing software could not be trusted. A little up-front education of that individual might have altered that course of events. It is important to teach the basic computer psychomotor skills of keyboarding and mousing.

| Level | Description |
|---|---|
| Ignoring | Person hopes that this ERP "fad" will go away. Doesn't feel impacted by implenetation because he is going to keep doing what he has always been doing in spite of the new software. |
| Receiving | Willing to give attention to the ERP implementation activity. Person doesn't ignore implementation or hope it goes away but doesn't participate. A wait and see approach. |
| Responding | Willing to participate in the ERP implementation at a basic level. Will participate when asked. Will provide information that is needed when requested. |
| Valuing | Sees the value of the implementation. Willing to accept the ERP implementation through the expression of a positive attitude toward the implementation. Volunteers to assist with basic implementation activities. |
| Organizing | Willing to make hard decisions regarding the implementation, willing to submit individual departmental desires for the good of the whole organization. |
| Championing | Believes that the ERP implementation is the right thing to do for the company and willing to champion the implementation. |

**Figure 6.5   ERP Attitude Taxonomy.**

When planning ERP instruction, each of the domains of learning must be considered both separately and in relationship to each other; each domain of learning impacts the others. As an example, when a production manager learns how to use a mouse to "drill down" on some detailed information about the number of labor hours applied to a work order, he is using psychomotor skills as well as cognitive skills to locate and properly use the information he has retrieved. In addition, the attitudinal domain may be incorporated because the desire is to have him look at this information voluntarily twice a day and to find the information of value as he monitors work in process on the shop floor. In another example, it may be necessary to motivate a learner to come to a class on a particular ERP topic or to motivate an employee who was required to attend the class by her manager. Therefore, the "soft" attitudinal domain may need to be the first item addressed, even if the lesson is covering "hard" MRP gross-to-net logic calculations.

The first step to incorporating the different domains of learning into the ERP training is to revisit the BOLs created under the Analysis step of LRP and to make sure that the objectives are written properly. ERP training should not have vague or unmeasurable goals. The learning occurring during the ERP implementation should be quantifiable. When written properly, the objectives classify the different levels of the BOLs into the different domains of learning. The first step toward designing quantifiable learning events is to develop effective objectives.

## *Objectives*

An objective is the final outcome desired from a learning event. Objectives are linked to each other in a hierarchical format in the BOL from the most basic learning objectives on the bottom of the list to the top learning objective, and ultimately to the strategic objective supported. Objectives need to be stated in a manner that is easily understood and measured by the designers and deliverers of the training. While objectives can be stated and developed using a variety of techniques, one of the most effective methods is to state an objective using the ABCD format.[4] ABCD is an acronym representing the words, *audience, behavior, condition,* and *degree*. Objectives written in this format are specific and measurable.

The audience is the group of individuals who are targeted for instruction. While at first this seems straightforward, many times employees will ask, "Will I get anything out of this training?" or, "Should I attend this training?" or, "Who is supposed to go to this training?" Without a clear-cut audience in mind, it is difficult to pinpoint exactly who gains from the class and who would be better served in a different class. The audience element of the objective is used to describe to managers which of their employees would most benefit from the achievement of this objective. Knowing the intended audiences is useful for the training developers; they need to understand the knowledge levels and aptitudes that must be accommodated in the training.

The behavior element of the objective indicates the desired outcome of the particular learning event. The behavior will be stated in the following form, "Will be able to enter a customer order" or, "Will be able to properly read an MRP report and determine what material to order." The behavior is what you want the person to be able to do as a result of the training. It is important to clarify the behavior because training programs can get off track when the desired outcome of the training activity is not clearly defined.

A behavior like "understand how to reduce inventory" is not effective because the actual desire is not an understanding of reducing inventory but a method for reducing inventory. A better behavior would be to "analyze excess inventory and implement an activity to reduce it."

The term "condition" describes circumstances under which the behavior should occur. An example would be "when a customer calls," or "upon receipt of a work order." The condition describes a trigger for the desired behavior.

The term "degree" represents how well the employee must perform to be considered acceptable. The degree of the objective is the measurable component. Measures can be expressed as level of productivity, quantity, quality, time, internal or external customer requirements, or other criteria gained from actual or anticipated work practices.[5]

There are basically two types of "degrees" for objectives: product and process.[5] A product degree describes the product of a task and the process degree describes how well the employee should perform the task. Examples of a product condition include "correctly completed order entry screen," "with no excess inventory remaining," and "within 0.5 mm of specification." Process conditions include "correctly following the MRP ordering recommendations" and "within five minutes of receiving the purchase order."

A completed objective would be something like "A buyer/planner, when given a Master Schedule printout produced by the ERP system will correctly order the quantity needed for production so that it arrives within the correct delivery window for production needs."

Other examples of completed objectives would include:

■ An order entry clerk, when receiving an incoming phone order from a customer, will correctly identify the needs of the customer and record the information into the automated order entry system with zero clerical or typographical errors.

■ An implementation team leader, when faced with a decision regarding prioritization of tasks for an ERP implementation, will correctly select the proper priority sequence as compared to a list developed by a panel of ERP implementation consultants.

■ On the last day of the month, the controller will properly execute the procedure for the month-end closing routine within the accounting module of the ERP system with no errors.

■ A shop floor associate will voluntarily inspect the parts received from an upstream operation and recommend changes to the production process on a monthly basis.

Objectives classify the information to be learned into its appropriate category. The verbs chosen to describe the behavior within the objective are indicators of the types of learning that must take place to achieve the desired objective.

| Domain of Learning | Action Verbs | |
|---|---|---|
| Cognitive | Allocate | Elaborate |
| | Calculate | Express |
| | Compare | Identify |
| | Cross-Check | List |
| | Define | Name |
| | Distinguish | Outline |
| | Divide | Recall |
| Affective | Attend Closely | Judge |
| | Acknowledge | Justify |
| | Assume | Obey Rules |
| | Believe | Offers |
| | Cooperate | Participate In |
| | Display Enthusiasm | Qualify |
| | Engage In | Shares |
| | Interpret | Take Charge |
| | Join | Value |
| Psychomotor | Click | Press |
| | Draw | Record |
| | Lift | Release |
| | Lubricate | Strike |
| | Move Mouse | Type |

**Figure 6.6  Domains of Learning and Action Verbs Useful When Developing Instructional Objectives.**

Once the objectives are properly written, they can be classified into the different domains of learning. The most effective method for classifying the objectives is to identify the action verb for each objective. The action verb within the objective identifies the domain of learning into which the objective falls. Figure 6.6 lists a number of action verbs and their associated domains of learning. Knowing which domain an objective is classified under helps determine which instructional tactics are best for teaching that objective to employees.

## Learning Names, Jargon, Facts, and Acronyms

There are typically four types of basic information that must be memorized at the early stages of learning in an ERP implementation. These types of learning are the basis for all future learning and understanding of the system. The types of information that must be learned are names, jargon, facts, and acronyms.

Much of what is known in an ERP implementation involves understanding jargon. For example, BOM, MRP, regenerative, APS, JIT, gross-to-net logic, and dozens of other terms are not typical in a non-ERP/MRP environment. Basic verbal information must be learned for employees to first understand the ERP system and how it functions.

Examples of having to learn names are the different types of Bills of Material. An employee may be familiar with the basic concept of a Bill of Material but now must learn the names and the associated look of the variations of the basic BOM. Bills of Material can have several variations:

- Modular Bill
- Common Parts Bill
- Super Bill
- Kit Bill
- Single-Level Bill of Material

- Manufacturing Bill
- Engineering Bill
- Indented Bill of Material
- Transient Bill of Material
- Costed Bill of Material

Learning jargon is similar to learning names, however jargon can be more obscure. For example, a novice learner may be able to deduce what an Indented Bill of Material is if he or she already knows what a Bill of Material is and what the term "indented" means. In contrast, an employee would have trouble deducing what "regen" means if he or she never before heard the term.

Another obscure term for someone not familiar with ERP systems or automated manufacturing would be "rough-cut." Although the term refers to capacity planning, no mention of capacity is associated with the term. Another confusing use of jargon is when the time fences in Master Scheduling are referred to as frozen, slushy, and liquid. Jargon cannot be easily figured out without direct teaching of the terms.

The next type of basic information that must be learned are facts related to the ERP system. Facts are simply the association of one piece of information to another. For example, the term "Master Scheduling" means, according to the APICS dictionary, a "process where the master schedule is reviewed and adjustments are made to the master production schedule to ensure that inventory levels and customer service goals are maintained and proper capacity and material planning occurs."[6] This is a fact. Facts are important because they allow information to be connected at a basic level and provide a foundation for understanding concepts, rules, and problem solving.

The final type of basic information is abbreviations and/or acronyms. An ERP system is a virtual alphabet soup of abbreviations. For an example, MRP,

ERP, MTO, ATO, MTS, FAS, PO, WO, DTF, MPS, PTF, and ATP are just a few of the hundreds of acronyms that must be learned for employees to interact with the system and each other.

For any type of learning that involves memorization of information, the following instructional strategy is the most appropriate. First, present the information to be learned to the student (name, jargon, fact, acronym). Second, allow the student to practice with the information. Third, provide feedback on whether or not the student is correctly learning the information. For example, a student may get confused between little MRP — Material Requirements Planning, and the so-called big MRP — Manufacturing Resource Planning. Incorrectly learned facts are difficult to unlearn. It is critical that they are learned correctly the first time. It is like learning an incorrect name of a person and then later learning the correct name. Every time you see that individual, you tend to use the originally learned incorrect name even though you have now learned the correct name.

The information can be presented using three basic tactics. The first is to "chunk" the information. The second is to provide mnemonic devices and visualizations; the third is to encourage repetition. Each of these tactics helps students to memorize and recall information.

Overwhelming students with items to memorize is a counterproductive practice during an ERP implementation. When students are given large doses of information, they master less than 30%. Information to be memorized must be provided to the learners in small pieces or chunks. Study after study has indicated that the average adult can learn best if presented with information in a logical group of approximately five to seven items. For example, the terms MTO, MTS, and ATO can be grouped together as product configurations. Students would have an easier time understanding that Make-To-Order, Make-To-Stock, and Assemble-To-Order are all methods of producing product to meet customer demand than simply learning the terms from a long list of "Terms to Know."

Once a chunk of information is learned, it must be reviewed regularly. A regular review of chunked information helps student to grasp the information without a need to stop and think about the term. For example, after a while the employee will no longer have to stop and think "now MTO means Make-To-Order and that means … ." He or she will just know that MTO means that a product is made based on the specific demands of a customer and is not preassembled or made and placed in stock.

Another technique that can be used to help memorize information is a mnemonic. Mnemonics are tricks to help enrich the information to be memorized and therefore make the information easier to retrieve when needed.

Research indicates that the more richly we encoded information to be memorized, the more easily we can retrieve the information when needed. Mnemonics should be given to the learner at the time the information is presented. Basically there are two types of mnemonics that are appropriate for learning ERP-related information. The first is the Acronym mnemonic and the second is the Phrase mnemonic.

The acronym is simply the first letter of the information to be learned arranged in an order so it forms a word. A basic example is the pronunciation of the word "WIP" pronounced "whip" which is a word formed from the first three letters of the words *Work-In-Process*. Another example is the word PERT which is the first letter from each of the words *Program Evaluation Review Technique*. PERT is a method for project management for a job shop environment or even an ERP implementation.

A variation of forming a word is the arrangement of letters in a logical grouping to convey meaning. For example, to learn about the proper order for the continuously rotating wheel of the Shewhart/Deming Circle, the four letters PDCA are frequently referred to. These letters are the actual order in which a team or individual should move around the Shewhart/Deming Circle. The four parts of the circle are plan-do-check-act (PDCA). The four letters help trigger in a person's memory both what words the letters represent as well as the order in which the Shewhart/Deming Circle should be followed.

Next is a phrase type of mnemonic. A phrase mnemonic occurs when the first letter of a particular name, jargon, fact, or acronym is placed into a phrase or term to aid in the retrieval of the restored information. An example would be ROY G. BIV as a term for remembering the order of the colors in a rainbow (red, orange, yellow, green, blue, indigo, violet). In the manufacturing arena, an example would be a phrase to help someone remember the five key dimensions of a supply chain that goes something like this: "I Stopped Poor Oliver's Truck." The first letters each represent the words *Infrastructure, Strategy, Process, Organization*, and *Technology*.[7]

In addition, a combination of a phrase and acronym approach can be used for the creation of mnemonics. For example, the phrase "STOP Waiting for M&Ms" is a combination of an acronym and a phrase for the seven types of waste identified in manufacturing organizations. The first word STOP represents the first four types, "W" represents another type, as do the two "Ms."

- Stock (inventory)
- Transportation
- Overproduction
- Processing

- Waiting
- Motion
- Making defective products[8]

These mnemonic techniques can all be employed to help employees learn the basic terms, jargon, names, and acronyms they will encounter during the implementation. Another effective method is to encourage the students to develop their own mnemonics and share them with others. This reinforces the learning for both the person who developed the mnemonic and the person who is learning the mnemonic. Working in pairs or groups can be an extremely effective method for memorizing information.

The old "drill and practice" technique is effective as well. This drill and practice technique involves repeating the same information over and over again until the learning has occurred. One particularly effective method of doing this is to have the learner read into a tape recorder the information he or she needs to learn and then to listen to the tape over and over again. The act of reading the words and pronouncing and then listening to them reinforces the learning through repetition using different mental capacities and senses.

Facts are the association of one piece of information with another. For example, a fact is that the term "Backflush" means "deduction from inventory records of the component parts used in an assembly or subassembly by exploding the bill of materials by the production count of assemblies produced."[6] It is not possible to understand the term unless you know the associated definition. Another fact is the idea that a hierarchy is used to display the items in a BOM for learning but not within an ERP software system.

The process of fact-based learning involves linking existing knowledge to new knowledge and constructing meanings for facts. Examples of tactics for teaching facts are associational, organizational, and elaborative techniques.[9]

Associational techniques primarily use analogies, metaphors, and images to convey meaning to a learner, for instance, the common image of inventory being like a stream and when the stream (inventory) is lowered, rocks (problems) are exposed. Effective organizational techniques include clustering facts by categories, placing the facts to be learned into the structure of a case study, and graphic organizers. An example of a graphic organizer is the MRP table; it displays the various concepts on the sheet and shows how they relate to each other. Placing facts to be learned into a case study means that the learner will learn the facts while he or she is reading the information without consciously attempting to learn the facts.

This technique was used in the book by Eli Goldratt called *The Goal*, in which Goldratt describes an elaborate story about an impending closure of a manufacturing plant, a failing marriage, and basic manufacturing facts, as well as concepts and techniques that should be followed by all manufacturing companies.[10] The reader becomes engaged in the story and doesn't realize he or she is learning Theory of Constraints fundamentals during the reading of the book but afterward realizes that learning, not just entertainment, has occurred.

Elaborative techniques are primarily generated by the learner but can be enhanced by the designer of the ERP instruction if he or she includes structures to aid the learner. These structures can include such items as chronology, comparison-contrast, cause-effect, and problem-solution. Also, encouraging students to fill in gaps, make inferences, and imagine "what if" scenarios are forms of elaborations.

Elaborating on a fact allows the learner to place the fact into a context that he or she understands. Well-designed instruction provides the learner with a predefined context so that the learner places the newly learned information into the correct place for future retrieval.

## Conceptual Learning

Concepts are the next level of knowledge that must be known and understood by the employees who will be utilizing the ERP system on a daily basis.

Underlying a successful ERP system are thousands of concepts that must be understood throughout the organization. A concept is a "name or expression given to a class of facts, objects, or events, all of which have common features."[11] For example, "finite capacity" is a concept that consists of related facts like the definition of "finite" and the definition of "capacity." The fact is there are only 24 hours in a day and not all of them can be productive. The fact is shop floor scheduling is needed to ship orders on time. The fact is that "load" is the amount of work to be performed at a work center.

Concepts can generally be divided into two types: concrete and abstract. Some concepts, such as inventory, are considered concrete concepts because an example of the concept can be easily shown. For example, a person can walk onto the shop floor of a metal-stamping operation and see sheets of metal and know that the metal fits the concept of inventory. That same person can then go to a manufacturer that forges axles for trucks and see the long metal bars shaped and sized differently, but still see the bars as inventory.

Other concepts are referred to as abstract concepts because they are not easily seen. A good example of an abstract concept is that of a BOM explosion or "manufacturing efficiency."

Teaching concepts involves two general strategies. The first strategy is one in which the learner is presented with examples and nonexamples of the concept and he or she is then prompted to induce or discover the concept. An example of this type of concept learning can be seen when individuals play a JIT game with interlocking blocks or some other item they must manufacture. First the learners are told to perform some task at their workstation and then they are judged on how many units they produce. Typically the game first uses a push strategy and only a couple of pieces are produced. Then the facilitator provides directions using a pull method of production. Many good pieces are then produced. The facilitator then asks the students to describe the characteristics or aspects of the pull method of production. The learners can then deduce attributes of a pull system of production.

A second method of teaching concepts is to first provide a "best example" of the concept and then discuss its attributes and characteristics. Learners are then asked to develop their own examples of the concept. For example, the instructor may discuss the concept of "value-added" by providing excellent examples of value-added processes and even providing one or two example of nonvalue-added work. The instructor would then ask the students to give examples of value-added work of which they are a part, within their own organization or process.

A third method is to think of the concept as an IF-THEN relationship. For example, to explain the concept of Net Requirements an instructor may walk a student through the following scenario,

> IF the Gross Requirements of item #4767 are 100 units
>    $\Rightarrow$ and the Scheduled Receipts are 55 units
> THEN the Net Requirements are 45 units.

Three effective teaching tactics used to help students learn concepts are graphical depictions of the concepts, analogies, and games. The first tactic is to provide a graphical representation of the concept showing its relationship to other related subordinate and superordinate concepts.[9] An example of using a graphical depiction of a concept would be an ERP flow chart showing the entire concept of an ERP system while simultaneously showing the relationships between the various modules (concepts) with the ERP system such as Master Scheduling and General Ledger.

The second tactic is to describe the concept in terms of an analogy. Analogies can help learners to remember concepts. This technique is especially helpful if the concepts are new or unfamiliar to the learner. An example would be the analogy of a cooking recipe to a Bill of Material. Understanding the concept of the recipe helps the learner to understand the concept of a Bill of Material.

The third tactic that can be used is in the form of a game. The learners can be involved in a game and not have the underlying concepts explained to them. The learners can then "discover" the concepts as they are playing the game. This technique is used frequently to help illustrate the concepts of a JIT or pull vs. push manufacturing environment.

One point to note is that when people first learn concepts, they tend to overgeneralize. For example, someone new to the concept of WIP inventory may assume that all material on the shop floor is WIP inventory when, in fact, some of the material could be maintenance, repair, and operating (MRO) items. Through the use of the various tactics for teaching concepts, an individual will learn to discriminate between examples and nonexamples of the concept and be able to provide examples independently.[9]

## Rules

The next type of information that needs to be learned during an ERP implementation are rules. Rules are a statement that expresses the relationships between concepts. Rules provide parameters dictating a preferred behavior with predictable results. For example, "i before e except after c" is a rule that provides predictable results. In manufacturing, lot-sizing choices such as Lot-For-Lot are rules. Rules are followed by an ERP system. In fact, an ERP system is mostly a collection of rules that are followed when certain events occur.

Rules can be used to predict the outcome of events and explain why certain events occur. Understanding the rules governing the operation of an ERP system is essential for understanding ERP dataflow and maximizing the use of the system.

One tactic for teaching rules is to state the rule and then have the learner work through several examples of the rule. When teaching a rule, it is necessary to ensure that the learner knows all of the prerequisite concepts to understand and apply the rule correctly. When a learner is having difficulty learning a rule, often it is because he or she has not fully grasped the prerequisite concepts.

A second tactic for teaching rules is to provide the learner with examples of the rule and allow the learner to determine the rule from those examples. This technique is not unlike the technique for teaching concepts.

## Procedures

When a series of rules is to be followed in a specific order, it is called a procedure. A procedure is a set of steps that must be completed to perform a task and achieve the desired results. Procedures are a vital element in the daily functioning of an organization. Teaching procedures is also an important element in ERP implementations. In fact, one manufacturer of cable wires estimated that for its new ERP system to function, it would have to develop 350 new procedures for the personnel to follow.

While initially difficult to learn step-by-step procedures, over time most people internalize procedural knowledge and are able to perform the procedure fluidly without thinking of the discrete steps. The best tactic for teaching ERP procedures like pegging a material purchase through to the ultimate customer order or a forecast driving the demand is to first provide an overview of the procedure and its desired outcomes and then to break the procedure into smaller steps and teach each step. Finally, the instruction must focus on putting the steps back in order so the learner can follow the procedure as it would happen on the job. Learners should have practice completing the entire procedure and evaluating the results a number of times. With a complex procedure, the practice might, after initial instruction, involve only simplified cases of the procedure. However, after instruction with more complex cases, the practice should review a range of procedural variations. Unfortunately, the tendency in many ERP training classes is to focus on the exceptions to a standard procedure instead of the more common occurrences within the procedure.[9]

Practice exercises should involve situations that require the simplest or most common path and some that require a more complex and extensive path.[9] After learners have practiced executing the procedure, it is critical that they practice recalling the sequence and the nature of the steps in the procedure. In addition, they should be able to recall critical keywords to ensure that they do indeed denote the entire procedure.

When the procedure is software related, as with ERP, do not simply allow the users to memorize a series of function key commands without thought to the purpose behind the function. Users need to know why they are performing a step in a procedure as much as they need to know how to perform the step. If a step within the procedure is not well understood, it tends to be ignored or changed to suit the needs of the employee. While the employee may be accommodated, the overall manufacturing data collection effort or customer service process could be compromised.

Procedures that are obscure or used infrequently, like a month-end General Ledger closing or annual physical inventory, need to be documented completely with a step by step description of what needs to be done. The procedures document or job aid should clearly name the procedure, the dates it is active, and provide a brief overview of the procedure followed by the step by step instructions. The job aid provides a quick refresher to the person who will be performing the procedure. Sometimes the refresher overview is all the person will need to recall how to correctly perform the procedure.

The procedures document does not need to be a piece of paper to be effective. Many ERP systems have incorporated help systems that allow an organization to place their procedures directly into the ERP system. The users can then access any corporate procedure with only a few keystrokes. Other organizations place their procedures online into intranets or knowledge management systems. These systems allow an employee easy and quick access to the information.

These simple, online solutions only have one caveat. The employees must know how to use the online help and the search functions. It is not uncommon for an employee to be unsure how to use the assistance built into the ERP system or into the company's intranet.

An important element in teaching procedures is to teach how to access information about those procedures. In the few short ERP classes typically attended, it is impossible to teach employees everything they need to know about maximizing their use of the new system. Therefore, time spent teaching how to learn from the information within the ERP system and/or a corporate intranet is time well invested. It is a simple thing to teach the layout of the job aid or help system and how to use it properly. This important step is often overlooked because it is assumed that everyone knows how to read the job aid or use the online help system. That is not always the case.

For example, in one organization employees complained that although electronic release notes were available for all new releases of the ERP software, the notes were simply a long list of statements. The employees did not like scrolling through 50 or 60 separate notes just to get to the ones specific to their department. They had been using the technique of scrolling through the notes for over a year. One day, a representative from the ERP software company was visiting the plant for another matter and noticed one of the employees scrolling through the long list of release notes. He was impressed that she was taking the time to read through all the release notes. She said she wasn't. She was just trying to find the notes specific to her department. He then showed her the search and sort features of the online release notes. She was grateful and spread the "new" technique throughout the company. It is hard to imagine just how many hours that buyer/planner and the rest of her organization spent searching through release note after release note n the capability to find and classify the information was there all along. Teaching employees the functionality, operation, and subtleties of any online help capabilities can save valuable time.

Software functionality changes from time to time because of upgrades, but fortunately the functionality of online help rarely changes. Once an employee knows how to locate on-line assistance, he or she can check for new procedures and information and even review existing information to find better ways of performing the procedures. Employees will be empowered to teach themselves about changes and improvements in the software.

Procedures are an integral part of any ERP implementation. Helping employees to quickly learn procedures and to utilize methods of retrieving procedural information aids in the ERP implementation and functionality process. When employees are comfortable with the requirements of their jobs, they can quickly and easily perform their required functions.

## Problem Solving

A myriad of problems are encountered and solved daily within any complex organization. A machine is running too hot; it is adjusted to run correctly. An incorrect customer order is changed. Inventory for a specific item runs out sooner than expected and a rush order is placed. Joe calls in sick and Harry covers for him. The primary vendor for part #2107 has run out; a new vendor is found. The lathe machine is over capacity and needs to be run on two shifts instead of one. The list goes on and on.

While an ERP system provides the critical data required to analyze and examine problems occurring within a manufacturing organization, it does not eliminate those problems. Employees must use the ERP system to effectively solve problems. Learning how to solve problems is the value-added education that occurs during an ERP implementation.

In educational terms, problem solving is the application of previously learned rules, procedures, memorized information, and concepts to remedy a previously unencountered situation or problem. Problem solving is different from rule or procedural learning because it involves the simultaneous consideration of multiple rules and procedures, the selection of the appropriate rules, and finally, the proper sequencing of the rules and procedures to achieve a satisfactory answer.

Teaching problem solving requires three elements. The first is to teach the underlying rules and concepts that can be generally used to solve problems. The second is to teach students how to look at the interrelated nature of problems. The third is to provide practice for the students to rehearse problem solving in a nonthreatening environment.

The first element of problem solving is actually knowing names, jargon, facts, acronyms, concepts, rules, and procedures. A learner must have prerequisite knowledge if he or she is going to be able to effectively solve problems encountered in the manufacturing arena. Most effective problem solving involves decomposing the problem into its subelements for the cause to be correctly identified. In fact, a common shortcoming among novice problem solvers in a given area of expertise is their ability to correctly identify the problem. Without fundamental knowledge of the environment in which the problem is occurring, identifying and eventually solving it becomes extremely difficult if not impossible. One cannot solve a problem involving incorrect planned order receipts if the concepts and rules of lot sizing, EOQ, time fences, demand fences, gross requirements, gross-to-net logic, and net requirements are not understood.

The second element of problem solving is to understand the interrelatedness of the elements of the problem. Most problems are difficult to solve because of the quantity of and interaction among variables. When one variable decreases, the other increases, when one process is in balance another is out of balance, when one element is favorable another is unfavorable. For example, when management dictates customer service increases within an organization, typically finished goods inventory increases. The problem in this situation is how to balance a high-level of customer service with a reasonable, manageable level of finished goods inventory.

The trick to problem solving is to understand how variables react with one another and consideration of multiple reactions prior to presenting a solution. The analysis of how variables react is important to the final answer to the problem. For example, a common problem in ERP implementations is that once the system is implemented the amount of inventory goes up. This is a troubling situation since one of the purposes of implementing an ERP system is to help reduce inventory. To solve this problem, an individual must first have considerable knowledge of inventory. Is there safety stock for certain inventory? Who controls inventory levels? Knowledge of how the BOMs are structured is required. Knowledge of inventory lot sizes and use of lot-sizing rules is also required. Even knowledge of human nature is needed.

The second element necessary to solve this problem is to understand the interrelatedness of an ERP system. A demand in the master schedule triggers a need for a subcomponent. The subcomponent most likely has a lot-sizing rule associated with it as well as a safety stock requirement. The subcomponent itself will most likely have its own subcomponents, also with lot-size rules and perhaps additional safety stock levels.

If each person responsible for an inventory item within the BOM puts in a cushion for both the lot size and the safety stock all the way down the BOM from the end item to purchased material, the ERP system will calculate the increased need for inventory. If these orders are acted upon, inventory levels rise. If unchecked, the inventory levels rise dramatically. This example illustrates how the first two elements of problem solving are used to analyze and solve a typical problem encountered within a manufacturing organization implementing an ERP system.

The third element in teaching problem solving can be summed in three words *practice, practice,* and *practice.* Errors in problem solving by novices frequently result from their unfamiliarity with the type of problem they are attempting to solve.[12] Experts have less trouble solving a variety of problems because, most likely, they have encountered those types of problems before. An expert problem solver in a particular area first reflects on the new problem and then uses existing knowledge to construct a solution. This means that instruction designed to teach problem solving in an ERP context must involve the presentation of a number of situations in which the learner has an opportunity to practice solving problems likely to be encountered. It also means that the novice must be taught the skills necessary to learn how to reflect upon both the new problem and previously encountered and solved problems. The novice must be taught to think about how he or she is thinking about the problem. The act of thinking about thinking is called metacognition.

Research suggests that emphasis on metacognition during training significantly improves the subsequent ability of the learners to solve problems.[12] Typically, an expert problem solver monitors his or her performance while solving a problem. The experts analyze how they are looking at the parts of the problem, assess the logic they are using to reach a conclusion, predict outcomes, compare and contrast with former problem-solving sessions, and weigh their conclusions.

An effective technique for teaching metacognition skill is to teach the act of self-questioning throughout the problem solving process. Effective metacognition questions to ask during problem solving are

- What did I do last time?
- Let me review what I already know?
- How is this problem similar to others I've solved?
- If there were no barriers to solving this problem, what would I do?
- Who is an expert in this area? What would she do?

- Am I applying the right steps to solve this problem?
- What might I do better to solve this problem?
- What am I not seeing?
- What don't I understand?
- What facts do I need to know to solve this problem?

The skill of metacognition is important to the process of solving problems. Most experts ask these types of questions subconsciously and are not even aware of the process they go through to solve a problem. Making the process overt helps a learner to understand what he or she must do to reach the level of an expert problem solver in a particular area.

An effective method for teaching problem solving and the use of the questioning technique during problem solving is to provide the learners with a number of case studies and ask them to solve those cases. During an ERP implementation, case studies should be designed and built to facilitate understanding of how to use the information from the system to solve problems encountered in the organization.

Building a case study involves working with material that closely approximates an actual situation that a student will encounter while using the ERP system. Case material typically can be found in three formats: factual or true information, disguised information, and completely fabricated information.

Research indicates that each of these types of case materials can be effective as long as the incidents occurring in the case could actually occur to the employee on the job. The fidelity of the case can be relatively low and still achieve the desired results. This is the same concept as watching a play and being startled by a character jumping out from behind a sofa. You know you are watching a play. Other people surround you. You are 50 to 100 feet from the stage, yet you still react.

A learner can know he or she is at a terminal, participating in a "staged" manufacturing case, yet still achieve the desired learning outcome because he or she can "suspend disbelief." Suspending disbelief is the concept that people can be emotionally and mentally drawn into a situation they know is contrived or false because they choose to be drawn in. This phenomenon occurs when someone is reading a book and gets really involved in the characters, and even starts crying although he knows it is just a story.

In a case-based learning environment, learners are presented with a complex but realistic problem environment in which they need to make decisions. The conference room pilot during the ERP implementation is an excellent place to develop and present a scenario of a typical situation and allow the user or team of users to work through the situation.

The learners are given specific details of the problem to be addressed. The learners must then use the information available within the ERP system to solve the particular problem they are encountering. For example, the problem might be to determine if the shop floor has enough capacity to take on a large order from a new customer and still meet the needs of existing customer orders, or the reason why a particular subassembly component is chronically unavailable.

Once the problem is presented, the learners are required to analyze the available information, develop a course of action, and explore their decisions as they relate to the case. During this process, the learners need to be encouraged to use metacognition strategies. The solving of the case and the use of the strategies enables the learner to apply the content covered in the case to the solution of realistic ERP problems. In addition, solving problems in a safe environment provides the learner with a high level of comfort when he or she actually encounters a similar situation on the job. The investment in time to develop and administer the cases is paid back in terms of increased employee morale, the proper resolving of ERP problems, and the higher level of productivity of employees working with the ERP system.

## Soft Skills

Soft skills deal with the development of communication, leadership, and team building. As stated earlier, the need for soft skills training is critical for implementation success. The interrelationship between people is what makes an ERP system function effectively.

Soft skills are best taught with a four-step method. The first step is to present the model for desired behavior to the learner. For example, in an opening lesson on team building the steps of *forming, storming, norming*, and *performing* would be presented. The model of the soft skill to be learned can be presented as written information, but is more effective if shown through a video, DVD, CD-ROM, or a live role-play. A video on team building could show the interaction of a successful team and how it was able to function effectively to solve a difficult ERP implementation problem. Soft skills have a variety of intricacies that must be observed firsthand to be fully understood and appreciated. The second step is for the learner to develop a mental checklist of the key behaviors of a particular soft skill. For example, in team building, the skill of active listening is important. Active listening involves paraphrasing, acknowledging, and understanding how something was said in addition to what was said. It is best when learners are asked to deduce those behaviors from the video model presented in step one. The third step is to provide numerous examples of the soft skill. This may involve case studies of the skills being applied in a variety of situations. It can also involve discussion of what the learner would do if confronted with a situation in which the particular soft skill was required. Finally, the learners need to have the opportunity to practice the skill in a safe environment that provides feedback on their actual behavior. This can involve role-plays of a particular scenario that is likely to occur. For example, two people could act out a team conflict situation while the learner attempts to settle the conflict to everyone's satisfaction.

An e-learning form of this type soft skill role-play is called "social simulation."[13] A social simulation or social simulator accomplishes for the soft skills training what a tank or flight simulator accomplishes for military training. The key feature of a tank simulator is that the soldier is allowed to practice a skill in an environment that mimics the real world as closely as possible, expect that in the simulated environment it is OK to make a mistake.[13] In an actual tank battle that same mistake may kill the soldier.

While not teaching life and death skills, a social simulator can play a valuable role in teaching soft skills. Social simulation software offers a work environment in which the employee can interact with simulated characters through conversations and on-line discussions. As students move around in the simulated world from the shop floor to the customer's place of business, images of the scenes and characters provide visual realism. The students using the social simulator apply multiple-choice options or pull-down menu choices to interact with the character on the screen, who may be an angry general manager or the upset customer. Characters visually respond to the user though digitized video displays or still photographs, showing a range of emotions and feelings depending on the choices of the employee in the simulation.[13] Figure 6.7 is a screen capture for a social simulator that teaches interviewing skills.

While not primarily considered the type of training necessary in an ERP software implementation, often, the soft skills of the implementation team and the key players within the organization make the difference between success and failure. Offering a well-designed off-the-shelf social simulator greatly increases the effectiveness of the ERP implementation.

## Attitudinal Learning

Attitude and employee morale play a large part in the implementation of an ERP system. As Malcolm Gladwell points out in his work *The Tipping Point*, it only takes one or two disenchanted employees to spread bad morale like a contagious disease.[14] Organizations must devote some of their resources to

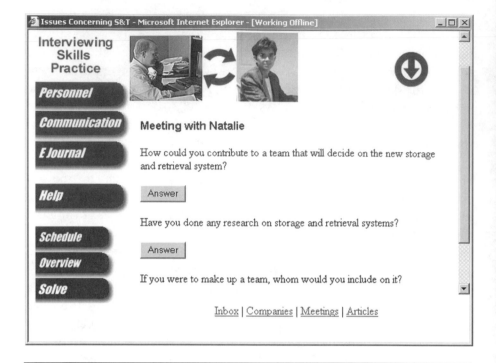

**Figure 6.7  Screen Capture from Social Simulator Used for Teaching Interviewing Skills.**

teaching a positive attitude toward the ERP implementation or at least in trying to influence the majority of employees toward a positive outlook on the implementation.

While most of the time we do not think of teaching attitudes, organizations like Habitat for Humanity and the United Way attempt to teach attitudes toward helping other people who are not as fortunate. Advertisers attempt to teach attitudes toward certain products. Public awareness groups teach attitudes toward smoking, drugs, and unsafe sex. Many of the same techniques used by these groups can be used to help influence the attitudes of employees toward the ERP implementation.

Several methods have been found effective in teaching and influencing attitudes. These methods include endorsement of the concept by credible role models, awareness of the likelihood of success, emotionally charged media events, a display of confidence and enthusiasm by those in charge, and active participation in the event.

One method used frequently by advertising agencies is celebrity endorsement of a product. Whether people like it or not, they are influenced by celebrities or people who have achieved a great deal of success. Companies have been known to hire individuals well known in the field of manufacturing resource management to kick off an ERP implementation effort or to serve as a consultant to the team. Hiring an individual of high caliber, an author of several books, the president of a professional society, or a well-known management guru adds credibility to the ERP implementation effort. It also sends a message to the employees that the company is not alone in the implementation. It projects a positive message that the company is seriously approaching the implementation and is seeking advice and council from some of the best minds available.

Another version of the celebrity endorsement concept is to utilize well-respected people within the company and ask them to endorse the concept and to openly convey the message that the implementation is a positive event for the company. Internal champions who are well respected greatly contribute to building a positive attitude.

A second effective method is to let the employees know that a successful implementation is not an impossible goal. In the 1950s it was thought that no human could break the four-minute mile barrier. In fact, at that time some physiologists claimed that it was impossible for humans to perform the feat. On May 6, 1954 Roger Bannister stunned the world by breaking the four-minute mile illustrating that the seemingly impossible task was, in fact, quite possible. While that news is fascinating and interesting, the really exciting result of Bannister's achievement was the next year, when 37 other runners broke the four-minute-mile barrier. What Bannister had done was shown others the feasibility of breaking the record. He provided proof that it could be done. Once other runners' attitudes changed from one of believing that breaking the four-minute barrier was impossible to knowing that breaking the barrier was possible, they too could break the barrier.

This same technique is effective for ERP implementations. Have a production worker from a company that successfully implemented an ERP system come and talk to the employees about achieving implementation success. When employees know that success is possible, they will work toward that success knowing it can happen at their company. The representative should be enthusiastic, energetic, and able to speak to the employees about what it took to be successful. The representative needs to send the message that if our company can do it, so can your company. Providing employees with an example of what is possible helps to influence attitudes and increase morale.

Having the knowledge that success is possible helps employees achieve implementation success. Software vendors are excellent sources for finding individuals from one of their successfully implemented customer companies willing to speak. The local APICS chapter is also an excellent source of individuals willing to speak about their ERP success stories. Check the last year's conference proceedings for authors of ERP case studies.

Emotionally charged media events can "fire up" employees and leave them with an enthusiasm that is lasting. Many major software organizations, sales conventions, and other big events typically have a multimedia show with music, entertaining light shows, and exciting media elements on the last day. The purpose is to send the participants out with a sense of excitement and energy that they will take with them back on the job and into the workplace.

This same technique can be used not only to kick off the event, but as a booster part way through the implementation when attitudes are sinking. It can even be done effectively in small doses during ERP implementation training classes. It is amazing how effective playing upbeat, exciting music can be at the end of a class period or during breaks. Music has a deep impact on our attitudes and can influence behavior dramatically. Today, with the use of presentation software providing the availability of digital images, music, and video, it is not hard to put together an engaging multimedia show which can present some of the benefits of the ERP implementation to the employees. A presentation like this can also be shown from time to time to the implementation team members to boost morale.

People constantly look to authority figures for cues on how to act and behave. During an ERP implementation, the implementation team is under considerable scrutiny by the employees. How is the team behaving? Is there infighting within the team? Do they believe in the direction of the implementation? Do they always look tired? Are they stressed? Like it or not, the implementation team must act as cheerleaders for the ERP implementation. Certainly there can be bad days, but the overall attitude and outlook of the implementation team must be positive because their attitude is contagious.

Finally, encourage as much participation in the implementation process as possible. Research studies have shown that if a person can be encouraged to perform an important act that is counter to the person's own private attitude, a change in the person's attitude can occur.[9]

Involving employees in different phases of the implementation process can be accomplished in a number of ways. One is to have the employees involved in the planning or analysis phase. Another effective method is to conduct train-the-trainer activities where some employees gain knowledge in an area and share it with others. Another technique is to have employees form into different teams for inventory accuracy, BOM accuracy, requisitions processing, etc. Each of these teams is then responsible for a different aspect of the ERP implementation.

A particularly effective but high-risk activity is to take the individual most adamantly opposed to the implementation and place him or her into a critical role. Many times this method has worked because the person begins to realize the benefits of the implementation and is able to have some control over the changes that are occurring. It doesn't work in every case, but when it does work it is highly effective. The biggest opponent becomes the biggest supporter and other former naysayers fall behind the now pro-implementation individual.

Teaching attitudes is not a familiar process and is not commonly undertaken in a manufacturing organization. However, the above ideas are proven techniques and methods for helping employees to develop a positive attitude toward the ERP system. The attitude of employees must not be overlooked during an implementation.

## Psychomotor

Not many psychomotor skills are required for an ERP implementation. The most important motor skill will be using the computer mouse and keyboard to enter information. Teaching a psychomotor skill involves showing an employee how to perform the function and then allowing the employee to practice, with immediate feedback on whether or not the task is being performed correctly.

For learning to perform mouse-related functions like clicking, double clicking, dragging and dropping, and left and right mouse clicking, a game that comes with Microsoft Windows called "Solitaire" is an excellent skill builder. In the game, the user must perform all of the basic mouse functions. Unfortunately, when a new computer is purchased, the first thing most IT departments do is remove the games. Leave the game of Solitaire on for a while and provide employees with time to play the game. Within an hour or so of playing Solitaire, the user will have mastered any mousing skill necessary for an ERP system. Then the game can be removed.

## Managing the Classification Process

While classifying the types of learning necessary to properly educate personnel prior to the ERP implementation is important, its effective management can seem daunting. Fortunately, a number of tools exist to aid in the process. One of the most effective tools is the "Learning Diagnostic Chart."

This chart provides a visual representation of the objectives that need to be learned, the classification of the objectives by learning domain, a method

| Learning Objective | Domain of Learning | How Assessed | Personnel with Mastery |
|---|---|---|---|
| Naming the parts of a lathe | Learning names, jargon, facts, and acronyms | Given a diagram of a lathe, an associate will correctly identify the parts with 100% accuracy. | Ray Harling<br>Doug Wilson<br>Allen Bradshaw<br>Lori Hollister<br>Lacy Hrynkiw<br>Mary Kay Smith |
| Comprehending which lot sizing method to use for make-to-order inventory items. | Understanding rules | When asked, a worker can articulate three reasons why a particular lot sizing method was chosen for a particular part within 5 minutes. | Ryan Emerson<br>Susan Peascie<br>Ray Harling<br>Doug Wilson |

**Figure 6.8   Learning Diagnosis Chart.**

for assessing the learning, and the names of the individual employees who have mastered that particular objective. This information can easily be entered into a spreadsheet and tracked by the human resources department or departmental managers. This chart can also be used as a guide for cross-training employees to be proficient in different skills.

The Learning Diagnostics Chart provides a quick reference tool for determining who has met which learning objectives, how the learning objective is classified, and how mastery will be determined. This tool becomes invaluable when tracking a large number of employees undertaking the LRP process. Many human resource (HR) software programs have the capability to track, sort, and monitor this type of information. In fact, some ERP systems have HR modules designed specifically for this purpose. These modules or a simple spreadsheet can transform the Learning Diagnostic Chart into a handy tool for assessing the learning needs of individuals going through the ERP implementation process. Figure 6.8 shows a completed Learning Diagnostic Chart.

## Motivation

An important aspect of any type of instruction is motivating employees to attend and participate in the instruction. A systematic method for designing motivational instruction for learners was developed by John Keller.[15] Keller proposed a four-step model. The steps of the model are *Attention*, *Relevance*, *Confidence*, and *Satisfaction*. The model is known as the ARCS model of motivation.

Another aspect of motivating employees within an organization is to examine how adults learn differently than children. In 1968, Malcom Knowles proposed an idea called Andragogy (as opposed to Pedagogy), which was a methodology for helping adults to learn. Knowles' basic premise was that adults have different reasons and motivations for learning than children and therefore must be taught differently. The combination of Keller's ARCS model and Andragogy form a strong foundation for teaching ERP concepts, rules, and problem-solving techniques to adults in a manufacturing setting.

The first aspect of the ARCS model is to gain the attention of the learner. Once the attention of the learner is gained, it must be sustained throughout the instruction. This is similar to Knowles' premise that adults need to know why they need to learn. The attention of the adult learner must be gained by both the content and the implication of the content upon that adult. Adults do not like being in a training class because they were "told" to attend. They need to understand the value of the class to themselves, their function, and the company.

One of the most effective methods of gaining the attention of an adult learner is to present compelling content either positively or negatively. For example, an ERP overview class could start with the instructor showing comment from a front-page article in the *Wall Street Journal* calling the implementation of an ERP system the corporate equivalent of "root canal." A statement of that magnitude would certainly catch the attention of the audience. The instructor could then explain how the company can avoid that fate by effectively learning the information presented in the upcoming ERP lesson.

On a positive note, the instructor could start the class with positive ERP implementation statistics such as implementations have improved corporate productivity by as much as 30%, reduced lead times by as much as 20 weeks, have decreased customer backorders by over $500,000. The instructor could then tell the class that in order to achieve dramatic results like these they need to learn how the ERP system functions and how to take advantage of the system's features and functionality.

The second aspect of motivational instruction is relevance. According to Knowles, adults are goal oriented and relevance oriented. They need to see a reason for learning something. It has to be applicable to their work or other responsibilities to be of value to them. During the ERP instruction, the instructors must clearly identify how the employees will be impacted by the system and what their expected roles will be.

Showing relevance to the employee can be accomplished in a number of ways. First of all, the president of the company could visit the class, or send a videotape or streaming video over an intranet, discussing the importance of the implementation to the organization as a whole and how much the company expects to benefit. Another method is to ask the class to write how they expect the ERP system to positively impact their roles within the company. Then the instructor could ask the learners to share their expectations and discuss what they need to learn to benefit from the ERP system. An effective technique is for the training department to send a letter or e-mail to the employee's direct supervisor once the employee is registered for a class. The letter should explain to the supervisor what the employee will learn in the class and what the employee should be able to accomplish once he or she has successfully completed the class. The letter should ask the supervisor to support the employee by discussing with the employee the upcoming class and its expectations. Once the employee returns to work from the class, the training department should again send a letter reminding the supervisor of what the employee was taught and asking him or her to monitor the employee to see if the learning had occurred. This method is highly effective for motivating employees.

The third element in the ARCS model is confidence. Learners must have a degree of confidence in themselves and the content of the instruction. No one wants to look silly in front of his peers. If the training environment is one in which a person unfamiliar with a computer is forced to use it in front of others or forced to show others a lack of knowledge, the person will not be motivated to continue.

A good methodology for designing instruction to build confidence is to provide small tasks which can easily be accomplished and then build upon those tasks to more complex tasks until the learner is confident in performing the easy and the difficult tasks. For example, establishing pricing policies within an ERP system can be difficult because of all of the variables, options, and algorithms used by the system to automatically calculate the price based on user-defined criteria. To teach the establishment of pricing policies, the instructor could start by showing the students how to establish an item that has the same price for all customers. Then the instructor could show how to establish a pricing policy based on the geographic region of the customer. Next the instructor could show how to set a price policy by combining the geographic region and product category of the item. The instructor could build on that knowledge and show how to establish the price for an item based on the geographic region, product category, and quantity price breaks. The level of detail can steadily increase until the learner has mastered the most complex sequence necessary.

What makes this method effective is that the learner masters each subset of information prior to moving to a more complex level. The learner gains confidence by moving from the simple to the complex. Since the learner gains confidence, he or she is motivated to keep learning. It has been said that good instruction leaves the learner feeling better about themselves.

Adults will not keep working at a task unless they are satisfied with the results. The satisfaction can range from the simple reward of learning new information, to the official recognition by the executives of the organization, to certification in some aspect of ERP. Adults are also satisfied when their input is acknowledged and implemented. If suggestions are made regarding the instruction or some functionality of the system and they are legitimate, they should be acted upon.

The four elements of *Attention, Relevance, Confidence,* and *Satisfaction* must be continually interwoven within the instruction to provide continual and sustained motivation throughout the ERP training process.

## Summary

ERP systems are carefully designed and programmed to perform specific functions to enhance the interaction between and among departments within the organization. The training provided to employees using an ERP system must also be carefully designed to provide the knowledge required to effectively use the ERP system. Many companies have achieved stellar results from mediocre systems because the people within those organizations were trained to use the system to its maximum potential. A large part of reaching that potential is well-designed instruction.

Once objectives are determined and the larger curriculum established, a sequence for the learning events established, the type of learning classified, and motivational events built into the instruction, the next step is to execute the instruction. When training information is presented to the employee, it should incorporate all the elements discussed in this chapter in the following order:

- Describe the objectives of the learning
- Attempt to motivate the learner
- Provide content overview
- Provide examples
- Describe prerequisite knowledge
- Provide the content
- Provide prompts and guidance through the content
- Provide exercises
- Provide feedback[16]

Regardless of the method of delivery of the instruction (instructor-led, e-learning, conference room pilot, or lunch meeting), the sequence should remain constant and the information should be presented according to how it is classified. This training sequence leads to both LRP and ERP success.

Training that is systematic and well sequenced provides employees within an organization with effective instruction. This, in turn, allows the employees to reach their full potential, which should be the goal of any change initiative within an organization. Good design is one of the most critical elements of good instruction. Employees can usually overcome poorly delivered training and even poorly timed training, but a poorly designed training program provides obstacles to learning that can be overwhelming.

## LRP Design Checklist

| Design Task | Completed Yes | No | Date |
|---|---|---|---|
| **Identify Types of Classes and Learning Events Needed** | | | |
| 1. Basic Manufacturing Training | ___ | ___ | ___ |
| 2. ERP Integration Training | ___ | ___ | ___ |
| 3. Soft Skills Training | ___ | ___ | ___ |
| 4. Basic Computer Literacy Training | ___ | ___ | ___ |
| 5. ERP Set Up Training | ___ | ___ | ___ |
| 6. ERP System Functionality Training | ___ | ___ | ___ |
| **Identify Delivery Strategy for Classes and Learning Events** | | | |
| 7. Instructor-Led Training | ___ | ___ | ___ |
| 8. Informal Lunch Meeting Training | ___ | ___ | ___ |
| 9. Conference Room Pilot Training | ___ | ___ | ___ |
| 10. e-Learning Training | ___ | ___ | ___ |
| **Develop Instructional Strategies and Tactics for Teaching** | | | |
| 11. Names, Jargon, Facts, and Acronyms | ___ | ___ | ___ |
| 12. Conceptual Information Related to ERP | ___ | ___ | ___ |
| 13. ERP-Related Rules that Must Be Followed | ___ | ___ | ___ |
| 14. ERP-Related Procedures that Must Be Followed | ___ | ___ | ___ |
| 15. Problem-Solving Techniques and Strategies | ___ | ___ | ___ |
| 16. Metacognition Strategies (thinking about thinking) | ___ | ___ | ___ |
| 17. Soft Skills (communication, leadership, teamwork) | ___ | ___ | ___ |
| 18. Emotional or Affective Domain Materials (what overall message does the company want to send concerning the ERP implementation) | ___ | ___ | ___ |
| 19. Psychomotor Skills (mousing and keyboarding) | ___ | ___ | ___ |
| 20. Motivational Techniques to Implementation Team | | | |
|     a. Gain Attention of Employee Being Trained | ___ | ___ | ___ |
|     b. Establish Relevance of ERP Training | ___ | ___ | ___ |
|     c. Allow Employee to Gain Confidence | ___ | ___ | ___ |
|     d. Show how ERP Knowledge leads to Satisfaction | ___ | ___ | ___ |
| **Develop Learning Objectives** | | | |
| 21. Write Objectives using the ABCD Format | | | |
|     a. Establish Audience for Training | ___ | ___ | ___ |
|     b. Determine Desired Behavior of Employee | ___ | ___ | ___ |
|     c. Establish the Conditions which Elicit Behavior | ___ | ___ | ___ |
|     d. Determine Criteria for the Degree of Behavior | ___ | ___ | ___ |

# References

1. Summerour, J., APICS education improves high-tech refrigeration production, *APICS~The Performance Advantage*, 8(11), 28–30, 1998.
2. Peters, T., *Circle of Innovation*, Alfred A. Knopt, New York, 1997.
3. Kemp, J. E., Morrision, G. R., and Ross, S. M., *Designing Effective Instruction*, 2nd ed., Merrill, Upper Saddle River, NJ, 1998.
4. Seels, B. and Glasgow, Z., *Exercises in Instructional Design*, Merrill, Columbus, OH, 1990, p. 135.
5. Rothwell, W. J. and Kazanas, H. C., *Mastering the Instructional Design Process*, 2nd ed., Jossey-Bass Publishers, San Francisco, 1998, p. 162.
6. APICS, *APICS Dictionary*, 9th ed., APICS — The Educational Society for Resource Management, Falls Church, VA, 1998.
7. Copacino, W. C., Get the complete supply chain picture, *Logistics Management & Distribution Report*, November, 1998.
8. Hall, R. W., *Attaining Manufacturing Excellence*, Irwin, Chicago, 1987.
9. Smith, P. L. and Ragan, T. J., *Instructional Design*, 2nd ed., Merrill, Upper Saddle River, NJ, 1999.
10. Goldratt, E. M. and Cox, J., *The Goal*, 2nd rev. ed., North River Press, Great Barrington, MA, 1992.
11. Kemp, J. E., Morrision, G. R., and Ross, S. M., *Designing Effective Instruction*, 2nd ed., Merrill, Upper Saddle River, NJ, 1998.
12. Leshin, C. B., Pollock, J., and Reigeluth, C. M., *Instructional Design Strategies and Tactics*, Educational Technology Publications, Englewood Cliffs, NJ, 1992, p. 230.
13. Burke, R. D., Representation, storage, and retrieval of tutorial stories in a social simulation, in *Inside Multimedia Case-Based Instruction*, 1st ed., Shank, R. C., Ed., Lawrence Erlbaum Associates, Mahwah, NJ, 1998.
14. Gladwell, M., *The Tipping Point*, Little, Brown, Boston, 2000.
15. Keller, J., in *Systematic Design of Instruction*, 4th ed., Dick, W. and Carey, L., Eds., HarperCollins, New York, 1996.
16. Hannum, W. and Hansen, C., *Instructional Systems Development in Large Organizations*, Educational Technology Publications, Englewood Cliffs, NJ, 1989.

# 7 | Implementation

## Introduction

The integrated nature of an ERP system makes it an all or nothing proposition. One department utilizing the system, partial adoption of a few of the features, or use of only a couple of modules is not effective. The entire organization must embrace and use the system to achieve success. This is the importance of "implementation" in the LRP process. Figure 7.1 illustrates the position of the implementation step within the LRP model and its significance in relationship to the other steps in the model.

Unfortunately, there is no guaranteed adoption of the ERP system. Examples of partial implementations, inadequate use of the system, and nonexistent ROI are available in every industry. Companies have even gone bankrupt because of mismanaged ERP projects. A front-page article in the *Wall Street Journal* claimed that the implementation of an ERP system was the corporate equivalent of "root canal."[1] Failure of an organization to fully adopt an ERP system is expensive, costly, and unfortunately too common.

Too often, failed implementations are erroneously attributed to poorly designed or overly complex software, lack of employee understanding, or failure of the software to conform to existing processes. The real reason ERP implementations fail is because employees resist the new ERP software rather than embrace it. As with any technological innovation, an ERP system must be adopted and used throughout the entire organization to achieve the desired results.

Vijay Jolly, a well-known expert in commercializing new technologies and a professor of strategy and technology management at the International Institute for Management Development in Switzerland, has studied how

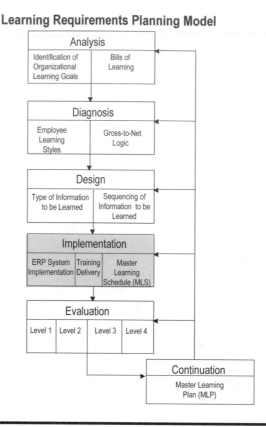

**Learning Requirements Planning Model**

**Figure 7.1  LRP with the Implementation Step Highlighted. Implementation Is the Fourth Step in the LRP Process.**

people adopt technology for many years. Jolly believes that resistance is encountered, not because employees are lazy or want to protect their own interests at the expense of the company, but because humans adapt only gradually to change, overconform to group and organizational norms, have various levels of tolerance for new technology, and tend to limit their focus to repetitive activities.[2]

To minimize this natural resistance to change, a successful ERP implementation requires an understanding of the employees' varying levels of technological acceptance, the proper approach to internally "selling" the system, assembly of a highly effective implementation team, and the proper method of bringing the system online. The team must use established techniques and procedures to help employees more rapidly adapt to the ERP system.

Figure 7.2   Depiction of an Implementation Triangle. This Triangle Illustrates the Critical Areas of Success for an ERP Implementation.

## Overview of the Implementation Process

LRP approaches organizational adoption of the ERP system from three sides. Each side is dependent upon the others. The interplay of the sides is what makes an ERP implementation a success. If any of the sides are ignored, the implementation cannot achieve the desired level of success. Figure 7.2 illustrates the interrelationship among the elements on the triangle which, together, lead to implementation success.

The first side is technological acceptance. This is the concept that employees within the organization will be inclined to use the ERP system with different levels of acceptance. Therefore, the task of the implementation team is to "sell" the ERP system to employees in the organization differently, based on the employee's acceptance level for new technology. The implementation team needs to understand the different rates of adoption and how to utilize techniques to accelerate the technology adoption process.

The process of people adopting the ERP system or any new technological innovation is called "Diffusion." The goal of an ERP implementation team is to diffuse the ERP system into the organization as quickly as possible. The faster the rate of diffusion, the more quickly an organization reaches full system utilization and an optimal ROI. In order to implement the ERP system, the organization needs to focus on how to get the users on board and help them to "buy in" to the new technology.

Diffusion of the ERP system occurs because its concept and practice is communicated from one person to another through both informal and formal channels over a certain period of time. If the diffusion process fails to be positively communicated in either channel, the rate of adoption of the ERP system will be slow. If the diffusion process is negative, the ERP system will be rejected by the organization and the implementation will fail.

The implementation team responsible for diffusing the ERP system into the organization is typically unaware of the process by which innovations are adopted by a group. Awareness and proper management of the adoption process increases the likelihood that the ERP system will be adopted and utilized by the entire organization.

The two key elements of the diffusion process that must be understood by the implementation team are the attributes of innovations that make them attractive to individuals and, secondly, the different types of employees within the manufacturing organization and their tendencies to accept technology and to pass on innovations to others.

The second side of the triangle is an effective implementation team. An effective project team must be assembled and empowered to make the implementation happen. Traditionally, ERP implementation literature focuses on the functional areas that must be represented on the team. While functional area representation is important, the more important aspects of the team are the technology acceptance level of the team members and the roles that each is assigned within the team.

The third side of the triangle is a systematic method of implementing the ERP system. Several strategies exist for actually executing the ERP implementation. These strategies include a parallel approach, phased approach, pilot approach, and a "big-bang" approach. The organization must choose the method that is most appropriate for its needs and then execute the method effectively.

## Side One: Technological Acceptance

The first side of the triangle is technological acceptance. An innovation is diffused throughout an organization because it is attractive to adopt. There are several universal attributes that make any technology attractive. The ERP implementation team must be aware of these attributes and present them to the user base. By presenting the attractive aspects of the innovation to the ERP users, they will be more inclined to adopt the system.

Everett Rogers, author of *Diffusions of Innovations*,[3] has studied technological innovations extensively and developed a list of "attractiveness" criteria
required to have an innovation diffuse throughout an organization. These
attributes are listed below.

## Rogers' Attractiveness Criteria

### Relative Advantage

This is defined as, "The degree to which an innovation is perceived as being
better than the idea it supersedes."[3] The employees must see the new ERP
system as having an advantage over the existing system whether it is a paper
system or a legacy inventory control system. If no advantage is seen, the rate
of adoption among the employees can be low. In fact, research has shown that
the concept of "relative advantage" is one of the best predictors of an innovation's rate of adoption.[3] This is basically the idea of "a better mouse trap."

The higher the perceived value of the innovation, the faster the innovation
is adopted throughout the organization. Therefore, if an organization is
trying to quickly implement an ERP system, the advantages of the system
must be clearly defined for the employees.

In addition, the advantages don't actually have to be real; the important
element for adoption of an innovation is that the employees adopting the
ERP system believe it has a tremendous amount of real advantage. The great
thing about an ERP system is that it typically does have real and tangible
advantages for the employees. The advantages are savings in time and effort,
a reduction in workload, better information upon which to make a decision,
ease of use, and many others.

The implementation team and upper management must develop a kind
of marketing campaign to display to the employees the advantages of the
new system. While many of the advantages will be geared toward the entire
organization, an effort must be made to personalize the advantages so each
individual within the company will realize a personal gain because of the
ERP system.

### Compatibility

This is the degree by which an innovation is perceived by the adopters as
being consistent with the current mission of the company, past experiences
of the workforce, and current needs of the employees. Employees want to
have something that is familiar to them even if it is new. The ERP system

must not be perceived as an overthrow of all that has come before (this was part of the reason why reengineering did not fulfill all of its promises). A complete overthrow is often too radical for most employees to accept. A display of compatibility can be achieved by illustrating how the new ERP system, in some ways, is like the legacy system, or how it is similar to the current practices of the company. The greater part of the system may in fact be radically different, but the implementation team needs to focus on the similarities to the existing practices for the majority of users.

For instance, if employees are now using a Windows-type operating system and the new system is similar, they will have an easier time adopting the ERP system than if the old legacy system is command-line driven and the new system is Windows driven. This level of familiarity will provide comfort to many employees. Even more difficult is introducing a non-Windows software into an organization that is accustomed to a Windows environment.

One aspect of compatibility is how well the innovation meets the needs of the current workforce. One method of determining this is to survey the workers and see if the needs that they are expressing can be addressed by the ERP system. Then demonstrate to the employees how the needs are addressed by the ERP system. This method highlights to the potential users the advantages of the new system and how it is compatible with their current needs.

One note of caution about this attribute, employees in the company who want change and enjoy new technology (there are always a couple) do not want to hear that the system is just a new version of the old way of doing things. Later in this chapter, the different types of employees will be discussed. Different employees will be attracted to the ERP technology based on different attributes. The team must be aware of the type of employee listening to the list of attributes and modify the message accordingly.

## Complexity

How difficult is the new ERP system perceived to be by the employees who will be using the system? If employees perceive the ERP system to be difficult to use or cumbersome then it will not be quickly adopted. The system must be seen as easy to use and understand. This is the KISS concept (keep it simple, stupid).

One method for accomplishing this goal is to provide a basic tutorial on navigating through the ERP system. This tutorial should provide information on how to access the online help system, how to perform basic functions within the system, and how to generate reports and conduct inquiries. The ratio of instructor to students should be low — only four or five employees per instructor. The training should not discuss specific transactions or functionality like MRP generation, rather it needs to focus on building a level of comfort among the employees in terms of navigation and seeking their own help within the ERP system.

Another effective method is to develop a number of system mentors or subject matter experts (SMEs). Each department or functional area can have a mentor who assists others in learning how to navigate and use the basic functions of the system. The mentors need to be trained to effectively use the system and be provided with a complete set of manuals in case a question arises concerning a specific part of the system with which they are unfamiliar.

Another effective tool for minimizing the complexity of the ERP system in the eyes of the general users is to develop "cheat sheets" containing quick reference information that can be distributed to the users. The sheet should contain a reference to which keys are for help, exiting, saving, and deleting. These sheets should be laminated and presented to the employees as part of the communication effort of the implementation team.

## Trialability

This is the degree to which the ERP system can be experimented with on a limited basis before being deployed throughout the entire organization. New ideas that can be tried out on the installment plan will generally be adopted more rapidly than ideas that are required to be accepted all at once. This is the idea of "kicking the tires."

This concept highlights the importance of the conference room pilot implementing a system that is tried and true. Later adopters of an innovation are influenced strongly by those who have adopted the innovation earlier. In some cases, the fact that an innovation has been tried out at another company or even several other companies is enough to persuade people to adopt the ERP system. For others, they must use the ERP system on their own to become comfortable with it.

A good example of encouraging trialability is one used by a tool and die manufacturer in Western Pennsylvania who sponsored a "Test Drive the New ERP System" day. Shortly after the ERP system was purchased, the implementation team contracted a trainer from the software vendor to set up a couple of modules from their company throughout the system and to spend two days helping any employee who was interested to work through a scenario of his or her choosing. The implementation team then "advertised" throughout the company that anyone who wanted to sit down in front of the keyboard and actually "drive" the new ERP system, with expert guidance from the software trainer, was welcome to do so. The test-drive program was a big success. Many of the employees came, two or three at a time, to either test-drive the system themselves or to watch co-workers test-drive it. Sometimes, they just asked the trainer to try a particular transaction. The test drive helped to demystify the new ERP system and helped the employees to realize that they could operate the system, with some training, once it was fully implemented.

## Observability

This is the degree to which the results of the innovation are visible to others. With ERP implementations, this occurs when the success stories of other companies implementing the ERP software are distributed and discussed. It also occurs in plant visits and other types of interaction between the employees of a company implementing an ERP system and those that have already done so successfully.

One problem is that plant visits and discussion with employees at companies that have successfully implemented the ERP system occur prior to buying the system but do not occur once the decision to purchase the ERP system has been made. Additionally, only a few people get to observe the system being utilized at another company. If more employees are able to observe the successful use, the faster the rate of adoption of the ERP system will occur.

An example of providing observability to an entire organization occurred at a company in Michigan that supplies electronic parts to major automakers. This company sponsored several corporate-wide demonstrations of the software product. The demonstrations where scheduled over a three-day period so that everyone who wanted to would have the opportunity to view the ERP system chosen by the selection team. This allowed employees to ask questions about the new system and to actually observe how the new system functioned. The implementation team even created packets of reports and screen captures that the employees could take with them to view at a later time.

The implementation team must present the ERP system to the users within the organization as having attributes that are attractive. They need to be assured that they will be able to use it properly and not be intimidated by its complexity, and that they are not the first ones to use it. If the implementation team can present these attributes favorably, the diffusion of the ERP system will occur more smoothly and quickly.

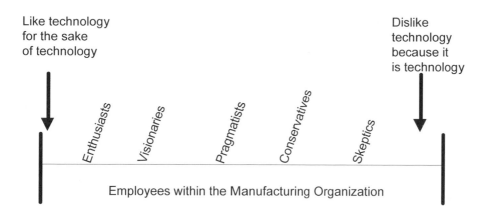

**Figure 7.3   Technology Adoption Continuum Showing the Different Types of Technology Adopters in an Organization.**

## Technology Adoption Continuum

While all the attributes discussed above are useful in "selling" the ERP system internally, certain employees in the company will be attracted to different attributes. In any organizational system like a manufacturing organization, there are four types of individuals on the technology adoption continuum. At one end are the technology enthusiasts who embrace, almost blindly, any new technology. On the opposite end are the skeptics who reject any new technology.[3,4]

In-between are technology visionaries, pragmatists, and conservatives. Each one is more hesitant to adopt the new ERP system than the last. The challenge for the ERP implementation team is to present the technology to the individuals within these different groups appropriately. The difficulty is that the sales pitch used for the technology enthusiasts and visionaries is exactly the opposite of the pitch that should be presented to the pragmatists, conservatives, and skeptics. The unique characteristics of each group need to be understood by the project team. Figure 7.3 illustrates the continuum and the various types of individuals on the continuum.

### Technology Enthusiasts

These people are known in many organizations as "techies." These employees have no problem adopting the new ERP system. They enjoy and are fundamentally committed to any new technology. They like to fiddle with new stuff and like to be the first ones to know how the system works.

When the implementation team is explaining the ERP system, the techies want to know all of the specifications. Does it use the latest and greatest technology? Does it use state of the art languages? Is it Internet compatible? Does it interface with the machines on the shop floor?

Many times, individuals within the engineering and information technology departments are techies. However, techies can exist in any part of the organization. The techies are not interested in the business advantages of the ERP system. Instead, they are interested in the "wow" factor of the technology. They want to see what the technology will allow them to do and what features are available. They are not really interested in translating the "wow" features into internal business practices.

## Visionaries

These are the individuals within the organization who are extremely interested in translating the new ERP technology into advantageous business practices. They are not interested in technology for technology's sake; they are interested in the competitive advantage offered by the technology. These individuals want to use technology to break from the past and start an improved future.

Visionaries are interested in the competitive advantage offered by the new ERP system. They want to know how the features of the system will make their job easier or allow them to do the things they have been thinking about but were unable to accomplish because of the limitations of the current system. They are also concerned with how the new ERP system provides an advantage over competitors.

When the new ERP system is being discussed, visionaries want to know how they can achieve a business or personal advantage with the system. Will the system let me sort customers how I would like? Will the system provide data on customer spending habits? Will the system provide me with information on the quantity on-hand at multiple locations? Will the system provide cost data from each level of an item's BOM? Visionaries are concerned with translating the technology into successful new business processes.

The visionaries look to the ERP system for certain features and functionality that provides unique insights into organizational data not otherwise available. The visionaries use those insights to increase productivity, sales opportunities, or product offerings to customers.

These individuals typically look to the techies for advice and information about new technology and about certain features of the technology. For the most part, visionaries are able to communicate with both the techies of the organization and the pragmatists. These individuals are important during an ERP implementation because they are the ones able to translate the technological advantages of the new ERP system from the technology-speak of the techies to the straightforward, business-oriented language of the pragmatists, conservatives, and skeptics within the organization.

Many times, visionaries are in the sales and upper-level management positions within the organization. These are typically positions of influence throughout the organization and visionaries are oftentimes the first group of employees to address the business needs of the company through the ERP system.

Techies and visionaries are highly interested in the new ERP system precisely because it is new. Taken together, these two types of people will be the first employees within the organization to adopt the new ERP system, oftentimes with great enthusiasm. The techies like the new technology because they like to check out the new bells and whistles, they want to know the Operating System, the database supporting the system, and all of the neat functions of the report writer. They are after the technology and will push to see that it is the latest and greatest.

The visionaries within the company like the new technology because they can see the advantage it provides. Visionaries will be able to see how their job will be simplified or their productivity improved. Visionaries will also be able to see how the system will help the company stay ahead of its competition. They will be pushing some of the unique and special aspects of the system in order to gain an advantage over others. They envision revolutionary changes occurring because of the ERP implementation. The will want to run the business with all the new features, functionality, and possibilities of the new ERP system.

When internally presenting the system to techies and visionaries, the implementation team needs to stress the technological advantages of the system and its ability to provide a competitive advantage above and beyond what can be accomplished with the existing system. Techies and visionaries like the "newness" of the system. The implementation team needs to convince these employees of the newness of the technology and functionality of the ERP system.

Unfortunately, the newness of the system is precisely what the pragmatists, conservatives, and skeptics dislike about the new ERP system. These individuals are not interested in pushing the envelope in either business practices or technological features. They would prefer the status quo and are not interested in the newness of the ERP system.

## Pragmatists

These employees prefer to see a tried and true technology introduced into the company. They want to know that the technology is used by hundreds of other users with no problems or major concerns. They are not technophobic; rather they want to see that the technology works and that it is worth the effort to switch from the old technology to the new before adopting the ERP system. Pragmatists tend to deliberate for some time before adopting the new ERP system. They want to see evolutionary changes within the organization, not revolutionary changes. However, the pragmatists also want to make sure they are not the last people in the organization seen to be adopting the new ERP system.

Pragmatists want to see that the new ERP system will make the existing functions that they use perform work more efficiently. They want one or two new features but really don't want to fundamentally alter the way in which they perform their job functions. On the other hand, if they see the tide going against them in terms of system use, they are able to adapt and adjust to the technology. They can make the change, perhaps not always willingly, from the old system to the new ERP system.

When the new ERP system is being discussed, pragmatists want to know how it is going to impact their daily jobs. Will the system allow me to enter orders like I have in the past? Are there functions able to make the data entry that I currently perform easier to do? How easy is it to find a vendor for a particular purchased part? How will the system know when the bill-to and ship-to addresses are different? Where do I enter special notes? Pragmatists are concerned with how the ERP system is going to make their lives easier and not add any work, yet still allow them to handle special circumstances within the system.

Many times the pragmatists are the order entry, inventory, or purchasing clerks who have developed elaborate systems and procedures for handling their daily tasks. They know the procedures are cumbersome and difficult, but they are the only ones who understand how the system operates and they do not want to alter what they have developed. However, they are willing to change if the new system seems to offer some advantages or more effective methods for accomplishing their daily tasks. The pragmatists are interested in the new ERP system if it clearly makes their job easier. If the implementation team can convince the pragmatists of time and resources savings for them personally, the pragmatists will adopt the new system.

One word of caution is that the adoption of the new ERP system by the pragmatists does not take place as quickly as it does for the techies and visionaries. Often an ERP system receives a tremendous amount of enthusiasm and energy as the project starts and then the enthusiasm dies down and the implementation slows. This is because the techies and visionaries will rapidly embrace the system and become highly vocal about its features and functionality. Once they have adopted the system and it is no longer new they tend to move on. This can occur while the pragmatists are still determining whether or not to adopt the new ERP system. It is important to take time to allow the pragmatists to digest the system and become comfortable with it rather than trying to rush the implementation past them. This is especially important because the next group on the technology adoption continuum is the conservatives, who will take even longer to adopt the ERP system.

## Conservatives

These employees are extremely slow to adopt the new ERP system and by nature are extremely cautious toward new technology. Whereas the pragmatists want to know that the ERP system is used by hundreds of others, the conservatives want to know that it is being used by billions of others. Conservatives border on technophobia. These are the employees who want the new ERP system to do everything the old system did exactly the same way — only better. Conservatives are a hard to please, highly skeptical group.

Members of this group will not adopt the new ERP system until the techies, visionaries, and pragmatists have all done so first. These employees are skeptical about their ability to gain any value from the ERP system and undertake the implementation only under extreme duress. In most cases, they begin to use the ERP system only because the alternative is to be passed by the rest of the organization, or they fear they will not be able to perform successfully and as a result not be of value to the organization. The method that works most effectively with this group is to demonstrate how the entire organization, except them, has switched to the new system and is now using it without any problems. This group certainly doesn't care about increasing their productivity through technology or bettering their positions. They simply want to be left alone and not burdened by the necessity to learn how the new system functions.

When the new ERP system is being discussed, conservatives want assurances that nothing about their present job will change. Of course, the way they perform their jobs will change to some degree. So the questions have to be handled carefully. Does the system have any bugs? How do we handle this (rare) exception? Can I override the price calculation on the system?

How many features can I override? What can I print out so I don't have to perform the function online? Conservatives are concerned with maintaining the status quo and in maintaining their work habits.

A mistake made by many implementation teams is to spend a great deal of time concentrating effort on trying to "convert" the conservatives to becoming enthusiastic about the system. The conservatives will eventually adopt the new ERP system but not until everyone else does. The team's efforts are better spent on the pragmatists. Once the pragmatists embrace the system, the conservatives eventually follow.

## Skeptics

Skeptics will never embrace the new system. The skeptics delight in challenging the hype and claims of the ERP system. "What is the big deal?" the skeptics continually ask. The skeptics are quick to point out problems with the system and exploit any weaknesses in the implementation. They are ever-present critics who are not likely to use the new system unless forced. Many times, it is the skeptics who will leave a company during the implementation process. Fortunately, there are usually only a few skeptics within any organization. Unfortunately, they tend to be highly vocal and they attempt to persuade both the pragmatists and the conservatives to become skeptics. The point of reference for the skeptics is in the past.[4]

Skeptics ask questions in an attempt to undermine the system. They will even try to locate implementation horror stories concerning the particular software purchased by the company. The questions will include, "How come the list of release notes is so long? Why does the system have bugs? Why is the system so slow (regardless of how fast it is)? What if someone enters the wrong information? How do you ensure that the system is calculating correctly?"

The implementation team should not spend much energy addressing the concerns of the skeptics. Because the one or two members of this group are typically very vocal a tendency is to try to address the concerns of these individuals. However, these individuals are not going to change their mind concerning the ERP system and any effort to convince them that the ERP system is good for them and the organization will go unheeded.

Once the implementation team is able to identify who falls into which technology adoption area, they can gear their message toward that individual or group appropriately. These different levels of technological enthusiasm must be handled carefully if the implementation is to be a success.

However, there is one more critical type of person who must be identified and brought onboard to the implementation. These individuals are critical to the success of the project because they are able to influence the opinions of others. These most critical individuals are called "Opinion Leaders."

## Opinion Leader

This person is the individual or individuals within the manufacturing organization who influence other employees' attitudes and/or overt behavior with relative frequency.[4] Opinion leadership is earned and maintained within an organization by the individual's technical competence, social accessibility, and conformity to the system's norms. These individuals are extremely important in the adoption and utilization of the ERP system. If the opinion leaders are enthusiastic and pro-ERP, then others in the organization will follow — if they are opposed to the implementation, others will be as well.

The most striking characteristic of the opinion leaders is their unique and influential position with the manufacturing organization's informal communication structure. The opinion leader's interpersonal network allows him or her to serve as a model whose behavior is imitated by many other employees within the company.[4] Figure 7.4 shows a network within a manufacturing

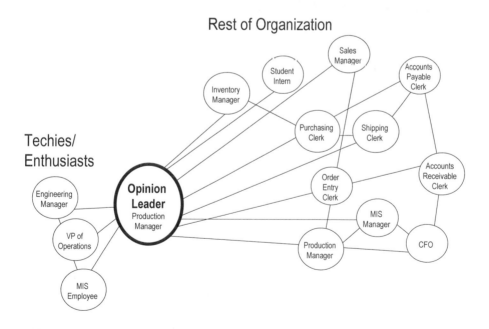

**Figure 7.4   Relationship of the Identified Opinion Leader with the Internal Network.**

organization with the opinion leader controlling the type of technology information that influences the majority of the organization.

Typically, the individual who is an opinion leader is well connected to several different departments within the organization. An opinion leader is the person who speaks informally to people in the order entry department and the inventory department, who is friendly with people in sales and in engineering. Organizations typically have more than one opinion leader: usually two or three. This generally is not a problem but can become an issue if one opinion leader is pro-ERP implementation and the other is opposed.

Early in the implementation process, the implementation team or, even upper management, must identify the opinion leaders of the organization. Upper management will want to place an opinion leader on the implementation team to more rapidly diffuse the ERP system into the organization. If the team has already been formed, the implementation team will want to quickly identify who the opinion leaders are and make a special effort to bring those people onboard. This may require special training or sending them to conferences. The money invested in bring an opinion leader onboard is well spent.

While critically important, the actual identification of an opinion leader is not a difficult process. It requires surveying employees and asking people who they listen to when deciding what actions to take.

There are three systematic methods for determining the opinion leaders within a manufacturing organization.[4]

## Organizational Survey

This method involves asking all employees of the organization whom they go to for advice and information about new ideas. It involves asking every employee in the organization to name a leader or number of leaders. The main question asked is, "Whom do you ask for information about innovations and new ideas?" Opinion leaders are selected the greatest number of times.

## Interview of Key Players

Employees of the company are selected and asked to designate opinion leaders. The question asked is "Who are the people in the company that have the most influence over others?" or, "Who are the people other employees go to for advice and council?" or, "Who would have the most informal influence over other employees?" This method requires that the employees interviewed are well connected to the informal communication network within the company and are insightful enough to recognize which employees are the opinion leaders.

### Self-Designating Survey

This method involves asking each person in the company a series of questions to determine the degree to which he or she perceives himself or herself as an opinion leader. The question asked of the individuals is "Are you a major influence upon your fellow employees?" This can sometimes result in misleading information depending upon the accuracy with which the employees report information.

Once the opinion leaders have been determined, they can be mapped onto a network diagram showing the interactions between and among members of the manufacturing organization. Figure 7.4 shows an opinion leader's position within the organization. This visual depiction of the manufacturing organization can serve as a road map for determining who to contact and who to attempt to positively influence in terms of ERP implementation.

Winning the opinion leaders over early in the organization is crucial to the overall success of the implementation. If the opinion leaders can be positively influenced, many "obstacles" to successful implementation will be overcome. The opinion leaders will influence others and the entire organization will work toward a positive implementation. One of the most effective methods of "selling" someone on a concept is to have them responsible for implementing the concept. Therefore, place an opinion leader on the team.

Unfortunately, in the assembly of ERP implementation teams, an opinion leader is usually not chosen for the team. Teams are usually chosen on the basis of functional position rather than position within the social structure of the organization.

## Side Two: Implementation Team

The second side of the implementation triangle is the assembly and function of the implementation team. The team chosen to implement the system must address several purposes. The first is to see that the various functional areas of the organization are appropriately represented. The inventory, sales, finance, production, engineering, purchasing, and information technology departments must all be represented. These various team members contribute their content knowledge to the project. Most organizations do an adequate job of making sure each functional area is represented.

Where organizations do not do an adequate job is selecting employees from those functional areas who represent the visionaries — those who see the value of the ERP system. As mentioned before, the organization must also include an opinion leader on the team.

Another purpose the implementation team must serve is recognizing organizational "champions," who are responsible for helping others within the organization adjust to the new ERP system. The team must exhibit a positive attitude about the process and encourage others to embrace the system.

The third, and perhaps most important purpose of the team, is to actually implement the ERP system on time and within budget. The team must take the proper steps to ensure that the system can be installed correctly, can be run properly, and can be integrated into the daily functions of the organization without too much interruption to the organization.

To accomplish these three purposes, the team must work together effectively to accomplish its goals. Unfortunately, one of the problems with implementation teams is that although they consist of members from the same company they have rarely had the opportunity to work together as a team. Often, the ERP implementation is the first time the team members are all working together focusing on exactly the same goal. A team naturally goes through a process prior to obtaining maximum performance. Members must become familiar with each other's habits, methods of thinking, and various communication strategies before undertaking the large, complex task of implementing the ERP system. This does not occur overnight. Developing an effective team takes time.

Throwing the members into the ERP implementation as the first team project means that time will be taken away from the project while the employees learn how to function together as a team. If no team training is provided the process will take even longer. The implementation team needs training on how to function as a single unit and how to ensure that they are working to their maximum capability. This type of training can be accomplished with role-play exercises and training simulations.

Simulations are an excellent tool because the process of going through a mock implementation helps team members gain insights into how each individual and the team responds to problems and setbacks. These exercises will help build the team to a level where it can focus on its goal and not on building itself into a working unit. As many "practice" tasks and training opportunities should be provided to the team as possible before giving them the assignment of implementing the ERP system.

## Implementation Team Characteristics

Once the team has worked together for a while and has learned how each member functions within the team, certain characteristics will arise. The following is a list of characteristics that make an ERP implementation team effective.

- Clear purpose
- Defined roles
- Established Process
- Communication
- Involvement

- Empowerment
- Commitment
- Accountability
- Trust
- Exit plan

### Clear Purpose

The goals and objectives of the implementation should be clearly understood by the team, upper management, and all other employees. As indicated in Chapter 4, Analysis, the team should have a mission statement. The development and adoption of a mission statement helps the entire team understand its goal. The mission statement should be written and distributed throughout the entire organization. The mission can then be revisited throughout the implementation process to make sure that the team is on track and focused.

Often, implementation teams can become overwhelmed and lose track of their purpose. Sometimes the implementation team becomes too focused on reengineering processes and not on implementing the software, or becomes so concerned about everyone "liking" the new software that it becomes bogged down in marketing it and doesn't spend enough time on executing the implementation plan. The mission statement serves as a clear reminder to the team of its purpose and direction.

### Defined Roles

Team members require roles in order to function effectively. If roles are not explicitly defined at the beginning of the project, unintended roles will develop that may be counterproductive to the mission of the team.

The team should include the following roles: project leader (traditionally called the project manager), team recorder, team facilitator, team champion, and team member. The members fulfilling those roles should have written job descriptions outlining their obligations and responsibilities concerning

| Name of Person | Name of Role | Expectations of Role | Location on Technology Adoption Continuum |
|---|---|---|---|
| Joseph Hall | Team Leader | Responsible for calling team meetings<br>Developing and monitoring the LRP plan<br>Required to meet monthly with executive management<br>Trouble-shoots implementation issues | Visionary<br>Opinion Leader |
| Nancy Loggins | Team Facilitator | Responsible for running team meetings<br>Required to assign tasks to individuals within the meeting<br>Makes sure input is received from everyone in the meeting | Pragmatist |

**Figure 7.5    Team Roles and Responsibilities of the Implementation Team and Its Associated Responsibilities and Attitude Toward Technology Adoption.**

their involvement on the team. While job descriptions are a common practice when hiring new employees, they are seldom used internally. However, when employees are placed into an unfamiliar job situation, a detailed job description can help them to understand what is expected of them throughout the process of the implementation. The roles work best when the individual team members define them. When the roles of each team member are written, the individuals can refer to their roles when discrepancies arise and team members can remind each other of their roles. Figure 7.5 illustrates a chart showing the roles and responsibilities of each team member as well as their team job description and location on the technology adoption continuum. These are all-important traits to know and consider when assembling the implementation team and after the team has been assembled.

A word of caution about the assigned roles; the roles should not be cast in stone. Allow flexibility within the team. Assigning roles and writing job descriptions for each role is an important component of team growth. It also forces the issue of accountability. However, the goal of assigning team roles is not to restrict the team members in any way, rather it is to allow the team to establish norms and parameters by which it operates. It is always acceptable to ease up on team roles and job descriptions after they have been firmly established. It is difficult to apply strict roles when a team has been run loosely for some time.

The first role to consider is obviously the team leader or project manager. The individual in charge of the ERP implementation must be more of a leader than a manager. A combination of a team leader and a project manager is a "project leader." A leadership emphasis is required since the mere management of an implementation is not enough. ERP implementation team leaders can "no longer update task lists and issue meeting minutes if they are to succeed."[5] Project leaders must inspire, cajole, and lead team members and the organization to success. Implementation of an ERP system is about working with people to accomplish difficult and challenging goals. Managers will not lead people to achieve those goals. All of the planning in the world will not lead to success unless the project leader can inspire his or her team to execute the plan with a clear focus, sound methodology, and a willingness to be flexible enough to fulfill the mission of the team. A team leader is required.

The team leader should be dedicated to the project and be able to devote the majority of his or her time to the implementation. A full-time project leader is most effective because of the large demands placed upon him. The project leader must plan the project, follow up on assigned tasks, spend time rallying the troops, solve process problems, communicate regularly with one or more representatives from the software vendor, report to upper management, keep the entire organization informed of progress, quiet the skeptics, inspire the visionaries, work with the opinion leaders, coordinate with the IT representatives, resolve unexpected conflicts or problems, and sometimes even enter data. This is a large job that can require up to 60 hours a week during critical times in the project.

Unfortunately, in many small and mid-sized companies the luxury of a full-time project manager doesn't seem feasible. If that is the case, the organization should really consider whether it can afford to not have a full-time project leader. An ERP system is, conservatively, a $250,000 investment that will impact the organization for the next 5 to 10 years. Why risk a possible failed implementation because of 20 hours a week? A full-time project leader is not torn between multiple responsibilities and is able to spend full time thinking about the project. The focus on a single purpose provides many intangible benefits.

While a full-time project leader is recommended, the unfortunate reality is that many project leaders actually work part-time because of the limited resources of the organization. If a part-time project leader is a necessity, the following guidelines can help him or her to effectively manage the ERP process and fulfill regular job responsibilities.

A part-time project leader should specify the number of hours he or she is available for the implementation project and the number of hours performing regular duties. These hours should be strictly adhered to, otherwise the project leader may become burned out trying to do 40 hours as project leader and 40 hours as a regular employee. Few individuals can stand to work 80 hours a week for too long.

The scheduled hours should be consistent for the duration of the implementation. The other project team members need to know when the project leader is available to work on the implementation project and when the project leader is not available. Team members, who are also working part-time on the implementation, need to plan their time schedules around the project leaders schedule. Many project leader's want to spend a couple of hours every day on the implementation project and the remainder working on their other job. In some cases this works; however, on days when the project leader starts working on the implementation project, something will come up and he or she will spend the entire day on the implementation. It may be a good idea to schedule one day a week that does not include any implementation duties. The "free day" will enable the part-time project leader to keep up with his or her regular job duties.

As a part-time project leader, not all of the time spent on the project should be tightly scheduled. Many times a project leader needs to react to a problem or situation that arises unexpectedly. These are the times when the project leader becomes most valuable since he or she must make important decisions or intervene in critical situations. This means that the project leader must have some unscheduled time each day to work on project emergencies. Some days the emergency time will not be used and some days it will be over-used.

The part-time project leader must effectively delegate tasks. There are literally thousands of discrete tasks involved with managing a large project like an ERP implementation. The part-time project leader must develop methods of delegating those tasks to others and then following up on those tasks to make sure they were completed properly. This means the part-time project leader will spend a great deal of time on task lists and follow-up meetings. If others could conduct some of those meetings and write some of those lists, the job of the part-time project leader becomes a little easier. To free up time to work on the ERP implementation, the part-time project leader must also delegate a portion of his or her regular duties equal to the time the ERP is expected to take.

The next person chosen for the team should be the project recorder. The project recorder is the person responsible for recording the decisions of the team. Every team needs a recorder because while teams make decisions in meetings, determine procedures to follow, and set policy, not every team member will remember exactly what was agreed upon. Worse, different team members sometimes remember the "facts" of the decision, procedure, or policy differently. To avoid these lapses in memory, a team recorder is needed. The job of the team recorder is to take notes during meetings and training sessions, assemble a list of action items for members of the team, record the rationale for certain controversial decisions, and write down policies and procedures developed during team meetings. The recorder can also be responsible for the implementation team newsletter that is distributed periodically to keep the entire organization informed of the progress of the implementation.

While the project recorder job may not seem like a critical position, it is extremely important. For example, in one ERP implementation in a resistor manufacturing plant in Ohio, no recorder was appointed for the project. The team was making a decision concerning how to code the product category in the item master. The team debated whether the code should reflect production's needs, sales' needs, or inventory department's needs. The first time, they decided to reflect the inventory department's needs. The implementation stalled and no progress was made for several months. When the implementation started back up, none of the team members could remember how the product category was to be coded. A long drawn-out meeting was held and the decision was made that the product category codes should reflect the needs of the sales department.

Again, the implementation was delayed and another meeting was held to determine which product category codes to use since, again, no one could remember the last decision. This time the codes ended up reflecting the needs of the production department. Yet, again, the implementation stalled, this time because the company was purchased. Another meeting was held to determine the product category code. It was unanimously agreed upon at this meeting that the product category code should reflect the needs of the inventory department. This time some one actually did record the decision and the implementation moved on. A lot of time, energy, and frustration could have been avoided if the original decision had been recorded. Appoint a project recorder.

The next position that needs to be filled on the team is that of the team facilitator. This person's duty is to keep the team process functioning. Effective teams require certain elements to be successful. These elements include such items as always having an agenda, giving someone the floor while speaking, not interrupting someone until he or she is finished, involving all team members in the decision-making process, allowing all members to express their thoughts, making sure comments are recorded, apply conflict resolution strategies, and other team maintenance issues. The job of the team facilitator is to sit back from time to time and observe how the group is functioning as at team.

The facilitator makes sure that the rules of proper teamwork, as originally agreed to by the team in its early meetings, are followed. Following the rules and concentrating on the needs of the team helps the entire process to run smoothly. The facilitator's role is to help avoid conflicts within the team that cannot be resolved. If the facilitator is enforcing the rules of the team and ensuring proper team processes, then even though everyone may not agree with a decision of the team, they agree with how the decision was made. Team facilitators are critical to the success of the team.

The next important role is that of the project champion. As stated earlier, a large part of the implementation team's role is to internally sell the ERP system to the users. A team needs a person to constantly consider the user and help them to become enthusiastic about the team. The team champion should also be an opinion leader. This will help tremendously to diffuse the ERP system into the organization. The champion helps to move the team toward its objectives and is the liaison between the team and affected departments. In another view, project champions are considered to be from the executive ranks. Their job is to keep the ERP implementation in front of the other executives and to ensure that the proper priority and funding is committed to the project.

Finally, the team requires members who can work together to accomplish the desired goals. The team members perform the specific tasks required to implement the system. While the team members perform certain tasks, they should not be the only people within the organization working on the implementation. Implementation team members must delegate certain tasks and responsibilities to employees outside of the team.

This is required for two reasons. The first is that the implementation team cannot possibly perform all of the tasks required to get the system up and running by themselves. The second is that even if the team could perform all the tasks themselves, they need to involve others because everyone in the company should own the implementation. If the only employees who feel a part of the implementation are the implementation team members then the implementation team will be the only people using the system once it is installed. The implementation team must strive to delegate tasks to other employees within the company.

## Established Process

Every team needs to have certain rules and parameters under which it functions. These rules and parameters, enforced by the team facilitator, will help the team function together as a cohesive unit. One method is to develop a list of working rules in the early stages of the project. The rules can then be posted and referred to when necessary. The rules can include basic "rules of fairness" like:

- Always respect another's opinion even it you disagree with it
- Do not speak while another person is speaking
- No idea is too outrageous to suggest
- If an idea is controversial a vote will be taken
- All votes are final and an issue may not be addressed again if vetoed
- Focus on the problem or behavior, not the person.

These types of rules help the team meetings to run fairly and they remind the team that basic rules are important for reaching decisions.

In addition to rules concerning fairness, rules of conduct should be established. The rules of conduct should include:

- Meetings will be held once a week on Monday at 9:30 for the duration of the project
- Have an agenda for every meeting
- Always start meetings on time
- Important items brought up but not on the agenda will be placed off to the side for later discussion
- Minutes will be taken at each meeting
- Action item lists will be generated within one day of a meeting

Without specific rules, when times are tough and the implementation is stalled team members may be at each other's throats. Without established rules, the team can become embroiled in its own problems and conflicts and lose sight of the ERP implementation.

## Communication

The team must establish methods of communicating between and among team members. The team needs to determine the best method of getting information to and from each member. In addition to the weekly meeting, communication channels must be established. The team can use written memos, e-mails, or voice mails. The team must use the communication channel that is most effective for all members. It is recommended that some sort of written communication method, like e-mail or memorandums, be utilized. If written forms of communication are used, the recorder should be copied on this information so it can be kept for team reference.

The team also needs to establish a method for regularly reporting to upper management. The team can be sure that any bad news concerning the implementation will travel quickly through informal channels. The goal of the team is to keep upper management informed of the progress on a weekly basis so that there are no surprises. Upper management must also be informed of any process that need to be changed or any obstacles that are stalling the process. The team can use e-mails or memorandums for many of the communications with upper management; however, some sort of regular face-to-face meeting needs to be established. Face-to-face meetings convey many feelings, emotions, and impressions that are impossible to express using other forms of communication.

Finally, the team must communicate the progress of the implementation to every employee within the company. Too often, the implementation team gets so wrapped up in the project that it fails to communicate to the rest of the company. One of the monthly tasks of the team should be to distribute a written or electronic update on the progress of the ERP implementation. A simple one- or two-page message will suffice. An "official" project status report will help to quash any rumors that may arise in the company because the other employees are not informed. The regular update can also serve to generate enthusiasm for the project.

Communication is critical to the success of the project team. The team must communicate continuously and accurately to the rest of the organization, to upper management, and among all the team members. A surprising number of implementations fail because not everyone in the organization is informed of the progress and requirements of the implementation. The team must make good communication a priority.

## Involvement

Each team member must be actively involved in the project. If a member is unable to be involved for any reason, then that member must be excused from the team. The project team has too many tasks and responsibilities to carry a noncontributing member. Even though it may result in more work for the other team members until a replacement is found, it is not an easy course but it must be done.

One method of making the removal process a little easier is to establish criteria indicating when a member should be removed from the team. If that type of rule is established, many times the individual who is not contributing will volunteer to leave the team out of regard for that rule. This allows for a graceful exit for the team and the individual.

Another method is to have the project leader speak to the person privately to avoid a situation where the entire team is confronting one individual. When an entire team confronts one person that person feels "ganged up on" and may resent the team for their actions. If this occurs, the team has just made a very powerful enemy. Imagine the impact on the rest of the company of having a former team member bad-mouthing the implementation. Handle team exits with care and only as a last resort.

The characteristic of involvement does not just center on the members of the implementation team. Employees not on the implementation team must also be involved in the ERP process. As mentioned earlier, the more involved everyone is with the implementation, the higher the probability of success.

## Empowerment

The implementation team must be empowered to make changes and quick decisions within the organization. In many companies, even the simplest decision can take days, weeks, or even months.[6] Implementation teams cannot afford these types of delays. If the project team is seen by the rest of the organization as unable to make decisions, it quickly loses credibility and momentum.

At times, users of an old system or an owner of an existing process will not "allow" a particular change. They will run to their managers or other authority and devise some reason why changes should not occur. If the manager has the authority to override the team, he or she may do so to please the employee. This can cause problems when a change is required to increase productivity or conform to the way the ERP system processes information. The implementation team must be on the management level in terms of authority and power. Being at this level enables the team to discuss the reason for the change with the process manager and gives it the authority to override the manager if necessary.

## Commitment

Members of the project team must be committed to the project. This means that upper management must allocate time for these people to work on it. An implementation is an ongoing process for at least several months and cannot be casually attended. Employees who are not given the proper amount of time to attend to the project will quickly get the impression that the implementation is not important enough to the organization for them to waste their time on it. These employees will not be committed to the implementation. It must be made clear by the actions of upper management that the organization is committed to the project.

The implementation of any ERP software package will not be easy for the implementation team. Members of the team must realize that frequently they will be required to go above and beyond the call of duty. Team members need to be enthusiastic about the project and able to persevere in the face of adversity.

One method to help foster a level of commitment is the process of developing the team mission and of writing the job descriptions discussed earlier. Another method of building commitment is to create incremental goals leading up to the successful implementation of the ERP system. If a team has a number of clear and explicit goals that it needs to achieve, members can become focused and committed. The team must also feel that they have ownership of the process and will not be undermined by upper management.

Upper management must be committed to the implementation since they control the staff, budget, punishment, and rewards within an organization.[7] However, once upper management decides upon the implementation team members and empowers the team, then the members should be allowed to pursue their own course of action to achieve the desired end. The team must own the implementation in order to be committed to the project. If upper management steps in from time to time with certain edicts or decisions in which the team has no say, problems will arise.

This type of situation occurred at a metal-stamping company in Michigan. This first-tier automotive supplier had formed a team to both choose a new ERP system and to then implement that system. The team had carefully deliberated over the decision, invited a number of vendors to demonstrate their product, and then made a final decision on which system to purchase.

In the meantime, a salesman from another software vendor bypassed the selection team and got the ear of the president of the company. Based solely on the input from the salesperson, the president decided to purchase that software system and not go with the recommendation of the selection team. The selection team was then forced to implement the system chosen by the president.

When the consultant from the vendor arrived on site to conduct the first class on the new software, the team leader said, "This is your software, you implement it." The implementation went downhill from that point. Eventually, the implementation failed, team members left the company, the project leader moved back into manufacturing, and the selection process was started over again. Of course, the new selection team chose the software that was originally picked by the first selection team.

Team members will be committed to the project as long as they are given ownership of the project and allowed to make their own decisions. This doesn't mean that upper management should be absent in the process. Upper management plays a key role in securing resources and removing high-level obstacles. Upper management needs to be an asset to the team and not an obstacle.

## Accountability

The team must be held accountable for its actions. Upper management will, and should, step into the implementation process if the team is not doing its job. Because an implementation is a complex process, teams can easily get bogged down and not make any progress. The implementation team members may be busy working on things related to the project, attending classes, and making plans, but the implementation is not moving forward. The team must develop or be given a timeline for the completion of the project and then be held responsible for meeting those dates. Upper management must then use the timeline as a tool for helping the implementation to proceed at a reasonable rate.

Often a "drop-dead" date is established for the team. The team should backward-schedule from that date by determining what needs to be done in what sequence to make that date. Upper management must then not allow the implementation team to push that date back unless a compelling reason is presented. This hard-line approach helps to keep the team on track and focused on achieving the goal.

For example, at one company the implementation had been bogged down for over 18 months, progress was extremely slow, and not much was being accomplished. The upper-management team finally sent down a drop-dead date that would not be moved for any reason. The implementation team responded by rallying the troops, putting in some extra time, and made the date. When the team had no date, it was not focused. When a date was presented as immovable, it made the difference.

This is not to say that upper management should dictate a date and then never alter the date. The management team must consider the actual state of readiness of the team prior to the ultimate decision of whether or not to go live. A blind adherence to any date without looking at the facts of the situation leads to problems. "A couple of month's delay is insignificant compared to the years of pain from a failed implementation."[8]

If the team sets intermediate dates or milestones, and is communicating regularly with upper management, then the state of readiness will not be a secret to upper management or the implementation team. The team and upper management should be working together to achieve implementation success, not just meet some go-live date for the sake of making the date. If used properly dates can be a powerful tool for gauging and making progress.

## Trust

Team members must trust each other and upper management in order to perform their jobs properly. It is trust that allows team members to take chances and to suggest radical new ideas. The team members need to know that what is said in confidence during a team meeting stays confidential. Members need to know they can count on each other for assistance. They need to know that upper management will not be reversing critical decisions they have made concerning the implementation. Team members must be honest with each other and take responsibility for their actions.

Mistakes, problems, and miscues will occur throughout the entire implementation. Each company has a unique and varied culture, and when people implement a new idea or new technology they are pushing the envelope for that organization and mistakes will occur because of the "newness" of the venture. Mistakes are OK. The team must realize that without mistakes progress cannot be achieved. The team must expect mistakes to happen, learn from those mistakes, and then not let them happen again.

Teams can build trust through experientially based learning. For example, the team can take an outdoors rope-climbing class or a white-water rafting trip together. The team can build trust by working on role-plays or simulations together. Playing games together reveals a lot and allows a level of informal knowledge about the other person to be created. A team naturally builds trust and understanding over time because of the close working quarters of an implementation project if everyone is honest, responsible, and willing to forgive mistakes. If the environment is not open or forgiving, progress will soon stop because people will quit taking chances.

## Exit Plan

There must be a light at the end of the tunnel. The implementation team will be working extremely hard during the implementation project and must be able to look to an end of the project. Many teams get burned out on the project because go-live dates are pushed back time and time again. The team eventually believes that the system will never get implemented. Once this feeling of hopelessness sets in, the likelihood of a successful implementation is close to zero. The team must have plans for disbanding itself and moving on to other projects or transitioning into existing or new positions.

The organization must also make plans for retaining employees after the ERP implementation. Organizations can lose their trained implementation talent after the project is completed because of the valuable skills team members will have developed. The organization needs to have clear successorship plans. Employees learn a great deal during an ERP implementation and will often feel stifled or constrained if they must return to the same positions they had before they joined the team. The organization needs to make plans to utilize the valuable knowledge and skills these people have gained and keep them employed with the company.

The implementation team must also plan to celebrate its hard-fought victory when the project is finally implemented. Once the system is in place, the team needs to take some time to reflect on the project, consider lessons learned, and enjoy the contribution they have made to the organization. However, just because the implementation team is disbanded that doesn't mean the job is done.

Keeping an ERP system running effectively is no small task. The team must have put into place procedures and policies to ensure the smooth running of the system. The goal of the team should be to transfer ownership of the newly implemented system to the users.[6] To facilitate the transfer, the team should appoint individuals to oversee various functional areas related to the system.

One method of accomplishing this goal is to develop internal superusers. The purpose of developing superusers is to provide individuals within certain areas of the company who are extremely proficient with the system both as it relates to their specific area and as it relates to the entire organization. Developing superusers who, in turn, pass on their knowledge to existing and new employees helps to involve the entire company in the implementation. Empowering superusers helps the implementation to move more smoothly and quickly.

The characteristics of having a clear purpose, defined roles, an established process, communication, involvement, empowerment, commitment, accountability, trust, and an exit plan helps an ERP implementation team to be effective. Without these characteristics, the team cannot fulfill its potential

## Side Three: Systematic Implementation Methodology

The third side of the implementation triangle is the strategy or method chosen for the implementation of the system. Each organization will decide to approach the process of going live using a different approach. There are four common approaches to the go-live milestone. These are a parallel approach, a phased approach, a big-bang approach, and a pilot approach. Each of the four approaches has certain advantages and disadvantages. The individual organization must determine which approach is most appropriate.

## Parallel Approach

This implementation strategy involves running the current system alongside the new ERP system. The two systems are running at the same time and then data from the new system are compared to the old system to make sure the systems are providing the same or similar information. Once the new ERP system proves that it is providing consistent and accurate data, the old system is turned off and the new system takes over.

During the parallel process the following data from the old system and new system should be compared:

- On-hand inventory balances
- On-order inventory balances
- Open production orders
- Open purchase orders
- Open customer orders
- Bills of Material/recipes/formulas
- Routings/process sheets
- Inventory, customer, and vendor master files
- Financial data including accounts receivable, accounts payable, and general ledger data

The comparison of the data from the two systems ensures that the new system and the old system are compatible. Once the implementation team is assured that the data are accurate in the system and that the information is similar, the cutover to the new system occurs. The parallel process provides the implementation team and rest of the organization with a high level of comfort.

Unfortunately, this method of implementing an ERP system is extremely difficult. It requires the organization to run two systems at once. The process burns out employees trying to keep both systems running if it continues for a long period of time. In many organizations, employees are already scrambling to keep up with their daily tasks. The parallel implementation essentially doubles the workload of these individuals. The implementation team must then review reports from both systems and then pick items to compare. The comparison of the items inevitably yields discrepancies that then must be investigated to determine if the differences in the data are due to problems with the new system or with how data are handled in the new system.

In addition, since the number of people available to rekey information into the system is often limited, the IT department can write computer routines to transfer data from the old system to the new system so the new system is using the data available from the old system. This process is cumbersome and requires a knowledgeable IT staff to create the routines to pass data back and forth from the old to the new system. These routines have to be written, tested, debugged, and implemented prior to the transfer of the data. If problems are found with these routines, time and energy must be spent to correct the data problems and then the information retransferred from the old system to the new system.

The use of the two systems also tends to confuse the employees. "Should I look in the old system or new system for the numbers I need?" "Is that data correct in the old system?" "Where did you get that report?" The confusion is then compounded by the fact that some of the employees in the organization are using the old system and some the new system.

The parallel process also makes training difficult because employees are trying to learn how to use the new system while still using the old. The employee will continue to rely on the old system and not put any trust in the new system because they are comfortable with the status quo. They won't learn to use the new system; they will tolerate it while they get the "real" information from the system they have been using all along.

However, the MAJOR problem with this strategy is that it assumes the organization wants the same data from the new system as it does from the old system. If all an organization wants to do is have the same data from the old system, then why is the organization implementing ERP? The purpose of the new ERP system should be to provide the organization with access to data, information, and knowledge not previously available. If the organization is focusing on simply having the same data, only delivered differently, then the implementation is probably not warranted.

## *Phased Approach*

This strategy involves bringing up one or two software modules at a time, fixing any problems with those modules, and then bringing up more modules. This process phases out the old system and phases in the new.

The first step in the phased process is for the company to select a set of modules that will first replace existing systems. Often, the Accounting modules are chosen since most organizations already have an automated accounting function and most accounting departments are familiar with automated transactions. While there are many positive reasons for phasing in accounting first, one drawback to this approach is that the least number of people are impacted. Rarely are accounting departments very large nor do they interface with many other people in the organization. The success of the accounting department in phasing in the new system is an excellent achievement but does not have the level of visibility needed to convince others of the need to proceed with the implementation. In many respects Accounting should be one of the last areas to implement since much of the accounting data is created by transactions elsewhere in the system. Payables, receivables, inventory valuation, WIP value, etc. will result from the implementation of Purchasing, Sales, and Production anyway. Until those areas are implemented, the Accounting people will need to manually enter a lot of data if they are implemented first. Alternatives to first phasing in the accounting department include

1. The inventory control modules, because of the far-reaching impact inventory control has over the rest of the organization
2. The order entry modules, because they most directly impact customer service and customer relationships; and
3. The production modules, because they are often the least automated and can benefit the most from the application of the rules and procedures imposed by the ERP system.

Another consideration is whether or not a particular functional area includes individuals who are considered techies, visionaries, pragmatists, conservatives, skeptics, or opinion leaders. A successful approach would be to target a highly visible area with a number of visionaries and techies and at least one opinion leader. If this area was successfully phased in, then other areas would follow.

Once the set of modules chosen for the first phase of the implementation is in place, the old method of processing transactions is eliminated and the new ERP software modules are put into use. The employees of that particular functional area then utilize the selected modules to perform their daily functions. The entire implementation team can then learn from the first phase of the implementation and apply those lessons in the next phase.

An example of this type of phased implementation occurred at a company called Westell Technologies.[6] Westell is a provider of high-tech electronic products to the telecommunications industry. The company was implementing SAP/R3 using a phased approach. Westell was able to leverage the experience and insights gained in the first phase of the project to improve and refine the efforts in phase 2 and phase 3. Further, the phased approach allowed Westell to begin receiving benefits earlier, which built momentum and support for future phases. By pausing between the phases, Westell allowed the environment to stabilize somewhat prior to introducing the next change. The implementation was "highly successful" and a "critical component" in the future successes of Westell.[6]

While the phased approach can lead to success, some difficulties can be encountered. One such difficulty is that ERP systems are highly integrated and when one or two modules are used in isolation, missing data, incomplete information, and erroneous results can occur. The integrated features of an ERP system — the features that make ERP so powerful — become burdensome to the implementation team when using a phased approach. For example, if the production modules are phased in first, the order entry information that drives the demand for the production module may have to be manually entered into the system instead of generated directly from the order entry department. This means that the data will need to be keyed in twice, once in the existing system and once into the new system, to feed demand for the work orders. This rekeying of data makes it difficult for order entry personnel to know quantity-on-hand information or the status of the work order unless they looked into the new system instead of the old system. The requirement to look into two different systems to find the information to respond to a customer can be confusing and requires training of the order entry personnel in how to use both the new and old systems. They will need to be kept informed throughout the implementation on which system contains updated and valid information and which system no longer contains the accurate data they need to respond to the customer request.

Also, once new modules are brought online, the data from the modules that have been used for a while must be synchronized with the new modules. This requires a great deal of effort from both the implementation team and the IT department to ensure that all of the data are properly synchronized.

## Big Bang Approach

This approach is also known as the "cold turkey" or "do or die" approach. This strategy involves completely shutting down the old system and bringing the new system online. The organization runs from that day forward without the benefit of the old system for reference or to serve as a crutch. Employees have no choice but to use the new system since the old system no longer exists.

Prior to implementing the big bang strategy, the organization conducts elaborate training, practice, and trial runs. In order for this approach to work, the data in the system needs to be accurate, verified, and stable. All of the customers, vendors, and item files must be checked and rechecked to guarantee integrity. The employees must be comfortable with the system and able to perform the required transactions without any major problems.

Trial runs in the format of conference room pilots, and a "play" database to practice and gain confidence, are essential to ensuring that the system is able to provide the types of results desired by the organization. Everything needs to be in place prior to the big bang. However, the organization must realize that problems will still occur no matter how complete the preparation. It is impossible for the implementation team and other employees to prepare for every problem that will be encountered when going live. The best approach is to try to implement the big bang during a slow period and then develop an ability to fix problems quickly. With the big bang, there is no phasing in of the system.

The big bang cutover typically occurs over a weekend or planned plant shutdown (although this week or two of opportunity is almost always missed). Employees then arrive for work, typically on a Monday, and are required to use the system to complete their daily work tasks. This is an extremely stressful situation for employees and the implementation team. Steps should be taken to reduce the overall stress level and to encourage employees to adequately prepare for the big bang.

For example, it may be better to schedule the big bang in the middle of the week rather than on a Monday. This provides people some time to get mentally prepared for the change and can help to reduce the combined stressors of heading to work on Monday and going "cold turkey" on a new ERP system. In fact, statistics show that more people commit suicide on Mondays than any other day of the week. Therefore, Monday is already a difficult day, do not add the ERP implementation — wait until at least Tuesday.

Another method of reducing stress during the big bang is to have roving response teams available the first week or two of the cutover. These teams should respond to problems encountered by employees using the system. These teams should consist of implementation team personnel, IT personnel, representatives from the software vendor, and perhaps an outside consultant. The role of these teams is to access the severity of any problems encountered, provide an immediate fix if possible, and then to repair any damage caused by the problem and to implement a long-term fix to ensure that the problem does not occur again. These teams help to provide a level of comfort to a workforce that will be understandably apprehensive about the big bang.

The big bang approach has a number of advantages in terms of the implementation as well as a number of extremely serious disadvantages. One advantage is that the employees of the company are forced to utilize the new system. This means that they will not be trying to refer to the old system while the new system is being put into place. The employees will have no choice but to rely on the new system. Another advantage is that prior to the impending big bang, employee motivation to learn the new system is extremely high. When employees realize that they have no choice but to learn the new system, they tend to learn what they need to know to perform their jobs. A third advantage is that data accuracy and integrity are usually checked and double-checked numerous times to help ensure that the data will be ready when the big bang occurs.

The big bang approach can be successful if the company has a single product line, a simple product, or a when several conference room pilots have been completed successfully within relatively small companies. The larger the company, the less likely a big bang implementation approach will work. However, it can work in big companies. For example, Amoco Corporation (now BP Amoco) successfully implemented an ERP system in all 17 of its business groups with a series of "little bangs."[8] The project was accomplished in five separate implementations. People walked out on Friday and walked into a new system on Monday. The implementation was not without minor problems, but overall it was a success.

The disadvantages include low employee morale. If the big bang is not handled correctly, the employees will resent the ERP system, upper management, and the software vendor. The system will be used grudgingly — if at all. The ERP system will not be as effective as it could if employees voluntarily bought into the system instead of being forced to use it. A botched implementation with a big bang does not lead to having the ERP system act as knowledge management system. At best, it will become little more than a database for company information.

Another disadvantage is that no matter how much planning, training, or testing of the data and the system, problems will arise during the initial few days and weeks of the big bang. The implementation team and the employees must be prepared for these inevitable problems and must be prepared to tackle them as they occur. The entire company must be flexible enough to develop contingency plans and work-arounds to keep the organization functioning as effectively as possible. Customers will be forgiving to a certain point and then will take their business elsewhere.

Once the big bang is used to implement the ERP system there is no going back. If the old system needs to be brought back online, the data in it will be weeks old. The inventory balances will be incorrect, the forecasts will be wrong, and the MRP reports will be hopelessly inaccurate. Even if the old system can somehow be salvaged and brought back online, the likelihood of the employees ever trusting either the old or the new system is extremely low.

The single, largest disadvantage is that if the big bang doesn't work, for any reason, the entire company can be placed in jeopardy. If inventory levels are not accurate, production scheduling is wrong, and capacity planning is nonexistent the company will not be able to function and a state of chaos will ensue. These problems could eventually lead to a situation where the company that implemented the big bang approach to the ERP system is not able to ship product. If the company cannot ship product, it cannot invoice; if it cannot invoice, serious cash flow problems result.

An example of this situation occurred at Hershey Foods Inc. who had problems shipping their product, candy, at Halloween time. Although Hershey eventually recovered, the financial losses that quarter were severe. Tom Wallace indicates in his book *MRP II: Making IT Happen*, "Although I'm not aware of any company that has actually gone out of business [because of a big bang implementation attempt] there are some who've come close."[9] The big bang strategy can be risky and the skeptics in the organization will be salivating at the opportunity to tell upper management how they thought that the ERP system was a dumb idea from the beginning, and now that the implementation has failed — they were right. Failed big bang implementations are how implementation team leaders get fired. However, a successful big bang installation is how legends are made within an organization.

## Pilot Approach

This approach is also called the "quick slice" or "slice" approach because it involves implementing the ERP system in a small manageable area (or slice) of the company. The goal is to put the entire system through all of its paces utilizing only a single product line or small area of the company. The concept is to choose an area small enough so that if problems arise, they will be dealt with quickly and effectively.

The pilot should function as a mini-implementation. The tasks accomplished during the pilot should be far-ranging, from order entry to final shipment of the product. Each step in-between, including scheduling, material requirements planning, releasing of a work order or the production of a flow order, purchasing, and logistics should all be handled, if feasible, with the ERP system. The pilot should truly test how the system will function when everyone is using it.

The area of the company into which the ERP system is to be implemented should be small enough to complete the job within three to four months. The product used for the pilot approach should be one that is fairly representative of the manufacturing process and procedures used throughout the company. Choosing an obscure product line that offers little chance to generalize the lessons learned during the implementation of that particular product line is a wasted effort, and a sure method of stalling the diffusion of the ERP system into the organization.

One of the first steps in choosing an area for the ERP pilot is to examine each product line to determine feasibility. One aspect to examine is the nature of the product line and the individuals responsible for that product. Is the product line run in a progressive or naïve manner? Are the employees schooled in manufacturing basics? Are outdated procedures in place? Is there another initiative such as cellular manufacturing also being implemented?

Visit the line supervisor or manager for each product line and determine his or her short- and long-term goals and objectives for the product, talk to sales and find out which product lines they would like to see connected to the ERP system, determine training requirements of the employees on each line and find out how similar a particular product line is to the rest of the organization. Receiving this type of input will facilitate the process of choosing which product line or functional area should first be piloted for the implementation.

Look for product lines with a progressive, educated workforce willing to take some chances and who have put some improvement processes in place. Although another initiative may be underway on that product line, it may be a good time to implement pilot ERP when everything is changing anyway. The employees may feel that one more item thrown on the fire won't matter or that the ERP system will help to achieve the other initiative.

One of the main advantages of the pilot approach is that it allows the organization to focus all of its implementation efforts, knowledge, and resources on a single area. This narrow approach means that the efforts of the implementation team will not get scattered throughout the organization. Any problems encountered can be addressed immediately and any data accuracy problem is contained to a few part numbers or one or two BOMs, and not multiplied exponentially throughout the organization.

At the end of each day of the pilot, the implementation team should hold a meeting to discuss problems, solutions, and any work-arounds required. The meetings should then designate action plans for addressing every issue that requires attention. At the end of each week of the pilot a longer meeting should be held to discuss methods of applying the lessons learned to larger areas of the organization. Careful notes and records should be kept at theses meetings to make sure that the organizational knowledge about the pilot implementation process is not forgotten or lost. Preparing "lessons learned" documents during the pilot will be most helpful when expanding to other product lines. Discussing what worked well and why, and what didn't work and why, will minimize problems and maximize implementation success.

Another advantage of this approach is that it allows the organization to quickly begin to receive ROI for the system. Often the full-blown implementation of an ERP system takes 12 to 15 months, sometimes longer. If the implementation team can get a quick victory by bringing up an important product line in three or four months, the organization will quickly see the advantages. When others see the success of the pilot, they will become enthusiastic about the ERP system and want their areas to be next.

One potential pitfall of this approach is that if the pilot fails for any reason, the entire organization will know of the failure and no one will step up to volunteer his or her product line for the next pilot. Careful consideration should be given to choosing just the right area and personnel to make the ERP pilot a success.

This approach builds ERP system knowledge and experience into a few employees within the organization and allows those employees to "cut their teeth" on the new system and to gain a firsthand understanding of the system and how it functions using actual data and products.

Choosing the correct implementation strategy for the organization depends upon a number of variables:

- Level of comfort the employees have with new technology.
- State of the old system.
- Familiarity of employees with ERP systems.
- Experience level of the implementation team.

All of these factors must be considered before determining which implementation approach is best.

## Summary

The successful implementation of an ERP system depends upon many factors. The employees of the organization must be assured that the ERP technology is going to provide them advantages over the older methods of doing business, but is not going to be so different and complex that they can't use it. The different levels of technology acceptance must be taken into consideration and accounted for when the implementation team is "selling" the system to the users.

The implementation team must be properly trained and have experience working together prior to tackling the formidable task of implementing the system. The team must have time to develop characteristics that will make it successful.

Finally, the team must choose the correct go-live method. The method chosen must reflect the characteristics of the organization and must provide the greatest benefit for the time and resources committed.

These three concepts are summarized in the idea of the implementation triangle. The LRP process uses this triangle as the basis for a successful implementation. The most important part of the implementation process, of course, is the training and preparation that precedes the implementation. The LRP process drives the preparation and training and helps the actual diffusion of the ERP system into the organization to occur quickly and effectively.

## LRP Implementation Checklist

| Implementation Task | Completed Yes | No | Date |
|---|---|---|---|
| **Identify Attributes of ERP Appealing to User Base** | | | |
| 1. Relative Advantage | —— | —— | —— |
| 2. Compatibility | —— | —— | —— |
| 3. Complexity | —— | —— | —— |
| 4. Trialability | —— | —— | —— |
| 5. Observability | —— | —— | —— |
| **Identify Employees on Technology Adoption Continuum** | | | |
| 6. Technology Enthusiasts | —— | —— | —— |
| 7. Visionaries | —— | —— | —— |
| 8. Pragmatists | —— | —— | —— |
| 9. Conservatives | —— | —— | —— |
| 10. Skeptics | —— | —— | —— |
| 11. Opinion Leaders | —— | —— | —— |
| **Identify Method of Determining Opinion Leaders** | | | |
| 12. Organizational Survey | —— | —— | —— |
| 13. Interview Key Players | —— | —— | —— |
| 14. Self-Designating Survey | —— | —— | —— |
| **Identify Employees For Implementation Team** | | | |
| 15. Choose Representatives from Appropriate Functional Areas | —— | —— | —— |
| 16. Choose Representatives from Appropriate Technology Adoption Continuum Location | —— | —— | —— |
| 17. Choose an Opinion Leader | —— | —— | —— |
| **Provide Team Training** | | | |
| 18. Give Team-Building Training to Implementation Team | —— | —— | —— |
| 19. Give Team-Building Experiences to Implementation Team | —— | —— | —— |
| 20. Allow Team Time to Work to Maximum Effectiveness Prior to Starting Implementation | —— | —— | —— |
| **Consider Pros and Cons of Each Go-Live Method** | | | |
| 21. Parallel | —— | —— | —— |
| 22. Phased | —— | —— | —— |
| 23. Big Bang | —— | —— | —— |
| 24. Pilot | —— | —— | —— |
| 25. Choose Go-Live Method | —— | —— | —— |

# References

1. White, J.B., Clark, D., and Ascarelli, S., This German Software is Complex, Expensive — And Wildly Popular, *The Wall Street Journal*, Friday, March 14, 1997, Vol. IC, No. 51.
2. Jolly, V. K., *Commercializing New Technologies*, Harvard Business School Press, Boston, 1997.
3. Rogers, E. M., *Diffusions of Innovations*, 3rd ed., Free Press, New York, 1983, p. 15.
4. Moore, G. A., *Inside the Tornado*, Harper Business, New York, 1995.
5. Smith, G. R., Project leadership: why project management alone doesn't work, in *APICS 1997 Int. Conf. Proc.*, APICS, Falls Church, VA, 1997, p. 285.
6. Marshall, B. A. and Uzkan, S., If ERP is the solution, what is the problem? A practitioner's approach to building a new model, in *APICS 1999 Int. Conf. Proc.*, APICS, Alexandria, VA, 1999, pp. 473–476.
7. Miller, G. J., ERP implementation lessons, in *APICS 1999 Int. Conf. Proc.*, APICS, Alexandria, VA, 1999, pp. 328–330.
8. Osterland, A., Blaming ERP, *CFO Magazine* [on-line], http://www.cfo-net.com/html/Articles/CFO/2000/00Jablam.html, January, 2000.
9. Wallace, T. F., *MRP II: Making It Happen*, Oliver Wight Publications, Essex Junction, VT, p. 171.

# 8   Evaluation and Measurement

## Introduction

The training program for an ERP implementation, as with any other form of corporate activity, must be held accountable for results. Unfortunately, the traditional methods of measuring the training do not work in the LRP model. Counting the number of hours a person was trained or the number of people trained, or even the dollars spent on training, is not effective. None of these traditional measures determine if learning has occurred or was translated into action. In fact, developing an elaborate ERP training program without determining whether or not the program is contributing to the corporate bottom line is simply poor management.

The Evaluation step of the LRP model, shown highlighted in Figure 8.1, forces an organization to seriously examine its delivery of training and determine whether or not the objectives of the training lesson, class, or learning event were met. The information gathered during the evaluation step is fed into the other steps of the LRP model. This continuous feedback shapes and molds the analysis, design, and diagnosis steps. This feedback cycle ensures that the learning process is continually refining and improving itself — built-in continuous improvement.

## Overview

Evaluation of the organizational learning process must be conducted both during the formation of the training program and at the end. While many

**Learning Requirements Planning Model**

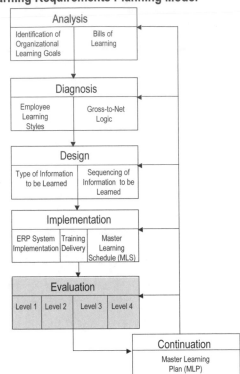

**Figure 8.1 LRP with Evaluation Highlighted. Evaluation Is the Fifth Step in the LRP Process.**

organizations provide cursory rating sheets for evaluations at the end of a training class or event, many do not carry the evaluation beyond the reporting of employee satisfaction with the presentation of the material. While this level of evaluation is important, it cannot be the final level. Traditional rating sheets never measure whether or not any learning has occurred. Without genuine employee learning, the ERP implementation will not succeed. Methods must be in place to measure what employees have learned during the training. These methods are called "summative" evaluations and are conducted at four different levels to determine the effectiveness of the completed training.

However, waiting until the training is complete, packaged, and delivered to the students in order to measure its effectiveness is not sufficient. Mechanisms for measuring the effectiveness of the training must be put into place throughout the training design and development process. This developmental training evaluation is called "formative" evaluation since it occurs during the formation of the training.

# Formative Evaluation

Formative evaluation shapes and molds the training so that it is easy to understand and helps employees learn. This level of evaluation ensures that the ERP training is effective when presented to the employees.

During the creation of training materials in the Design phase of LRP, as strategies and tactics are applied it is important to test the actual instruction for accuracy, completeness, and content integrity as well as for basic quality assurance issues. Nothing undermines the credibility of instruction more than misspelled words, misrepresented facts, and wrong or incomplete information.

During the formative evaluations the emphasis ranges from simple quality assurance to issues like strength of instructional strategies and tactics used, ability of learners to learn from the information, and the motivation level of students as a result of the instruction.

Formative evaluation can be divided into four different types. Each of the four types is used to provide both the basic evaluation of the materials as well as a more in-depth evaluation. The four types are Subject Matter Expert (SME), One-on-One, Small-Group, and Field Trail evaluations.

## *Subject Matter Expert (SME)*

This label is somewhat of a misnomer. The individual reviewing the material is not necessarily an "expert" in the traditional sense of the word, he or she is simply someone who knows the process, procedure, or content and can easily share that knowledge with others. It is important that this person can easily share knowledge, because often, a true expert unconsciously knows so much about a topic that he or she has trouble bringing the knowledge down to a level that novices and instructional designers can understand.

During the review, the SME reads the materials and determines if the information is factually and conceptually correct. Unfortunately, this is not always as easy as it sounds.

In some cases, the SMEs provide information about how a process currently functions and not how the process is supposed to function. For example, a SME may describe the shipping process as one where materials are packaged to forecast and not to actual customer demand. The implementation team may want to change the shipping practice to packaging finished goods for customers only after the customer has ordered the product, and not rely on forecasting. The designer(s) of the instruction for the ERP implementation must make sure that they are developing instruction based on input from the correct people — the SMEs and the stakeholders who are driving the implementation.

One method of eliminating the need for a SME to review all of the materials is to purchase already existing materials from a credible source. A variety of training materials exists for basic manufacturing training or system overview training. These types of training materials are readily available and do not need to be recreated by a short-staffed training department. Basic manufacturing training can be supplied by professional organizations such as APICS~The Educational Society for Resource Management or from qualified, well-known consultants in the field of production and inventory management. Also, software vendors are usually capable of providing overview and some basic manufacturing fundamentals training as it relates to their products. However, it may be best not to go with the software vendor for basic manufacturing concepts training. The reason is that when another organization presents the basics of manufacturing to employees; it reinforces the universality of capabilities of the vendor's software.

In some cases employees are so used to performing a function incorrectly that they believe that is the way that function is supposed to work. When the ERP software functions differently, they want the software changed — not their incorrect procedure. For example, one company wanted to modify the ERP software so that after the material was received into the plant the ERP system would automatically create a requisition for the material. The reason — their requisitioning process was so convoluted and slow that the paperwork was not complete until after the receipt of raw material. Unbelievable, but true.

In these types of cases a neutral third party describing the preferred methods of running a manufacturing organization can eliminate or mitigate potential conflicts about the "best" or "correct" manufacturing or business control methods.

Third-party endorsement of manufacturing methods is also important because sometimes two SMEs have very different opinions about how a process is to be performed. This can be difficult when material is based on the input of one SME and another individual within the manufacturing organization openly disagrees with how a process or procedure is being trained.

## One-on-One

This type of evaluation involves the selection of one member of the target training population to serve as an evaluator. The evaluator is then asked to act as a student and to receive the training that has been developed to this point. The role of the evaluator is to simply learn from the material and to write comments during the learning process. The evaluator is to provide feedback to the designer of the instruction about ease of understanding the materials, ease of use of the materials, readability of the materials, and overall effectiveness of the materials.

At this point, the evaluator can even be tested to determine if the instruction had any effect on the learner's knowledge in a specific area or on his or her ability to perform a specific task. Part of the responsibility of the evaluator during this task is to "think aloud" about the process and comment as the instruction is unfolding. This allows the designer of the instruction to determine where learners may get confused or where the material is not logical. The evaluator also, inevitably, finds typos and other simple items that can be easily addressed.

If the evaluator has major problems with the training material or is totally stumped, the instruction may need to be redesigned. In that case, the good news is the ineffective training has only been delivered to one person and can be modified prior to presenting it to a larger group.

The process of the one-on one evaluation should occur at least three times to obtain the opinions of three different people. On occasion, a person will have an impression about the training based on a personal idiosyncrasy. Having two other people validate or not validate the impression helps with the overall design. The one-on-one evaluation process does not mean that every little thing a person doesn't like gets changed, it is meant to gather an overall impression of the effectiveness of the training and to resolve minor aesthetic or usability issues and discover any instructional flaws.

One element the instructional designer should focus on during the one-on-one evaluation is the clarity of the message. Does the evaluator understand what is being presented? Does it make sense? Are certain topics confusing or hard to follow?[1]

Another element is the impact of the instruction on the evaluator. Ask about the usefulness of the information, how easy or difficult the information was to learn, was the learning enjoyable, was he or she satisfied with what was learned?[1] These types of questions help with the formation of the instruction and can help the designer build the ERP instruction to more closely address the needs of the organization.

## *Small-Group*

The small-group evaluation primarily has two roles. The first is to determine if the changes made as a result of the one-on-one evaluation had the desired outcomes and the second is to identify any remaining problems with the ERP instruction. The designer of the instruction typically performs the small-group evaluation.

The small-group evaluation consists of approximately 8 to 10 students who are employees of the company implementing the ERP system and who all proceed through the training together. This group is then debriefed after the training process to determine what did and didn't work during the instruction. The debriefing can be conducted by personal interviews of the students as well as written surveys to gather impressions of and attitudes toward the instruction.

The types of questions to ask at the conclusion of the small-group evaluation include:

- What materials were most helpful to you during the instruction?
- What additional materials would have been beneficial to you during the instruction?
- Was the instruction interesting?
- Did the tests/quizzes test your knowledge or understanding of the material appropriately?
- Did the tests seem fair?
- Did the material have enough examples?
- Were the examples clear and easy to understand?
- Were the examples relevant?

At this stage of the development process, changes can still be made to the materials. The small-group evaluation allows the designer to get a range of opinions concerning the ERP instruction and to determine how the instruction was perceived by a group of employees. The impressions of the group can be used to strengthen the ERP training materials for the presentation at the next level of evaluation — the field trial.

## *Field Trial*

Often, during an ERP implementation training is performed in a train-the-trainer approach. Supervisors or managers are trained and then they are expected to train their subordinates. The purpose of the field trial is for the designer of the instruction to observe the instruction as it will be delivered. In the field trial, the designer becomes a student in the class while the supervisor or manager conducts the ERP training class.

The designer of the instruction then takes notes about the possible modification of content or the addition of more examples or exercises. This approach helps the supervisor or manager to become familiar with the material prior to a major rollout and allows the "instructors" to have input into the materials they are going to be using to present ERP information to their learners.

In the field trial, both students and the instructor are asked for final opinions and input into the instruction. The major advantage for the designer is that this is the first time he or she will receive feedback from the people using the material about how they liked the material and what improvements should be made in the material from an instructor's viewpoint.

The various levels of formative evaluation are not always feasible within a manufacturing organization. The realities of time and budget constraints as well as a lack of personnel too often cause the formative evaluation stage of training to be set aside. In many cases instruction is not designed internally at all, the manufacturing organization simply purchases "canned" materials from the software vendor, consultant, or a professional society like APICS.

Parts or aspects of the formative evaluation process can be combined or used in isolation to provide some level of formative evaluation. While not ideal from an instructional design standpoint, this selective formative evaluation process can help to avoid major instructional mistakes and help the ERP training proceed more smoothly.

For example, if material is purchased, the training or HR manager can establish a "dry run" environment in which a supervisor or manager can teach three or four "friendly" people to get used to the material and how it should be presented. Or a SME from the production department can read the vendor's materials and make specific notes about the internal process that need to be highlighted or further explained during the training class. A one-on-one evaluation can be conducted for the training on manufacturing basics that is going to be presented to all the production employees.

## Summative Evaluation

Once training is developed and has passed the formative evaluation stage and is delivered, then the next step is the summative evaluation. This level of evaluation determines if the instruction accomplished the goals for which

| Evaluation Level | What it Measures | How to Measure |
|---|---|---|
| Level 1 | Reaction to Training | Rate Sheet at End of Instruction |
| Level 2 | Knowledge Gain | Paper and Pencil Test, Hands-On Performance Test |
| Level 3 | Behavioral Change/Transfer of Learning to the Job | Supervisory Reports, On-the-Job Peer Surveys, Action Plan Reports, Observation, Self-Reports |
| Level 4 | Financial Impact on Organization | ROI Analysis, Benefit/Cost Analysis |

**Figure 8.2   Levels of Evaluation. The Four Levels of Summative Evaluation for LRP.**

it was developed or delivered. "Was the instruction effective?" is the question answered by a summative evaluation.

The results of the summative evaluation can justify the need for training. If the training is effective and solves the problem, then similar training may be needed in other places within the organization. For example, if the production employees in a manufacturing plant are trained in the basics of manufacturing and tangible improvements were found during the summative evaluation, then the training program could be transplanted to another plant within the company to achieve similar results.

Summative evaluation is used to quantify the impact of the training program on the ERP implementation process. It puts cold, hard numbers to the often vague and fuzzy concept of corporate learning. Evaluating the effectiveness of the training delivered to the organization allows the training department or human resources department to speak in terms that managers in the financial department, production department, and sales department understand — numbers.

In 1959, Donald L. Kirkpatrick, then a professor at the University of Wisconsin, developed a four-level framework for evaluating the effectiveness of training.[2] Kirkpatrick's classification scheme is an effective framework for determining training's impact on the enterprise. If measurements are not taken at each level of the training process, it becomes difficult to attribute any improvements to the Learning Requirements Planning process.[3] Figure 8.2 identifies the various levels of training evaluation and how to measure each level.

## Level 1 Evaluation

A *level 1* evaluation measures a trainee's reaction to the training. Level 1 determines the initial impression of the learner. These evaluations are typically conducted by handing out questionnaires at the end of the training session. Some training professionals sneer at these "smile sheets." These professionals insist that evaluations at the end of instructor-led or computer-based training only measure the entertainment value of the course and not its quality.[4] Not entirely true — what is actually measured is initial customer satisfaction. And initial customer satisfaction is an important measurement. Only when level 1 evaluations are used as the sole criterion for evaluating the effectiveness of training should the level 1 evaluations be called into question.

To ensure the collection of valuable information from a level 1 evaluation, certain standards should be followed. The first is that the information measured should be of value to the organization and the designer of the instruction. Collecting information because it "should" be collected wastes employee time. Only collect what will be used.

Second, design the level 1 evaluation instrument (written or electronic) so that the information collected can be tabulated and quantified. Quantifying the data provides a base of information upon which to make decisions. Quantified data allow for comparisons across classes and student populations. Quantified data also help to avoid rash or unsubstantiated claims by employee managers.

Occasionally, a supervisor will ask an employee, "How was the training class?" and the employee will answer off-the-cuff, "Not very good, we didn't learn anything." If this feedback gets to upper management, they may decide not to continue with the training because "people" aren't learning anything, even though the information only came from one disgruntled employee who never has a good thing to say about anything.

If level 1 information is collected at the end of the training class and overall ratings for the class are good, then the credibility of the training class cannot be called into question. The existence of empirical, quantified data indicating that the majority of attendees liked the class and said that they learned new information during the class is invaluable for making a business case. The quantification of the data can be used effectively against a random, off-the-cuff comment from one employee. If level 1 information is not collected, no evidence is available to substantiate the fact that most students learned during class. Relations can become strained between the training department and the first-line supervisor who doesn't want to send people to class because of a false perception that they aren't learning anything.

Level 1 end-of-course evaluations are typically divided into four sections, instructor ability, materials quality, learning environment, and information learned. The instructor ability section measures items like:

- Was the presenter knowledgeable?
- Did the presenter carry himself well?
- Did the instructor clarify difficult topics?
- Did the instructor keep the class interesting?
- How well did the instructor use the instructional media (overhead, whiteboard, computer display)?
- Were summaries conducted at appropriate places throughout the lesson?
- Was the pace of the instruction too fast or too slow?

Determining the effectiveness of the instructor delivering the training message is important because employees need to believe that the instructor is knowledgeable and credible in order to for them to gain the most from the ERP training session. In addition, these types of questions and their answers provide an organization with insight into the motivation of the learners to attend another class with the instructor. This becomes especially important for companies using a front-line supervisor to train fellow employees. Some supervisors may be naturally good trainers and some will not be effective. The ones that are found to be lacking in some way can use the feedback from the level 1 evaluations to improve their delivery approach. A "Train the Trainer" course will benefit most people with their training delivery skills.

The next set of questions found on a level 1 evaluation relate to the quality of the material. The materials section asks questions like:

- Was the student guide easy to use?
- Did the illustrations used in the class convey the correct message?
- Could you find information you needed in the handbook?
- Were the PowerPoint® slides easy to read or too crowded?
- What was the overall quality of the course materials?
- Did you find the handouts useful?

Instructional materials are the only tangible items students have when they walk out of a training class. Often these items are used as references and as quick look-up guides for specific pieces of information. If the materials are of high quality and contain useful information they will become indispensable to the employees. If they are useless or not very effective, they will end up in the trash.

Often, the level 1 evaluation sheets will ask about the training environment itself: questions like: Were the seats comfortable? How was the temperature of the room? Was the room too dark or too cold? While these questions seem basic and inappropriate on an evaluation sheet, at times they can have merit. For example, at one manufacturing plant, the ERP training classes literally took place in a back hallway. People walking past the training session were constantly interrupting the classes. The message to the employees in those classes was that this training was so unimportant to the company that an empty conference room couldn't even be located or schedules changed to find a more suitable location. If the trainees then reported to their supervisors that the training was horrible and they didn't learn anything, the training might be cancelled. A level 1 evaluation containing comments about the physical atmosphere of the training area might be enough to convince management that the training classes would be more effective if held in a room instead of a hallway.

Another section typically found on a level 1 evaluation sheet concerns the issue of what information was learned. This section of the level 1 evaluation asks for students to report on what they have learned during the training class. The idea is to get an impression from the students on what was actually learned. This section contains questions like:

- Was the information presented in the class related to your job?
- Will the information covered in class help you to perform your job better?
- Will you be able to use this information on the job?
- Did you learn new concepts?
- Did the course help you to comprehend ERP terminology?

Unfortunately, the responses given by students to these types of questions are not good indicators of what was actually learned. Students leaving a training class tend to either overestimate or severely underestimate what they have actually learned. Students don't really know what they have learned in the class until they attempt to apply the information directly to their job.

It is important to note that the level 1 evaluations should be conducted for online learning as well. As more and more ERP vendors offer online learning options, these must be evaluated with the same rigor as instructor-led learning experiences. Some questions to ask of online learning include:

- Was the online learning easy to navigate?
- Were the ideas presented on the computer screen easy to understand?
- Was enough time given for each exercise?
- Could you learn from the material while at your desk?

- Did you get lost in the software program?
- Could you find online help when you needed it?

The questions should also address the learning environment in which the training is delivered. For instance, if the training is being delivered to the PC at the employees' desk and the employee cannot concentrate on the instruction because of constant interruptions by co-workers, an alternative location may need to be secured. Many companies have learning stations separate from an employee's main work area so an employee can attend training without leaving the office and not be faced with constant interruptions.

While level 1 evaluation questions are important for gauging the initial impact of the learning experience on the students, they should not be cited as the only evidence indicating that students learned. Determining what students have actually learned requires a level 2 evaluation.

## Level 2 Evaluation

A *level 2* evaluation tests participant learning. At this level, the evaluation of the learning is not a self-reporting instrument like in level 1; it is the administration of an objective test. The idea behind a level 2 evaluation is to see if the student can demonstrate what he or she learned. The fundamental question behind a level 2 evaluation is, "Did learning occur?"

Level 2 evaluations serve a number of purposes. One is the identification of employees who may need more practice or training in a specific area. By identifying and then retraining individuals who need additional assistance, an organization can maximize the potential of its employees by making sure everyone learned the skills and knowledge needed to be successful on the job.

A second purpose is that adding a testing "milestone" in the ERP training program provides an extra incentive or motivation factor for employees. If employees know they will be held directly accountable for the information that will be presented to them in the training classes, they are more likely to ask questions, pay attention to details, and learn the information to be successful on the test.

Not only are employees more motivated to perform because of a testing milestone, but the trainers are more likely to "go the extra mile" to help all employees do well on the test. Pass and fail rates can be looked at for an entire class and the effectiveness of the instruction can be assessed. Again, this is not only applicable for instructor-led training, online training should also be examined to determine if students are able to pass tests based on the information presented online.

The main consideration when developing a level 2 evaluation is to make sure the test measures a trainee's performance on a job-relevant task, skill, or behavior. The test must measure what is actually needed in order for the person to perform well on the job. For example, during a class on master scheduling, the instructor may give a brief history of how the MRP process started, when it was first used, and why it was a better solution than older reorder-point-based systems. However, none of that information is relevant to the daily tasks that a master scheduler must perform. A person training for a master scheduler position can be tested on pegging an item's ultimate demand, but not on when the first MRP system was used in a manufacturing organization. The latter has no direct impact on the employee's ability to perform the job although it may be interesting trivia.

Level 2 evaluations can be divided into two categories. The first is a written or electronic test and the second is a practical or hands-on performance demonstration. The written exam is the typical multiple choice, fill-in-the-blank, true/false and other common formats used to assess knowledge acquisition by a trainee. The same methods can also be utilized online with today's modern e-learning software.

For example, a distance-learning education program called "Blackboard" has the built-in capability for creating online test questions in a variety of formats and an assessment pool where different learners receive different questions based on a randomization process provided by the software. The advantage of online testing is that the learner receives feedback immediately on whether or not the answer is correct. In a traditional paper-and-pencil environment, feedback is delayed while the instructor marks the test answer.

The proper development of the online or paper-and-pencil test requires following some basic guidelines. Guidelines are important because the assessment of employees must be fair and accurate.[5] Employees are typically not comfortable being tested on their knowledge and often view tests as a threat. Adhering to fair, objective guidelines can help to alleviate some of the fears.

The first guideline to follow is to develop questions that are "definite, precise, and objective."[5] An objective test is one in which multiple people scoring a test can all agree on the correct answers. Avoid ambiguous or subjective questions. Answers should be clear and not open to debate. One method to make sure the questions are clear is to test the test. Select other trainers or a small group of people from the intended audience to take the test before it is generally offered. This will help ensure that the test is fair and easy to use. A good population to use for testing tests is an operations or management class at a local college or university. This population is used to taking tests and can provide objective feedback.

Questions like, "What is the number one benefit of an ERP system?" are not good. A number of benefits can be obtained by implementing an ERP system and what one individual may see as a benefit may not be the same for someone else. A better way to phrase the question may be as a true/false item asking, "True or False: Inventory reduction is a possible benefit of a successful ERP implementation?"

The next guideline is to develop questions using a reading and vocabulary level understood by the employees who will be taking the test. This item is especially important in production environments where English is not the only language spoken. For example, in a plant in Saint Louis, the production workers are mostly Vietnamese who speak and read little English. Administering a test to them in English does not test their knowledge of ERP concepts, only their ability to understand English. To test this group of workers, either the test must be written in Vietnamese or the students should be allowed to take the quiz/test with an interpreter. Even in plants where English is the only language spoken, varying literacy levels may pose a problem.

The third guideline is that the questions on the test should not merely be items copied from the handouts or classroom materials. The test should not measure a person's ability to memorize. Tests need to determine what knowledge has been gained. Simply memorizing information does not mean that it is understood or acted upon. The test must measure more than simple memorization.

The next guideline is important from a motivational and educational standpoint. Start the test with a few important but relatively easy questions. This will help build the confidence of the employee and not cause panic when he or she first sees the test. Often, if the first couple of questions on a test are difficult, a person will "freeze" or panic and not be able to complete ANY of the questions even though the answers are known. Many employees in a working environment have been out of the classroom for over 20 years and have not taken a test or quiz in quite some time. Making the test as anxiety-free as possible will help them perform to their true potential. Keep the beginning of the test simple and easy.

Make sure the questions on the exam do not provide answers for other questions on the exam. In some cases, a question can hint at an answer for another question or provide information needed to answer a question somewhere else on the exam. This can be avoided by carefully reviewing the test. In addition, have a person unfamiliar with the material take the test to see if they can determine any of the answers from the test itself.

The final guideline is not to use any trick questions. Trick questions do not check knowledge, they simply check to see if a person is paying attention to the test or to the way questions are worded, or is good at solving puzzles.[6]

Trick questions can make students feel uneasy about the entire test. The idea behind the test is not to trick the students but to see if they actually learned what they needed to learn to perform their job. Trick questions do not help determine the extent of ERP knowledge gained by employees.

Test questions in a paper-and-pencil or electronic format can be constructed in a variety of ways. Each method has advantages and disadvantages and each can be used to measure different types of learning.

The first type of question format, and perhaps the most well-known and versatile one, is the multiple-choice format. This format consists of a question (known as a *stem*) and then a list of possible answers to complete the stem. The incorrect answers from which a student may choose are called *distracters*. Typically, most multiple-choice questions contain three distracters and one correct response, for a total of four possible answers. One typical mistake made on many multiple-choice items is that the correct answer tends to be the longest answer available. When creating a multiple-choice question, keep in mind that each of the four possible answers should be approximately the same number of words in length.

Multiple-choice questions can test four levels of learning: memorization, comprehension, application, and analysis.[6] Each of these levels of learning should be included on a test designed to measure employee ERP learning. Figure 8.3 illustrates the various types of multiple-choice questions and the levels of learning they are capable of measuring.

Multiple-choice questions have three advantages over other types of questions. The first is that they are easy to check; simply match the number written or circled on the paper with the correctly numbered or lettered response. The second is that they are able to measure a variety of types of learning. The third is that they are familiar to almost everyone taking the test. At one time or another, from driver's license tests to school exams, almost everyone has taken a multiple-choice test.

However, multiple-choice tests are not without disadvantages. One major disadvantage is that they allow for guessing. If a student doesn't know the answer he or she can make a guess. Also, if multiple-choice questions are not created correctly, they can end up testing only memorization and not the higher-level skills of comprehension, application, or analysis.

Another type of assessment question that can be created is a true/false question. This format asks the student to read a statement and determine if the statement is correct (true) or incorrect (false). True/false questions are easy to create and can be graded quickly. However, they should be used sparingly since they have a guess rate of 50%. At such a high guess rate, it is difficult to determine whether students are guessing or if they really know

### 1. Memorization
In terms of inventory control, what does the term MRO represent?
a. Maintenance, Repair, and Operating supplies
b. Manufacturing Resource Operations
c. Mechanical Regulation of Operations
d. Material, Resources, and Other supplies

### 2. Comprehension
If the ERP software scheduler program continued to add load to a work cell regardless of the capacity available, what type of scheduling would be taking place?
a. Finite
b. Backward
c. Infinite
d. Forward

### 3. Application
A buy/planner encounters an unusually high demand for a particular purchased item. What should she do?
a. Ignore the demand and order, the system is never wrong.
b. Peg the demand to determine what is driving it.
c. Call the order entry people to see the cause of the demand.
d. Call the vendor to see if the demand can be met by current supply.

### 4. Analysis
Examine the above SPC chart. What type of condition is it describing?
a. A process out of control
b. A process in control
c. A process with one outlier
d. A process trending upwards but still in control

---

**Figure 8.3   Types of Multiple-Choice Questions.**

the correct answer. Also, the statements that are used must be 100% true or false. This tends to limit the content that can be used for true/false questions.

Matching items is another form of assessment that can be used for testing ERP knowledge. These types of questions require the student to identify the relationship between two items. An example would be a list of terms and the corresponding definitions, as shown in Figure 8.4.

The main advantage of a matching test is that by carefully selecting terms and responses students have a substantially lower chance of guessing the correct association than on multiple-choice or true/false questions.[6] When

**Matching**

Match the term on the left with its definition on the right.

1) JIT

    A. The quantity shown on the ERP inventory record as being physically available.

2) Scrap Factor

    B. A philosophy of inventory management that emphasizes zero inventory and tight vendor/customer relations.

3) FAS

    C. A schedule of end items whether to replenish finished good inventory or to finish the product for a make-to-order product.

4) On-Hand Balance

    D. A percentage used by an EP system to increase gross requirements of a given component to account for loss of material during the manufacturing process.

    E. A philosophy where customer demand is pushed onto the top floor from workstation to workstation based on forecasted demand from customers.

---

**Figure 8.4    Example of a Matching Type ERP Evaluation Test.**

creating a list of matching items, keep the number of items to match at about four or five. More than seven items are hard to track; too few items make matching too easy. Also, be sure to provide one or two distracters so the number of answers and the number of terms are uneven. This helps to minimize the impact of any guessing by the student.

A less-frequently used form of test item in an ERP training program is the use of essay questions. Essay questions are easy to create but difficult to evaluate. It is also difficult to have one or more people who evaluate an essay concur on the result. Even an instructor will assess the same essay differently if he or she reads the essay at different times with ill-defined assessment criteria. Due to the subjectivity of an essay and the time commitment necessary to evaluate it, it is not recommended that many of the ERP tests used to judge or certify learners be essay based.

However, essay questions can be valuable in some cases. For example, if one wants to see the depth of understanding an individual has concerning a particular ERP topic and how the employee has related one concept to another, essays can provide that level of analysis. Also, at the executive or managerial level essays may be valuable in helping individuals to articulate their thoughts and understanding of a concept. Often, the process of writing something down tends to clarify thinking and generate new ideas and insights. These types of insights are valuable to managers and executives responsible for integrating the ERP system into their corporate strategy.

Paper-and-pencil and electronic tests provide a valuable tool for assessing the learning that has taken place after an individual has attended ERP training. Another important type of test used to determine how well a person has mastered a specific type of task is a hands-on performance assessment.

Hands-on performance tests require the employee to actually perform a task or series of tasks in a controlled environment. In this controlled environment, the instructor can determine the ability of the employee to perform the task. Hands-on performance assessments provide several advantages over written paper-and-pencil exams.

One such advantage is that employees can be tested in a situation closely resembling the job situation in which they will be using the skill. If the employees perform well on this assessment they are likely to feel confident and able to perform the task while actually on the job. This level of confidence often translates into better job performance.

Another advantage is that if the employee performs poorly, both the employee and the trainer know exactly the areas in which the employee is having problems. The trainer and the employee can then work on methods to help the trainee become more proficient. Hands-on tests are an excellent diagnostic tool for determining the need and focus of future training efforts.

A third advantage is that the employee receives immediate feedback on his or her ability to perform. The employee doesn't have to worry whether or not he or she can actually perform the task. The assessment indicates if the task has been learned or not.

A number of guidelines have been developed to create effective hands-on performance tests. These guidelines can serve as a basis for developing and delivering effective performance-based tests during an ERP implementation.[5] As well, they are effective for other performance-based learning events in the organization.

The first guideline is to simulate the actual work function as closely as possible, for example, if a person was being tested on how to enter a customer order. The performance test should involve supplying the student with a paper copy of the customer order and requiring the student to process the order. Or have an audiotape of the order to mimic a phone order. It is even possible for a trainer to role-play with the student and act as a customer when placing an order.

The student should then be required to independently enter the correct information into the ERP order entry system. Along the way, other tasks or skills that were taught to the student could be assessed. For example, the student could be asked to check the customer's credit or revise a shipping address. Using real information and real customers helps reinforce the learning by the students. It also provides the students with a level of confidence knowing that they can perform the task on the job. The assessment task should, as closely as possible, mimic the work environment in which the task will take place. If documents or manuals are available on the job, make them available during the assessment.

The second guideline is to have multiple assessments for the student. One hands-on performance test is not an adequate indicator of ability. Most trainers would never think of having a one-question paper-and-pencil test, but performance assessments often are just one-time events and then they are finished. A variety of approaches to a particular task needs to be assessed to ensure that the student has achieved an appropriate level of mastery. Adding a few exceptions to the usual task help the learner to generalize the information learned while performing one element of the task to other, possibly less frequent, elements of the task.

For example, while assessing the employees' ability to read a typical master schedule and determine material requirements, the instructor may want to add the element of a vendor not being able to deliver a promised amount of inventory. The instructor can then observe how the employees reacts during that part of the performance assessment. If the employees perform well on such items, they will gain confidence in their abilities. If the employees do not perform well, additional training can be arranged. Often, learning occurs when employees see the results of incorrect actions. The employees will remember what happened and not let it happen again.

A third guideline is to introduce the element of time to the hands-on performance assessment. Many people can plod through a task and complete it reasonably well, given a large amount of time. Unfortunately, in the hustle and bustle of today's business environment, time is not always available in large quantities. A student must feel some pressure when performing that task to get used to doing the steps of the task automatically and not need to think through every step before acting. A good way to gauge the student's "internalization" of a task is to add a time limit. The added pressure clearly demonstrates how well he or she has mastered the task.

The fourth guideline is to develop objective criteria in the form of a score sheet or checklist. A checklist provides a quick and easy method for determining whether or not all the correct steps were followed during the completion of the hands-on assessment. A glance at the checklist quickly reveals opportunities for improvements and areas to focus on in future training sessions. The checklist assessment can also be used by the student as a list of which items to practice and know prior to being assessed.

Remember, the idea behind ERP training is not to have an evenly distributed learning curve with an equal number of passing and failing students, but to have everyone perform their jobs effectively and efficiently while using the new system. Letting students know how they are going to be evaluated provides a roadmap for the students to study and prepares them to do their jobs better in the future.

Finally, make sure the directions for performance are clearly explained to the trainee taking the test. The objective of the performance test is to see how well a person will perform in a simulated work environment. Testing the ability to follow directions should be saved for a later time. Make sure the directions are straightforward and don't contain any ambiguous or vague instructions.

Level 2 evaluations are often used as certification. Successfully completing a hands-on performance assessment certifies that a person is able to perform a particular job function. At one plant in Northeastern Pennsylvania, every person within the organization must become ERP-certified for their particular job. The company wants to ensure that each employee can perform the right functions and processes within the ERP system. Once the employees have successfully demonstrated their ability to utilize a certain portion of the ERP package, they are certified for that particular module or task. Certification works well since it provides recognition to the employees and is a visible sign that they have mastered some ERP knowledge. Plus it acts as a motivator. "If even Jimmy H. can get certified, then I can get certified."

However, the testing milestone or end-of-class certification is not a panacea. Testing is not appropriate in every manufacturing organization. Problems can be encountered in a union shop where testing of individuals may be forbidden. Certain nonunion shops may also have a corporate culture that makes testing difficult.

Testing within a manufacturing organization must be approached carefully. The idea behind level 2 evaluations is to see if learning has occurred and not to fail or fire people who do not learn the information. Level 2 evaluations must be handled with care; information must be kept confidential concerning actual scores. Scores should not be posted for the general population to see and the tests must be conducted in an ethical manner. Also, consider embedding the tests throughout the instruction so that a huge end-of-course test is not waiting for each employee as he or she completes training. One method to ensure the fairness of the exams is to use a third party such as APICS for the content, administration, and scoring of tests related to the ERP body of knowledge. The content may not be 100% applicable to your manufacturing environment but the hassle saved by having the testing and certification performed by an outside agency may be worth it.

Passing a test does not ensure that the employees will apply what they learned in the training class on the job. For example, a typical inventory manager knows, intellectually, that he should keep minimum safety stock. However, many inventory managers have secret little stashes of inventory hidden around the plant to avoid stock-outs. More training is not going to help eliminate the excess hidden inventory. The inventory managers already "know" they shouldn't have secret stashes. What needs to happen is a change in the behavior of the inventory managers, not a change in knowledge.

## Level 3 Evaluation

*Level 3* evaluations deal with measuring whether or not the behavior of the employees has changed as a result of attending the training class. This is one of the most difficult training levels to assess. Measuring a person's change in behavior means that the behavior before the training had to be measured so it could be compared with the change in behavior that occurred after the training.

Level 3 evaluations check to see if the skills taught in the training are actually being used on the job. Is the employee exhibiting behaviors that were part of the online class or part of a traditional training class? Did the behavior change as a result of the learning experience?

The fundamental question answered in a level 3 evaluation is, "Did the on-the-job behavior change to the desired behavior after attending the training class?" Level 3 evaluations are concerned with transferability. Transfer of training is defined as the effective and continued application of knowledge and skills gained in training to the trainee's jobs function.[7] The answer sought by a level 3 evaluation is, "Did the training transfer from the classroom to the shop floor or the office?"

There are five methods that can be used to measure the transfer of training from the classroom to the work environment. These methods can be employed individually or combined in various formats to get the most useful evaluation cross-section. The five methods are supervisory reports, on-the-job peer surveys, action plan reports, observation, and self-reports.[7]

The first method of measuring the transfer of training is to ask for supervisory reports. Supervisors are well positioned to observe employees and to recognize whether or not training has had the desired impact. Requesting information from a supervisor engages the supervisor in the learning process. The supervisor becomes concerned with what the employee learned and how that learning is being applied.

When asking a supervisor for a report, it is not a good idea to simply say, "Hey, give me a report on John Smith." Provide the supervisor with a list of questions or specific behaviors to observe. This will help to ensure more accurate and unbiased feedback. Not all supervisors in a manufacturing organization will have the motivation or desire to complete written reports, so this process cannot be universally relied upon for information about the transfer of learning.

In addition, some bias may enter into the process. This could occur if the supervisor doesn't particularly like the subordinate or is particularly impressed with the subordinate, or even if the supervisor has strong misgivings regarding the ERP system. One method to avoid bias is to combine the supervisory report with other methods of determining learning transfer.

Another method of collecting data on the transfer of learning is to conduct peer surveys of performance. Keep in mind that most training occurs with a group of trainees and often the trainees are from the same peer group. A peer survey will not yield credible results if an individual was sent to a training class and is the only one who is supposed to be exhibiting the new behavior. The key to a peer on-the-job survey is to ask group questions about the behavioral change. The following types of questions should be asked of the group:

- Do most people seem to be implementing the concepts covered in the Cycle Counting class? Why or why not?
- Do you feel that you face any obstacles in implementing the concepts from the training class?
- Do you feel your peers are facing similar obstacles in implementing Cycle Counting?
- Have the behaviors of your peers changed as a result of the training?

The results from this type of survey can reveal why a particular group is not implementing what they learned in class or why changes are not occurring as predicted. This method is helpful when a group has attended training but no results are apparent.

The next method is the use of action plan reports. These start at the end of the training class when employees are asked to develop an action plan for implementing what they learned in the class into their daily job function. These plans are then sent to the supervisors, who can review the plans and help the employees implement the plan to maximize the learning from the training class. The creation of a written plan by an employee increases the likelihood of the behavior change occurring on the job because the plan is in writing. Items that people write tend to be accomplished because of the visibility and the mental energy it takes to put words to predicted actions. The employee can refer to specific action items within the plan. If the employee shares the plan with a supervisor, the supervisor can help to reinforce the learning by focusing on the plan and holding the employee accountable to the action plan. However, if the supervisor doesn't buy into the new ERP system or to the topics covered in training, the employee will have a difficult time implementing the action plan.

Another method of determining the level of the transfer of learning from the classroom to the work environment is to actually observe the employees on the job to see if they are exhibiting the desired behavior. Observation is good because it avoids the possible bias a supervisor may have when reporting on a subordinate. One caution is that when employees know they are being observed they may tend to act differently. It is preferable that the employees do not know that they are being observed.

Observations can also be obtained by looking at data contained within the ERP system. For example, if training was conducted for a purchasing manager, a comparison could be made of the MRP order reports vs. the actual inventory ordered. The results of this analysis could determine if the purchasing manager was following the recommendations from the ERP system or doing his own thing. If the two match, then the training was successful.

However, if the two do not match, the analysis cannot stop at mere observation. It must be determined why the MRP order reports are not being followed. If the reason is legitimate, the transfer of learning may have occurred for the purchasing manager but not for the buyer/planner, who could be entering unrealistic forecast data that is driving the bogus purchase requests.

The final method of measuring the transfer of learning is through self-reports. This method involves either interviews or surveys distributed or conducted two to three months after the training session. The questions asked revolve around whether or not the concepts taught in the training class are being applied on the job. Sample questions include:

- Have you implemented any of the BOM accuracy checks discussed in the training class?
- Have you conducted any BOM auditing meetings in the past two weeks?
- Do you feel you are able to implement what was discussed in class? Why or why not?
- What is the largest obstacle you face in implementing what was covered in class?

Employees can be accurate judges of their own achievement and transfer levels and will tend to tell the truth, especially if the results are kept confidential. This process can also reveal organizational issues that are impediments to the ERP implementation. The reasons why the concepts from the training class are not being implemented may reveal underlying issues in management, process procedures, or corporate policies.

Determining if training has transferred from the classroom to the work area is important. If learning is not transferring to the work environment, then the training program is not working. Effective LRP plans ensure transfer of learning by conducting level 3 evaluations. The evaluation of LRP cannot stop at assessing learning transfer. The learning must be measured to ensure that bottom-line results were achieved.

## Level 4 Evaluation

A *level 4* evaluation measures the bottom-line result of training. Did the training positively impact the company? Have sales increased because salespeople are now using the new automated sales system? This level of evaluation is difficult to obtain, but must be measured to ensure that the company is not wasting its training dollars. The level 4 evaluation asks the following types of questions:

- Did the training positively impact the company?
- Are trained workers producing more effectively because they can now schedule with the finite scheduler?
- Have sales increased because the salespeople are using the quote-tracking feature of the ERP software taught to them via an online training class?
- Has inventory been reduced because of the ERP training?

A level 4 evaluation compares the monetary benefits of the training with the costs. This level of evaluation is difficult to obtain but must be measured to ensure that the company is not wasting its training dollars.

Conducting a level 4 evaluation in conjunction with an ERP implementation is difficult. One problem is determining if the productivity increases are a result of the training or because of the use of the new ERP system. Are BOMs now more accurate because of the built-in change order function or because of the training conducted on ERP-based engineering change management? While complete separation and quantification of the direct financial results of training during an ERP implementation may be difficult, an attempt must be made.

One reason to attempt to financially measure the results of the ERP training is that course content will become more lean, relevant, and behavioral with a focus on monetary results.[8] Both supervisors and employees will take the individual action plans developed by trainees more seriously if they are tied to dollars.

Positioning ERP training as a business issue and not a "nice-to-do" issue brings legitimacy to the need for human resource development during the ERP implementation process. Most people agree that ERP and basic manufacturing training is needed but cut it when budgets are tight or implementation time lines are not met. Conducting an ROI on training justifies why it should be conducted. If the training can be shown to have a positive return on investment during the ERP implementation process, training will less likely be cut. Additional training classes may even be justified if the data can support the investment.

The easiest method for determining the ROI of an ERP training class is to simply ask former students of the class to meet with their managers and estimate the ROI from the training. First, send the training costs for that student to the manager. Then the student and the manager should discuss the actual improved performance that has taken place since the ERP training and agree on a dollar value of the improvement or cost savings. The manager and student should also write a brief paragraph or two discussing how they arrived at their ROI estimation.[8] A comparison and averaging of all of the responses from managers and trainees can result in a crude estimate of ROI on ERP training.

While this is not the most scientific method of determining ROI, it does give a chance for the manager to sit with the employee and discuss the value of the training experience. These discussions can be valuable in helping the employee apply what was learned during training. It also helps employees to think in terms of dollar benefits to the company. Employees who are aware of the financial accountability will tend to act in fiscally responsible ways.

Identifying the costs of training is easy: course development or purchasing expenses, material expenses, instructor salary, and online course fees. Quantifying the dollar value of the benefits is more difficult. There are four areas that can be quantified in terms of accessing the benefits of ERP training. The areas are timesaving, increased productivity, improved quality, and better employee performance. The quantification of these ERP items is outlined in Figure 8.5.

| Type of Savings Attributable to Training | Savings Formula |
| --- | --- |
| **Time Savings** | |
| Short lead time to reach proficiency with system | (Hours saved × dollars per hour) |
| Less time required to perform operation | (Hours saved × dollars per hour) |
| Less supervision required of employees | (Supervisory hours saved × pay per hour) |
| **Increased Productivity** | |
| Faster work rate | (Dollar value of additional units, sales, etc.) |
| Time saved by not waiting for help or being idle | (Hours saved × dollars per hours + hours of helpers time saved × dollars per hour) |
| Time saved searching for and retrieving information | (Hours saved × dollars per hour) |
| **Improved Quality** | |
| Less data entry mistakes | (Dollar value of mistakes × decreased mistake level) |
| Reduction of setup errors resulting in business problems | (Dollar value of error × decreased number of setup errors) |
| Increased customer service | (Percent increase in market share × dollar value of increase) |
| **Better Employee Performance** | |
| Avoiding need to hire new employees with desired skill set | (Recruiting salary and benefits savings) |
| Better utilization of time | (Hours freed × dollars per hour × opportunity cost of freed hours) |
| Less absenteeism due to frustration with system | (Hours of increased productivity × dollars per hour + cost of hiring a temporary worker) |

**Figure 8.5  Quantifying the Benefits of Training.**

$$\text{Benefit/Cost Ratio} \;=\; \frac{\text{Total Dollar Value of Benefits}}{\text{Cost of Training}}$$

**Figure 8.6    Benefit/Cost Ratio Formula.**

More rigorous measurements of ROI can be determined by borrowing calculations from the accounting department. Prior to using any dollar figures in these calculations, it is important to get the accounting department involved in the ROI discussion. If the accounting department develops the numbers and the formulas, they will stand behind the data when it is reported at the executive and managerial levels. The last thing a training manager needs is for someone from the accounting department questioning ROI numbers. The accounting department wins that battle every time.

Two common formulas for calculating return on investment are a benefit/cost ratio and ROI. To find the benefit/cost ratio, divide the total dollar value of the benefits by the cost. See Figure 8.6 for the benefit/cost ratio formula.[9]

ROI is determined by subtracting the costs from the total dollar value of the benefits to produce the dollar value of the net benefits, which are then divided by the costs and then multiplied by 100 to develop a percentage.[9] Figure 8.7 contains the formula for determining training ROI.

For example, to determine the ROI for an inventory fundamentals training program at a large manufacturing organization, the first step is to determine the benefits produced by the training and the cost of conducting and/or developing the training. In this example, the training produced benefits of $450,600 with a cost of $50,449. The benefit/cost ratio is 8.93 which means that for every $1.00 invested, $8.93 in benefits is returned.

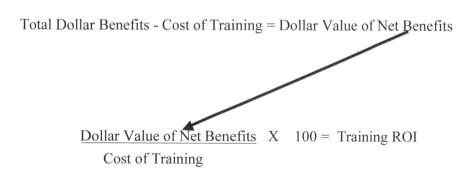

Total Dollar Benefits - Cost of Training = Dollar Value of Net Benefits

$$\frac{\text{Dollar Value of Net Benefits}}{\text{Cost of Training}} \;\times\; 100 \;=\; \text{Training ROI}$$

**Figure 8.7    Training ROI Formula.**

To determine the ROI for this same scenario, we must know the net benefit. To calculate the net benefit, one needs to know the total savings from the training and the cost of the training. The difference between the two is the net benefit. Performing the calculation, the net benefit is $450,600 – $50,449, or $ 400,151. To determine the ROI, divide the total net benefit by the cost of the training and multiply the result by 100 to get a percentage. The calculation is ($400,151 ÷ $50,449) × 100 which is 793%! Using the ROI formula, for every $1.00 invested in the training, there was a return of $7.93 in net benefits.

Conducting a level 4 evaluation of the ERP training program will ensure that training is contributing to the competitive position of the company. Conducting evaluations will focus the offerings of the training department and help shape the learning infrastructure of the organization. It is the job of every person within the organization to help ensure that a training evaluation program is in place and that the training is positively impacting the bottom line.

## Summary

No longer is the old "butts in seats" (BIS) an adequate method of evaluating the effectiveness of training. What organizations need are methods to accurately measure the gains in learning by employees. Training needs to be evaluated as it is developed to ensure that trainees receive the highest-quality training available. Good training is a result of a complete formative evaluation and understanding of the goals and objectives of the training.

The LRP process forces organizations to evaluate training at various levels. In turn, each of these levels of evaluation must feed back into the analysis step in the LRP model. Organizations must change their ERP educational approach if the training and education are not obtaining the desired goals. An evaluation of the training at all four levels ensures that the company's investment in LRP is profitable.

## LRP Evaluation and Measurement Checklist

| *Evaluation and Measurement Task* | *Completed* | | |
|---|---|---|---|
| | *Yes* | *No* | *Date* |
| **Conduct a Formative Evaluation** | | | |
| 1. Subject Matter Expert Review of Training Materials | | | |
| 2. One-On-One Review of Training Materials | | | |
| 3. Small-Group Review of Training Materials | | | |
| 4. Field Trial Review of Training Materials | | | |
| **Conduct a Level 1 Summative Evaluation of Training** | | | |
| 5. Develop Evaluation Criteria | | | |
| 6. Distribute Evaluation Sheets to Trainees | | | |
| 7. Review and Quantify the Results | | | |
| 8. Use Results to Strengthen Training | | | |
| **Conduct a Level 2 Summative Evaluation of Training** | | | |
| 9. Determine if Paper-and-Pencil or Performance Test | | | |
| 10. Develop Test Questions or Performance Tasks | | | |
| 11. Construct Test with Easier Questions/Tasks First | | | |
| 12. Administer the Test | | | |
| 13. Review and Quantify the Results | | | |
| 14. Use Results to Strengthen Training | | | |
| **Conduct a Level 3 Summative Evaluation of Training** | | | |
| 15. Determine what Behaviors Should Be Observed | | | |
| 16. Solicit Supervisory Reports | | | |
| 17. Conduct On-the-Job Peer Surveys | | | |
| 18. Review Trainee's Action Reports | | | |
| 19. Observe Trainees Back on the Job | | | |
| 20. Solicit Trainee Self-Reports | | | |
| 21. Review and Quantify the Results | | | |
| 22. Use Results to Strengthen Training | | | |
| **Conduct a Level 4 Summative Evaluation of Training** | | | |
| 23. Send Training Costs to Manager and Ask for Estimation | | | |
| 24. Develop a Benefit/Cost Ratio for the Training | | | |
| 25. Calculate ROI for the Training | | | |
| 26. Review and Quantify the Results | | | |
| 27. Use Results to Strengthen and Justify Training | | | |

# References

1. Dick, W. and Carey, L., *Systematic Design of Instruction*, 4th ed., HarperCollins, New York, 1996.
2. Kirkpatrick, D., Techniques for Evaluating Training Programs, *Training & Development*, January, 1996, p. 54.
3. Kapp, K. M., Moving training to the strategic level with learning requirements planning, *National Productivity Review*, Spring, 1999.
4. Gordon, J., Measuring the goodness of training, *Training*, 28(8), 19–25, 1999.
5. Smith, J. E. and Merchant, S., Using competency exams for evaluating training, *Training & Development Journal*, August, 1990, p. 65.
6. Kemp, J. E., Morrision, G. R., and Ross, S. M., *Designing Effective Instruction*, 2nd ed., Merrill, Upper Saddle River, NJ, 1998.
7. Garavaglia, P. L., How to ensure transfer of training, *Training & Development*, October, 1993, p. 63.
8. Parry, S. B., Measuring training's ROI, *Training & Development*, May, 1996, p. 72
9. Kapp, K. M., Transforming your manufacturing organization into a learning organization, in *APICS 1997 Int. Conf. Proc.*, APICS, Falls Church, VA, 1997, p. 288.

# 9  Continuation

## Introduction

Using LRP to implement an ERP system is not a one-time event. While the initial installation, setup, and utilization of the ERP system is important, it is the long-term use of the system that provides the greatest advantage. Organizations must learn how to continually refine and improve the ERP system to provide maximum advantage. Figure 9.1 shows the location and importance of continuation. Without the step of continuation, the model would not properly function or facilitate the ERP implementation.

LRP includes the continuation step in the model to ensure that the organization does not lose sight of the need to continually learn even after the ERP system is integrated into the organization. It is important for employees within an organization to realize that the other steps of the model must flow through the continuation step to be effective. The model can be cycled through many times to achieve desired results.

Organizations must use the foundation of learning established during the ERP implementation process to become a learning organization. Once an organization begins to focus on learning, it can use the LRP model for quality initiatives, e-commerce implementations, productivity improvements, new product development, and countless other improvement programs that require employees to learn on the job. Organizations that transform themselves through LRP into learning organizations receive tremendous benefits.

Learning organizations promote learning as a tool for getting results. Learning organizations weave a continuous, enhanced capability to learn into their corporate culture. This capacity to learn allows the organization to quickly and effectively react to competitors' changes in the marketplace, and to new technologies. Learning organizations continually exploit the features

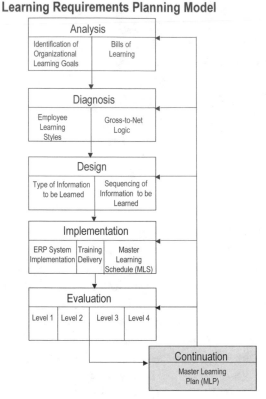

**Learning Requirements Planning Model**

**Figure 9.1 LRP with the Continuation Step Highlighted. Continuation Is the Sixth Step in the LRP Process.**

and functionality of their ERP systems to achieve an advantage in the marketplace, as well as to develop new methods of competing such as e-supply chain integration.

Transforming itself into a learning organization requires it to integrate learning into all of its processes even after the ERP system is up and running. During an ERP implementation the need for training is clear: the system is new, procedures are new, and change is obvious. After the ERP implementation, the need for continuous learning does not disappear, however, organizational focus tends to move away from training. The need is not as apparent.

The goal should be to remain committed to learning and constant improvement in spite of daily pressures and distractions. Often, the day-to-day tasks of running an organization overshadow the critical, but not urgent, need to educate the shop floor workers, upper management, and the support staff.

Organizations that have integrated learning into their processes and procedures come to view training, education, and learning as part of the daily routine and do not find it obtrusive or difficult to make learning a priority.

## Overview

In order to continue a learning focus beyond the ERP implementation, LRP requires consideration of three areas. These areas are planning, allocation of resources, and the use of a rewards and incentives program. If these three pieces are in place, an organization can use learning as a continual advantage, however, simply focusing on these three areas is not enough. The organization must practice five different disciplines in order to transform into a learning organization and continue a focus on learning after the ERP implementation has been completed. These disciplines are Systems Thinking, Personal Mastery, Mental Models, Shared Vision, and Team Learning.[1] Using these disciplines as a basis, an organization concerned with continuation learning and thus receiving a competitive advantage can establish benchmarks and milestones for achieving its goals.

## Planning

One of the most important elements in developing a learning-focused organization is the effective planning of formal and informal learning events. Informal learning within a manufacturing organization occurs on a daily basis. Employees learn how to complete time cards, how to turn a piece of metal, how to shortcut procedures, and how to improve production. Most of these events are not formal training situations. They are simply exchanges between two employees who are trying to make each other's lives a little easier. One employee develops a technique or reads something about manufacturing and tells other employees who decide to adopt the idea.

Formal learning occurs on a less-frequent basis when employees attend quality, manufacturing techniques, team building, and APICS-developed classes. Employees also receive formal education if they attend corporate-sponsored courses at a local college or attend workshops on particular topics.

Organizations must learn to plan for the formal and informal learning events. Careful planning ensures that both types of learning events are of value — not only to the individual employee, but to the organization as well. The goal for upper management is to have most of the learning occurring within the organization focus on the items that are critical to the strategic goals.

The way to ensure that strategic goals are met is to develop a Master Learning Plan (MLP). The MLP starts with a list of learning objectives derived from the strategic objectives of the organization. Once the learning objectives are established, resources that are appropriate for teaching the concepts and ideas required to reach the goals are gathered or identified. It is best to choose several forms of a message since each employee learns differently. The various types of resources include:

| | |
|---|---|
| Books | Presidential addresses |
| Article reprints | Meetings |
| Audio tapes | Lunch-time events |
| Video tapes | Formal classroom events |
| Magazines | Job aids |
| Newspapers | Mentoring |
| Newsletters | Computer-based training (CBT) |
| Letters from customers (good and | CD-ROM |
| bad) | Web-based training (WBT) |

Once the list of available resources is identified, the next step is to determine how the materials can be used to support the objective. Does the material provide background information, critical information, or how-to tips? The information should then be plotted onto a chart showing the learning objective, the type of material used to support it, and the time when the material will be presented or released to the employees. Figure 9.2 provides a sample of a Master Learning Plan showing learning objectives supporting the corporate strategic objective of "increase sales to existing customers by 10%." A carefully crafted educational campaign can prepare employees for change and teach them valuable skills through repeated exposure to the idea over a long period of time.

Adult learners learn best when exposed to a little bit of information at a time. The MLP provides this type of time-phased exposure. Information from the most abstract to more concrete can be presented over time until it actually becomes time to implement the change or idea into the organization. As an example, the Sweetheart Cup Company, Inc., which produces fast-food containers, straws, ballpark drink glasses, and ice-cream cones, was having some performance problems in its bakery division in 1994.[2] Prior to the improvement effort, the main thrust in the bakery products areas was labor efficiency rather than eliminating waste; in some areas the only measure-

Today's Date: 06/01/00

| | | | Delivery Media | | | |
|---|---|---|---|---|---|---|
| | WBT | CBT | Classroom Training | Lunch-Time Meetings | Video Tapes | Mentoring Program |
| **Learning Objectives** | | | | | | |
| Learn to use sales automation system | B | | CI | | | |
| Understand concept of selling a "solution" | | | CI | T | B | |
| Learn to use sales automation system | | CI | | | | T |
| **Availability Time Frame** | 06/01/00 | 06/15/00 | 06/25/00 | 06/05/00 to 09/15/00 | 06/01/00 | 08/01/00 |

*Note:* B = Background Material and Information. CI = Critical Information (main form of training), T = Tips and Techniques.

**Figure 9.2 Example of a Master Learning Plan (MLP).**

ments centered on how fast people could pack cones. Data accuracy was not even considered. The scheduling was in the hands of oven operators and plant mangers who had little or no real connection to the customer.

The first step in the improvement process was formal. The company held meetings with employees to inform them of the new effort. The CEO developed a list of "Business Imperatives" to be accomplished by the organization. These were posted for all employees to see. One of the initiatives on the list was for all employees to receive a minimum of 40 classroom hours of education per year.

Informal methods of education were also used. Employees recorded and then distributed a musical jingle describing the benefits of belonging to a small-group improvement team and sent it company-wide to other employees via voice mail. Pictures were hung along the cafeteria wall to illustrate team membership and accomplishments.

Little by little, employees were exposed to new ideas through training classes, meetings, posted imperatives, voice mails, pictures, and a constant communication of ideas and concepts from upper management. Formal and informal channels of learning were utilized. The results were dramatic. The scheduling process now yields a 99% performance of orders shipped complete to customers, while inventory has decreased significantly. Employees report that their quality of life has improved and that they are having fun while getting better.[2] A carefully developed campaign of meetings, education, and presidential imperatives can focus an organization in a particular direction. Once this focus occurs, individual employee initiatives become powerful informal learning events that build momentum and lead an organization toward its goals.

The planning and coordination of events is not something that can be accomplished in an employee's spare time or through the part-time effort of an implementation team leader. Someone within the organization must be appointed to the position of Chief Learning Officer (CLO). Appendix B contains a sample job description for a Chief Learning Officer.

The CLO is responsible for managing the informal and formal learning events within an organization and sits at the same level as the Chief Financial Officer. The CLO oversees the human resource interests of the organization. He or she makes sure that employees are treated as appreciating assets. The CLO participates in discussions about R&D commercialization, new product development, the strategic vision of the company, and increasing shareholder value.

The job of the CLO is to monitor internal training practices, position training to support the ERP implementation, participate in planning the education of the organization's workforce, and championing organizational learning and employee development during and after the ERP implementation.

The CLO makes sure that "learning" is written into the vision statement of the company, that job descriptions include the concept of continual learning, and that employees are properly educated. The corporate asset of "employee" must be planned and monitored with as much care and attention as the purchase of a major software system.

A large part of the responsibility of the CLO is to develop, administer and monitor the Master Learning Plan (MLP). The MLP is a visual depiction of all the learning that is to occur within the organization. The plan projects future needs and can be used to coordinate major educational initiatives with major improvement efforts. If a new piece of equipment is scheduled to arrive on a particular date, the CLO makes sure that the operator(s) of the equipment are trained by that date so that production time is not lost after the equipment arrives. The MLP should be reviewed monthly by the operations team to ensure that training is targeted to the needs of the employees within the organization. The executive team, to ensure that it meets the strategic needs of the organization, should also review the MLP monthly.

The CLO should also plan and develop an internal learning infrastructure to support the various learning efforts throughout the organization. The learning infrastructure developed by the CLO should consist of several interrelated systems encouraging learning and providing information on an as-needed basis. Many hi-tech and low-tech tools are available for building a learning infrastructure.

Intranets are excellent hi-tech tools for providing a common means for learning materials and online job aids. An intranet can serve as a collective corporate memory, capturing and distributing policies, procedures, and centralized online training. A collective corporate memory helps an organization avoid relearning information over and over again. Electronic networks and software tools provide a central exchange for the discussion of ideas, competitor actions, and new product launches.

An example of a successful use of online tools is the Hewlett-Packard plant in Roseville, CA. The company found that a key reason for employee turnover was the lack of career development and advancement opportunities for traditionally underrepresented groups like females and minorities. Hewlett-Packard initiated an online mentoring program whereby mentees are matched, via an online mentor database and a mentor-mentee matching software program, with qualified, experienced mentors. The program and its online facilitation of mentor-mentee relationships is a win-win for both the employees and Hewlett-Packard. Benefits to the company include reduced

better-prepared workforce, and increased employee productivity.
ages to the employees are a broader perspective of the company, improved skills, and easily obtainable coaching and guidance. The program was so successful that it received a 1999 "Excellence in Practice Citation" from ASTD (formerly known as The American Society for Training and Development, now known as ASTD).[3]

In addition to high-tech infrastructure projects like an intranet, many low-tech solutions are also available to build a learning infrastructure. Low-tech solutions include a corporate learning library holding trade journals, competitive information, and audio-taped seminars. An old-fashioned push-pin bulletin board can be an excellent place to exchange information or ideas. For informal learning events and impromptu brainstorming, white boards, flip charts, and markers should be readily available. As mentioned earlier, brownbag lunchtime training sessions can serve as excellent forums for the exchange of knowledge and information.[4]

Whether a learning infrastructure is built with high-tech or low-tech tools, careful planning is required to ensure that the learning goals of the organization are supported. The appointment of a CLO will help to allocate resources to the learning process and ensure that after the ERP implementation learning will continue in a focused, deliberate manner.

## Resources

All the planning in the world will not result in favorable results if the proper resources are not allocated to the project. ERP systems are effectively implemented when proper learning occurs in an organization because proper resources are dedicated to the process. This means that learning must be made a daily priority and not a one-time event that occurs in a training class and is "not really" part of the job. Learning must be made part of the job.

Training is often ignored or even discouraged when no major needs such as an ERP implementation are taking place. In fact, less than 13% of American workers have ever received extensive training in how to do their work better.[5] Employees cannot help to transform their organization into a learning organization with no training on how to improve their existing work practices.

Therefore, the first resource to allocate to continuous learning is time. Employees need time to learn. Most managers or supervisors would not look favorably upon an employee reading a magazine or surfing the web. However, an opportunity to learn new information or an innovative technique can come from magazines or web sites. Allowing an employee an hour or two a day to explore new possibilities improves the learning of the employee and prepares them for the future.

What type of learning should employees focus on? Any type of learning! The simple act of engaging the mind in an activity stimulates the brain and allows innovation and creativity to flourish. However, most organizations want an employee to attend a training class that will directly and quickly benefit the organization. Unfortunately, when employees become busy in their daily tasks they feel that time cannot be spared to attend training. Managers and supervisors must make sure that employees' work is covered so employees will not be swamped when they return to their jobs. The managers must also articulate to the employees that attendance in training programs is expected and required. When employees understand that training and learning is truly respected, then they will seek training opportunities.

While sending an employee to training is important, it must be noted that poorly designed and delivered training will sabotage any continuous training effort. Employees will value training only when it is well designed and delivered. The explanation of training throughout this chapter assumes that the training has been designed effectively using the strategies of LRP and Instructional Systems Design. If training is poorly done, employees will not respect learning and training, instead, they will reject it.

Once the employees are trained, they need to have time allocated to the process of thinking so they can practice what was learned. Time cannot just be granted for a training class, time must also be granted after the training class for rehearsal and re-enforcement of ideas and techniques. Time should also be allocated to employees to allow them to "think" and to be creative. Most managers would discipline an employee staring off into space and not working. Time should also be allocated to the employee for sharing his or her new insights. The sharing of ideas and training of others are two highly effective methods for reinforcing learning.

Another valuable resource to allocate is training space. Often, in manufacturing organizations the space for training is inadequate. Stories of trainers conducting classes in truck bays, unused warehouse sections, hallways, and other strange places are more common than one would expect. If space is not available on-site for adequately conducting a training class, then the organization should find nearby locations for this purpose. Many libraries, chambers of commerce, schools, and hotels have good facilities available.

Organizations must also allocate areas for employees to participate in on-line learning. Often managers expect an employee to sit at his or her desk and take an online course. This will not be effective. The constant interruption of the phone, fellow employees, and even the boss make learning at one's desktop difficult. The problem is further compounded on the shop floor where employees are expected to stand at a terminal and concentrate on a lesson when noise, fellow employees, forklifts, and countless other distractions occur all around. A designated place that is quiet and out of the way needs to be created for online learning to occur. The employees should be able to sequester themselves in the room and not be interrupted. This means that a computer and a space will need to be dedicated to online learning — that is good.

The final resource to allocate to continuous learning is money. In corporations, little is accomplished without the commitment of funds. However, money should not be committed unless it can be shown that the organization will receive a return on its investment. LRP provides the tools to show the return. The organization, in turn, must commit funds in order to see the results. If training outcomes positively impact the bottom line, then management must commit to working with the CLO to make sure that future money is available to continue the training and learning efforts.

Tom Peters in his landmark book *Thriving on Chaos* invites executives and managers to take a bold step. He writes, "consider doubling or tripling your training and retraining budget in the course of the next 24 to 36 months. Less serious consideration means a failure to come to grips with both the nature of the issue and the magnitude of the opportunity."[6] While this suggestion was bold in 1987, it is as relevant today as it was then — maybe even more so with the current half-life of most learning being between 8 and 36 months (less than 6 months for Internet-based technologies and highly competitive industries).

The half-life of learning simply means the time after completion of training when, because of new developments, the employee who attended training has become roughly half as competent as he or she was upon graduation. This means that a continuous effort needs to be made to ensure that employees have relevant skills. This effort requires an organizational commitment of money. While training is typically the first area to be cut when times are tight, the impact of the learning half-life means that 8 months after training is cut, half the employee's learned capabilities are no longer relevant. Instead of cutting training budgets in tight times, the budgets should be increased.

Organizations tend to give a great deal of lip service to training and education. However, employees quickly learn what is important to an organization and what is mere rhetoric. If an organization is truly committed to organizational learning and to continuing the learning process after the ERP system is implemented, resources will be allocated accordingly. Employees watch to see where resources are allocated and what items are given priority. An organization can claim to value human resources, but the allocation of resources either confirms or denies that claim. If learning is a priority, it will receive the resources it needs.

## Rewards and Incentives

Employees tend to perform most effectively when rewards are directly tied to their performance. Organizations that are able to foster continuous learning develop cross-training programs, pay for skills programs, and various employee recognition programs. Innovative companies use a combination of these techniques.

Cross-training programs allow employees to receive training in a variety of skill areas that are valuable for their immediate job as well as for performing work in other areas. Pay for skills programs provide monetary rewards to employees who learn a new skill above and beyond their current job requirements.

A TRW Occupational Restraints System plant in Mexico reports that its pay-for-skills program provided multiskilled workers who could rotate among various workstations. This allowed the plant to keep a highly flexible structure to meet dynamic customer demands.[7] Other organizations report that having flexible, cross-trained employees makes it easier to redeploy displaced workers when process improvements reduce staffing requirements in a particular area.

The learning focus of the organization should not change to a reward focus. Employees should understand that the value of the learning should be reward enough. Unfortunately, the reality of today's workforce is employees seldom voluntarily learn new skills. Upper management must find methods to motivate employees to continue to learn. A pay-for-skills program is an effective motivating technique.

Not all motivational programs need to be tied to monetary rewards. A vital way of reinforcing learning and training within an organization is to provide plaques or certificates for learning, free dinners, days off, tickets to a big game, or other rewards that are relatively inexpensive, but highly visible to the majority of employees.

Rewards and incentives must be handled carefully. Too much emphasis on the rewards and the purpose for the learning becomes overshadowed by a what-do-I-get-out-of-this mentality that does not foster learning but reward-seeking. Learning can be its own reward and motivator, and for many employees it will be. Increased knowledge and empowerment help employees to enjoy their job more and to feel more a part of the organization. However, not every employee responds favorably to the opportunity to learn. Some see it as boring or distracting from their "real" work. The organization will need to put some sort of reward and incentive structure in place to help all employees acclimate to the process of continuous learning.

# The Five Disciplines

To gauge success of the continuous learning efforts, an organization needs to have areas on which it should focus. Peter Senge offers a set of disciplines to put into place to become a learning organization. Senge is the author of *The Fifth Discipline.* He is also the Director of the Center for Organizational Learning at MIT's Sloan School of Management. His disciplines can be used to determine if an organization is on the right track toward transforming into a learning organization through the application of LRP.

The five disciplines are Personal Mastery, Mental Models, Shared Vision, Team Learning, and Systems Thinking.[1] Each of the five disciplines is briefly described below.

## *Personal Mastery*

This discipline involves an individual's ability to know what he or she wants and to work toward that goal. In a learning organization, creating an environment in which members can develop themselves toward the goals and purposes they choose and the organization chooses, like an ERP implementation, encourages personal mastery.

An organization cannot force its employees to learn. An organization can only set up conditions that encourage and support employee learning. A learning organization encourages managers and supervisors to serve as coaches and mentors. Learning organizations do not require employees to complete reams and reams of paperwork to attend a personal improvement class or to partake in company-sponsored learning events. Organizations that value personal mastery encourage diversity and discourage "group think." Successful organizations need and value the opinions of all employees.

Employees in a successful organization, in turn, value the organization and work on contributing positively to the organization in many ways. Tom

Peters in his book *The Circle of Innovation* lists eight items that one should consider when thinking about their own personal growth:

1. I will be known for what (2–4 items) by next year?
2. I am challenged by my current project in the following (1–3 ways).
3. I have learned the following new things in the last 90 days.
4. My organizational/local/regional/national/global "visibility program" consists of the following (2–4) items.
5. I have added the following contacts to my "contact list" in the last 90 days.
6. I have nurtured the following relationships in the last 90 days.
7. My principal "resume enhancement activity" for the next 60–90 day is (1 item).
8. I have the following (2–4) new items on my resume since last year at this time.[8]

These points can prompt employees to think about their own ability to manage their career and to focus on their own personal mastery. This list can be modified or altered as needed.

In many traditional organizations, the old "What if we train our employees and they leave?" question arises. It is an irrelevant question because studies have shown that participation in employer-sponsored training actually reduces the likelihood of an employee leaving. Ironically, as an organization focuses more on personal development and employee empowerment, employees are less likely to seek employment elsewhere. An exception to this is when a company is encouraging people to learn but then not allowing those people to use the new knowledge. If employees learn better ways to run the business and are thwarted in their efforts, it will be a demotivator that can result in departure. When a company helps employees to grow, employees will help the company grow.

Learning organizations ask a far more important question, "What if we don't train our employees and they stay?" Only stagnant or mismanaged organizations need worry about a large number of employees leaving after being trained. In any organization, some employees will leave in spite of good management, excellent reward systems, and numerous opportunities to learn. However, learning organizations have cross-trained, flexible individuals at all ranks of the organization and should be able to easily move employees around to satisfy personnel needs within the organization while providing those motivated employees with yet more opportunities to learn.

## Mental Models

Mental models are an organization's and an individual's internal picture of the world — a paradigm. Paradigms must be constantly evaluated, analyzed, and clarified to ensure they are as accurate as possible. An organization can easily get caught in an old paradigm and have trouble reacting to change. Old paradigms are frequently uncovered during ERP implementations. Once discovered, old, ineffective paradigms should be shattered and new ones put into place.

An organization that is working to become a learning organization must develop a formal method for examining the assumptions under which it performs. Too often, procedures remain in place while the conditions prompting the initial development of the procedure have long since disappeared.

One of the most valuable techniques for revealing an organization's mental model is to slow down and dissect our thinking to reveal the model. For example, an ERP software development company was finding that it had terrible relationships with its clients. The clients did not receive return phone calls in a timely manner, bug fixes were not always effective, and improvements to the software were driven by the software engineers — not customer needs. A team examined all of the symptoms of poor customer service and ultimately determined that the root cause of the problem was an underlying assumption throughout the software company that the clients were adversaries. The mental adversarial model was reinforced throughout the organization by the actions and words of the president and top management. Clients were constantly referred to as "dumb" or "uninformed" and even language in the sales agreement reinforced the negative mental model. Once the adversarial mental model was exposed and brought to the attention of the organization, changes resulted. Everyone in the organization attended training focused on the good aspects of the client organizations, rewrote contracts, and sent the software engineers to client sites to meet and mingle with the clients. The organization did not turn around overnight, but the mental model was slowly changed.

Organizations must make a conscious effort to continually review practices and procedures to determine the cause of actions and reactions to both internal and external events. The combination of actions can review the underlying model that is governing the organization. If the model is flawed or incorrect, then actions will not be appropriate. A formal process for reviewing underlying assumptions must be put into place.

## Shared Vision

This discipline embodies the idea of an organization building a sense of common commitment by developing shared visions of the future. This includes developing the principles and guiding practices used to reach the goal. During an ERP implementation, the mission or vision statement is often a tangible symbol of the shared vision of the future.

A shared vision allows all employees within the organization to work toward the same goals. Employees will strive for achievement when they know where the organization is headed.

## Team Learning

Skills learned through teamwork and team involvement enable employees to reliably develop intelligence and abilities greater than the sum of the individual members' talents. Team learning is geared toward developing collective thinking skills.

Manufacturing organizations can benefit greatly from a team-based approach to production. For example, TENNALUM, a Division of Kaiser Aluminum located in Jackson, TN uses a self-directed team approach with no supervisors. The teams are empowered to make operational and quality decisions, perform preventative maintenance and quality control decisions, and even develop minor equipment design modifications. Teams at TEN-NALUM are also empowered to make product quality decisions with the authority to put suspect material on stop, or to stop a process if they decide inferior product is being produced.[9]

The teamwork at TENNALUM has been extremely successful. The company has won the 1995 Shingo Prize for Excellence in Manufacturing, the 1995 Tennessee Quality Achievement Award, and countless other manufacturing excellence awards. The teamwork that is fostered throughout the organizations a major source of the results that have positioned them to win the awards.[9]

## Systems Thinking

This discipline is most critical in terms of helping an organization to successfully achieve ERP implementation success. Systems thinking is a way of thinking about and understanding the forces and interrelationships that exist between all of the different functional areas within the manufacturing organization. This discipline helps manufacturers to see how to change the systems more effectively and to act more in tune with the larger processes of the economic and industrial world.

When individuals begin to think about the entire organization and the integrated nature of a manufacturing plant, then decisions that were formerly made in isolation are now made with consideration to the impact on the whole organization. A focus on systems thinking helps all members of the organization to focus on the good of the many as opposed to the good of the few.

These five disciplines can serve as guidelines for developing a learning organization. Using the steps of the LRP model and the five disciplines, an organization can begin to work on the difficult but rewarding task of becoming a learning organization. As the global business marketplace becomes more and more competitive and margins are driven lower and lower, the advantage of learning and employee flexibility becomes, not a luxury, but a necessity to compete.

## Summary

Manufacturing organizations cannot stop their learning or improvement efforts simply because the ERP system is successfully installed and up and running. Once ERP success is achieved, the organization must remain focused on learning and continuous improvement. The ability to provide the proper rewards and incentives is critical to long-term organizational success. When organizations focus on learning, they are unstoppable, but if the focus wanes, competitors and market forces quickly AND WITHOUT MERCY negate past advantages. Continuation is an element in the Learning Requirements Planning process. Without continuation, the process is an event with limited scope and impact.

## LRP Continuation Checklist

| Continuation Task | Completed | | |
| --- | --- | --- | --- |
| | Yes | No | Date |

**Planning Tasks**

1. Determine the best method of conveying desired message to employees

2. Develop formal methods of conveying training message to employees (training classes, meetings)

3. Encourage the development of informal methods of conveying training message to employees (pictures, impromptu events)

4. Hire a Chief Learning Officer (CLO)

5. Develop a Master Learning Plan (MLP)

6. Develop a corporate learning infrastructure

**Resource Tasks**

7. Make training and learning a corporate priority

8. Allocate time for employee training

9. Allocate time for employee thinking

10. Allocate the space necessary for classroom training

11. Allocate a space and equipment necessary for online learning

12. Allocate the necessary money to support continuous learning

**Rewards and Incentives**

13. Consider cross-training the majority of the workforce

14. Consider instituting a pay-for-skills program

15. Develop nonmonetary methods of recognition

**Learning Disciplines**

16. Put incentive program into place to encourage employees to reach the discipline of Personal Mastery

17. Develop a process for examining the Mental Models present within the organization

18. Implement a program to provide a Shared Vision within the entire company

19. Initiate a program to develop a focus on Team Learning and teamwork within the organization

20. Initiate a program to develop Systems Thinking at all levels of the organization

# References

1. Senge, P. M., *The Fifth Discipline*, Currency Doubleday, New York, 1990.
2. Altomonte, W., Mooney, W., and Sheldon, D. H., Cultural change — empowerment at Sweetheart Cup Company, Inc., in *APICS 1997 Int. Conf. Proc.*, APICS, Alexandria, VA, 1997, pp. 187-189.
3. The ASTD Awards 1999, ASTD, Alexandria, VA, 1999, p. 17.
4. Kapp, K. M., Transforming your manufacturing organization into a learning organization, in *APICS 1997 Int. Conf. Proc.*, APICS, Falls Church, VA, 1997, p. 288.
5. Senge, P. M. et al., *The Fifth Discipline Field Book*, Doubleday, New York, 1994, Chap. 13.
6. Peters, T., *Thriving on Chaos*, HarperPerennial, New York, 1991, p. 386.
7. Sheridan, J. L., Lessons from the best, in *APICS 1997 Int. Conf. Proc.*, APICS, Falls Church, VA, 1997, p. 126–130.
8. Peters, T., *Circle of Excellence: You Can't Shrink Your Way to Greatness*, Alfred A. Knopf, New York, 1997, p. 193.
9. Swick, L., Team-based organization:the fruits of employee empowerment, in *APICS 1996 Int. Conf. Proc.*, APICS, Falls Church, VA, 1996, p. 209.

# 10 The ERP/e-Learning Connection

## Introduction

Over the past few years corporate training and, in particular, ERP education have begun to take on an interesting form. Because of the reduction in hardware costs, the compatibility and platform independence of browser software, and the difficulty software vendors have of sending their people all over the world to conduct training, ERP vendors are using e-learning to deliver ERP training.

e-Learning, distance education, web-based training (WBT), virtual learning, online learning, and other terms are all used to describe the delivery of training to employees over a distance via the Internet. This relatively new method of delivering training has been quickly adopted by the major ERP vendors and is dramatically changing the shape of ERP training.

The promise of anytime, anywhere, 24/7 ERP training is appealing to executives, managers, and employees. The ability to sign on to a class without the restrictions of time and space is exciting. Employees can literally attend an ERP training class at their desktop delivered by a trainer located anywhere in the world.

In addition, traditional methods of ERP education and training do not seem to be effective. In fact, an article in *CIO Magazine* titled "ERP Training Stinks" illustrates just how frustrated many companies are with traditional ERP training.[1] Employees are bombarded with millions of pieces of new information daily. Some of the information is critically important but much is nonessential. Yet it all must be processed. Add on top of all that information an eight-hour ERP training class in which the instructor dictates the pace of the learning and the information doesn't seem relevant to the employee's current job, and you have a recipe for disaster. Little effective learning takes place in that type of environment.

In addition, instructor-led training is costly. Flying in consultants and vendor trainers to an organization from across the country is not cheap. Airfare costs continue to rise, hotels are getting more expensive, and meal costs are skyrocketing. In addition, because the training is only available one time, all the employees in the organization must stop what they are doing to attend the class. Most of the classes also require a minimum number of students so some employees end up in a class they don't really need just to make the class "go."

ERP software companies like Baan, SAP, J.D. Edwards, Oracle, and PeopleSoft have adopted e-learning for the delivery of much of their training. These vendors are able to maximize their training resources by offering web-based training. However, the concept of distance training is not new to ERP vendors. The options of video-based training and CD-ROM-based training have been around for years. And their existence has not dramatically changed ERP training. Employees still want an instructor rather than sit in front of a CD-ROM or video. These two training methods are not effective.

The reason these two options pale in comparison to web-based instruction is because of the interactivity of the web. A CD-ROM or a video are one-way delivery vehicles. If an employee watching a video or clicking through a CD-ROM has a question, he or she is stuck — no one is there to answer questions. With the web-based delivery of training the option exists to have a trainer "live" online to answer questions through a virtual chat room or even through e-mail almost instantaneously as soon as a question is asked. In addition, some Internet training applications allow the trainers to "take over" an employee's computer screen and walk him or her through the correct steps. Trainees also have the option to contact other students at other companies via e-mail or chats to see how other companies are using the software or working through functionality issues. The web also allows employees to instantly link to additional instruction or information and to have instant training whenever a related topic interests them.

If an employee is working within an ERP application, he or she can simply open a web browser, type in some keywords into a search engine, and instantly find the training on the topic they need. The employee can then review the training and continue on with his or her job without ever leaving the desk. Contrast the web-based training scenario just described with having to wait for a training class or having to go find a VCR and fast-forwarding to the correct spot on the tape, or having to find the correct CD-ROM.

e-Learning holds many promises for ERP training. e-Learning reduces travel time, increases access to ERP experts, provides on-demand education, and allows employees to learn at their own pace.

## Defining e-Learning

e-Learning is the presentation of training materials, information, and content via the Internet or through an intranet. More specifically, it has been defined as "any purposeful, considered application of web technologies to the task of educating a fellow human being."[2] e-Learning takes advantage of web browser technology to deliver the training to any computer.

Several technological features of the web make it effective for instruction. These features include interactive web pages, chat rooms, threaded discussions, whiteboards, application sharing, web-casts, testing programs, and links to additional pages. Figure 10.1 shows a screen capture of a threaded discussion from an ERP implementation discussion group. Threaded discussions, as well as other types of e-learning communications, can cover a variety of topics and allow people to respond and post information when it is convenient for them.

Interactive web pages can have many different forms ranging from clicking different areas of an image, to completing a lengthy fill-in-the-blank form, to drag-and-drop exercises, to multiple-choice questions. One of the primary advantages of e-learning is that instruction encourages the user to become involved. Good e-learning programs require that learners interact with the instruction by performing various tasks online. Passively reading a computer screen is not good e-learning.

For example, a web-based training program can be developed to mimic an order entry screen. The learner can be required to enter information into the mock order entry screen just as he or she would on the job. The difference would be that if the learner didn't follow the correct sequence or forgot to perform a certain task, the computer would coach the learner through the exercise with screen messages and prompts.

Several products have been developed to assist with the process of creating interactive web pages quickly and easily. One such product is Macromedia's DreamWeaver. This package enables the user to create WYSIWYG (pronounced "wizzy wig") web pages. That means What You See Is What You Get. When you program an e-learning web page with DreamWeaver or Microsoft's FrontPage, the page looks similar to the way you type it. This is unlike straight HTML code that has a variety of special codes and characters in it, which

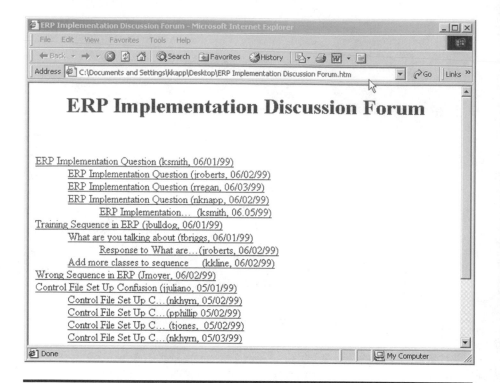

**Figure 10.1 Screen Capture of a Threaded Discussion Page on ERP Implementation.**

makes it difficult for someone unfamiliar with HTML to read and understand what the page will look like until it is actually "published" onto the web. Macromedia has added another piece of software called CourseBuilder that helps the DreamWeaver Package to create interactions such as multiple-choice, true/false, and fill-in-the-blank questions. The combination of these two software packages makes effective web-based training possible.

Another interactive feature is the chat room. A chat room is simply a typed conversation between two or more people conducted in real time over a web connection. A chat allows learners to ask questions of an instructor who is miles away and almost instantly receive an answer. Chat rooms also allow users to discuss topics among themselves over the web. One nice thing about computer chats is that they can be recorded and then reviewed at a later date. This is a tremendous benefit over classroom conversations, in which sometimes only half of the conversation is remembered.

Similar to a chat room is the threaded discussion. A threaded discussion is a typed conversation between two or more people, but it is not conducted in real time. The advantage of a threaded discussion is that the learners can log onto the instruction and read or post a message at any time. Most threaded discussions have an indented discussion format. This means that the first question (which starts the thread) is far to the left on the screen. Subsequent responses to the first question or comment are then indented under the original questions. This allows someone reviewing the threaded discussion to see what was initially said and then see all of the responses. If a response occurs to a response, it is indented under the comment or question to which the learner is responding. The result is something that looks similar to an indented BOM.

A whiteboard in an e-learning program is similar to the actual whiteboards found in offices and boardrooms across the country. A whiteboard is simply a white area on the screen in which anyone viewing the training can take a drawing tool from the whiteboard software and draw on the white area, type comments onto the white area, and highlight certain areas of images on the white area. Many whiteboard programs have the ability to import images of screens or documents so that groups of people can see a document at once and all comment on the document as well as interact with each other and the document over the web.

A whiteboard is a great tool for an ERP instructor who wants to illustrate a certain concept. The instructor can draw the concept on the whiteboard and then learners can type questions, circle areas that don't make sense, and draw extensions (in a different color) on the instructor's image. A whiteboard allows a space where ideas that cannot be easily expressed in words can be drawn.

Application sharing is the ability of a program to let learners see an application that is running on the instructor's program or allow the instructor to "take over" an application running on a student's terminal. This allows the ERP instructor to show how to enter a purchase order to students by actually entering a purchase order on a test system on his computer. It also allows that instructor to show a student the results of performing a certain function by "taking over" the student's computer, entering in the desired information, and then "releasing" the computer and asking the student to proceed. The student can then see the results right on his or her computer and will have the data that the instructor entered on the computer in the program.

A web-cast is similar to a live television broadcast. Both a moving picture and sound are sent over the web directly to the desktop of the students. This is great for hearing an expert on a particular topic speak or for receiving a high-level overview of a topic. Most web-casts even have mechanisms for feeding back questions and comments to the persons participating in the web-cast. The technology has even advanced to where the web-cast can be coordinated with presentation software like Microsoft PowerPoint so the person is seen speaking on the left side of the monitor and the presentation is appearing on the right.

Most e-learning environments have the ability to test or assess the learning by the students; this is commonly done in the form of a quiz or embedded questions. Embedded questions are questions that are placed throughout the instruction rather than being all bunched at the end like a quiz. One nice thing about e-learning is that students can receive instant, private feedback on their performance. The computer, based on previously defined test answers, will automatically grade the test and even provide preprogrammed feedback based on the wrong answer provided by the user. This type of personalized interaction provides highly focused feedback to the learner. If set up properly, students can receive corrective feedback on every question they answer.

The testing is not limited to a multiple-choice format. True/false, fill-in-the-blank, drag-and-drop, matching, and sequencing action are all options in e-learning testing software. The software will also let the test designer assign a randomly chosen pool of questions to minimize cheating, and even provide feedback on how long it took a person to take the quiz and how many answers were correct and how many they missed. e-Learning systems can even provide remedial feedback to students when they fail to pass the test.

Another effective feature of e-learning is the ability to link to additional pages. What makes this aspect of the web so exciting for learning is that it allows the user to learn only the information he or she needs to perform their job. The web can be made to lock-step a student through certain portions of the instruction, but it can also contain a number of different links that the student can be free to follow should he or she desire.

For example, if the instruction for a certain module was about production activity control, the system could contain a link for rate-based production and another for job-shop production and even a third for project-based production. The learner could then choose which link to follow. If the learner wanted, he or she could follow two of the links or even all three.

These elements of e-learning can be configured into two basic types of delivery. One is synchronous or live training and the other is asynchronous or self-paced training. Each of these configurations has certain advantages and disadvantages.

## Synchronous e-Learning

Synchronous e-learning means that all the students must be logged onto the computer and attending the training at a designated time. This is analogous to classroom training, where all the students must be in the classroom at a certain time for the class to start. Synchronous e-learning events include live web-casts, chat rooms, application sharing, and whiteboard sessions.[3]

For example, PeopleSoft offers live web-casts with real-time scheduled access and interaction with their instructors on a subscription or pay-per-use basis. These types of sessions are also provided by SAP, who offers live web interactions with learners through a software called InterWise.

The InterWise software not only has whiteboard features, chat rooms, and application sharing, it also has the ability to provide real-time, two-way audio exchanges. This means that a student anywhere in the world can ask the SAP instructor a question, all the students logged on the session can hear the question, and the question can then be answered over the Internet. The sound quality is surprisingly good in these situations. The use of the two-way audio provides a connection between the learners and the instructor that is not always available in a chat room where the users are typing messages back and forth.

The InterWise software uses a classroom paradigm for the presentation of information and the structuring of the interactions between the students and the instructor. For example, an icon exists that allows a student to virtually "raise her hand" if she has a question or comment to contribute to the class. An instructor can "call on" students. Students can even anonymously indicate to the instructor if the pacing of the class is too fast or too slow.

A program similar to InterWise is Centra Symposium, which offers capabilities similar to the InterWise product in terms of allowing two-way audio and having a classroom paradigm as the software interface. Each of these software products offers an organization a tremendous tool for delivering ERP training to geographically dispersed workers

The advantages of synchronous learning are that learners can discuss issues with other learners and the instructor at length, the motivation level of the class is high because it occurs at a certain time, and, most likely, peers will be involved, and learners can share ideas and thoughts about the instruction with others involved in the process at the same time.

A disadvantage of synchronous learning is that all of the learners need to be online at the same time. This means that the learners can not take the class whenever they want since they are dependent upon an instructor. An example of one of the difficulties of synchronous e-learning is when the instructor is in one time zone and the students are in another. Also, it has been found that learners who are unfamiliar with keyboarding skills are somewhat reluctant to participate in online chats because their peers, who type more quickly, leave them behind.

**Figure 10.2 Asynchronous e-Learning Screen Capture of an Accounts Payable Training Program.**

## Asynchronous e-Learning

The other type of e-learning that is available is called asynchronous or self-paced web instruction. An example of a screen capture from an accounts payable module is shown in Figure 10.2. Asynchronous instruction involves the use of interactive web pages and allows the student to participate in the instruction whenever he or she has the time. Since no instructor is involved in this training, the user can proceed at any pace he or she wants, unobstructed by others participating in the training.[4]

This training must be carefully constructed and created because the learner does not have the benefit of asking an instructor any questions. The people designing the instruction must anticipate as many questions and concerns as possible and make sure that the e-learning program addresses as many of the issues that may arise as possible.

Asynchronous learning means that a class can have a student body of one. Once the initial development costs of an asynchronous e-learning class is covered, it is inexpensive to have more people take the class or even to have only one person at a time take it. This is of tremendous benefit for training the occasional new employee or for training employees on the second or third shift.

Not only can the training be made asynchronous, but the testing can be as well. Many e-learning software packages like Blackboard and WebCT have the ability to automatically score objective tests. This means that a user can take a test and not have to wait for it to be scored by an instructor.

The primary advantage of asynchronous training is that it can be taken anywhere at anytime. One disadvantages of this type of instruction is that if the user has any questions, an instructor cannot individually address them. Also, most people have not had the experience of learning online in a self-paced environment. Therefore, they are not familiar with how to learn using this type of approach. Time must be taken to teach employees how to learn using this approach.

## Common Problems with Traditional Training

First of all, e-learning is not a complete replacement for instructor-led training. There will always be a need for instruction delivered by a knowledgeable, patient, and effective instructor. However, there is also a need for alternative forms of instruction. ERP training needs to be delivered to employees in as many different forms as possible. Having ERP training available in many formats allows employees to take the training when and where they need it and to learn in a style that is most appropriate for them. e-Learning and traditional instruction need to coexist during ERP implementations. Unfortunately, in most implementations instructor-led classroom training is the only educational alternative.

While traditional instructor-led classroom training has been around for literally thousands of years and has achieved a certain level of effectiveness, it still has a number of shortcomings. This is especially evident in ERP classroom training, where some individuals understand the information right away and others do not, or when the topics covered in the class do not apply to all employees sitting in the class.

The advantage of e-learning is that it addresses a number of the shortcomings of traditional training methods such as inefficient use of time, lag time between training and the go-live date, finding an appropriate level of instruction for the entire class, and inability to repeat the classroom instruction.

## Inefficient Use of Time

Not all of the time spent in an ERP classroom is totally devoted to instruction. During any classroom situation, interruptions occur. For example, one or two students arriving late from a break can slow down a class, or one particular student asking a series of questions can slow everyone else's learning.

Interruptions also occur due to one student not understanding the instruction or because of an emergency meeting or phone call. e-Learning eliminates typical classroom interruptions. Each student learns in his or her own environment and they do not have to worry about interruptions caused by other students.

On the other side of the efficiency coin, some students may be concerned that not enough time is dedicated to certain topics. Each employee within an organization has a slightly different role and, therefore, different ERP training needs. Employees would like the time spent in training to be directly related to what they are going to be doing on the job with the system.

It is clear from attending any training class that a wide range of learning speeds and needs are present. ERP instructors are constantly challenged with pacing the class appropriately while trying to cover an enormous amount of information.

e-Learning proceeds at the pace of the learner and provides numerous branches to additional information. One e-learning student may take advantage of a particular branch of instruction pertaining to inventory management while another may pursue lot-sizing rules. Still another student may ignore a particular instructional branch entirely because he or she already knows the information or that information is not relevant to his or her current job.

Another frequently encountered problem occurs during ERP software functionality classes when one student gets stuck or lost on a computer screen — the entire class must wait until the instructor can get the lost student back to the proper screen. e-Learning prevents this situation because it can provide students with a mock version of the software programmed to allow the student to proceed in only one direction. All the keys are not activated. This allows the student to learn what they need to learn without the frustration of getting "lost" in the ERP software because they hit the wrong key and were unable to proceed.

e-Learning provides a method of presenting instruction in more easily digestible chunks at a pace appropriate to each student, which aids student retention and increases learning. In addition, automating instruction eliminates student pacing problems because the entire class is no longer tied to the instructor. Each student is responsible for his or her own ERP learning and can proceed independently.

Student knowledge can be checked and verified during instructor-led sessions, either online or in a classroom. If the sessions are online, e-learning software exists that will allow the instructor to "look over the shoulder" of each learner to see what he or she is typing into the ERP system. The instructor even has the option of "taking over" the student's screen. He or she can then enter in the correct information to show the learner how to perform a particular operation or execute a transaction.

In addition, a number of studies have revealed that computer-based training actually requires less time for training when compared to instructor-led training and the training is usually of equal or higher value than instructor-led classes. This means that the same amount of material can be covered in a shorter period of time with e-learning than in instructor-led classrooms.[5]

## Lag Time between the Training and the Go-Live Date

In some cases, there is a lag between the time an individual attends ERP training and the time when the ERP system goes live. This delay can be due to a variety of factors such as problems with the software, lack of trainer or classroom availability, and the need for business process reengineering. Whatever the cause of the delay, the training occurs weeks or even months before the users will see the ERP system at their desks or workstations.

It is difficult for an employee to remember everything taught in class when weeks or months pass. The employees are expected to know the information because "it was taught in class" but they have trouble remembering the intricacies of the ERP program. This means that an employee either muddles through the system alone, re-training is scheduled, or the employee's manager must develop training within the department as a refresher. These instances are not efficient or effective for helping employees utilize the system properly.

Also, many employees in an organization will be using a computer for the first time and others will be highly proficient with a computer. This means that once a student is actually in an instructor-led ERP software training class, the instructor has to deal with a wide range of computer experiences.

e-Learning can provide background or preliminary training that can assist a student to learn about his or her job and its integrated nature on an ERP system and teach the requisite computer skills. This frees valuable corporate resources or expensive consultants from having to conduct the basic computer and integration training. e-Learning means the training can be conducted cost-effectively for even one employee who inevitably misses the scheduled instructor-led classroom training.

## Finding an Appropriate Level of Instruction

The students in the classroom dictate the pace of the ERP training. Instructors attempt to teach to the middle of the group, however, this means that some trainees are bored because they have already "gotten" the concept and are waiting to move on, while others are behind and are unable to catch up. The pace of the instruction is only appropriate for a few. Self-paced web-based training proceeds at the pace of the student taking the class, not at the pace of an instructor. Web-based training lets employees find the appropriate pacing level for the material they are learning.

Web-based training also allows the individual learner to determine his or her own content level. Not every job within a manufacturing organization requires the same skills or knowledge and different employees may already know how to perform certain aspects of their jobs. For example, a customer service job may involve interview skills as well as ERP computer skills. Some individuals who are excellent at interview skills may require more individual time to work on computer skills than what is available in the classroom, while other customer service employees may know computers but not be as comfortable with interviewing. e-Learning allows students to focus on their individual areas of need.

An employee who needs to know about inventory control can focus on that area of the item in master training with e-learning, while the person from accounting can focus on assigning cost codes to the item and determining the proper accounts to credit and debit when the inventory item is moved from WIP to finished goods.

Self-paced e-learning creates the appropriate level and pace of instruction based on how fast an employee moves through the information and what he or she decides to focus on in the course.

## Inability to Repeat the Classroom Instruction

If a student arrives late for class or steps out of class to solve a "crisis," the instructor rarely has the time to repeat what the student missed. Or if a student simply didn't "get" a certain idea or concept, the instructor is not able to stop the entire class until the student finally understands the material. Web-based training is repeatable and recordable. An instructor-led web-based class, an online chat, or a threaded discussion are all recordable and can be viewed later by the learner.

If the web-class is self-paced, the user can log onto the training and go through the information in whole or in part as many times as he or she desires. In addition, the training can be accessed at a PC at anytime.

## Cost Savings

There is a growing body of evidence that computer-based training reduces the total cost of training when compared to instructor-led training.[6] The lower delivery costs for online training are a result of a reduction in training time and the elimination of travel.

# Benefits of e-Learning

While typical lectures are good for the delivery of information, they are passive learning experiences, they proceed at the pace of the instructor, they assume everyone in the class needs and wants all of the information, and they cannot be accessed repeatedly once delivered.

By contrast, when you convert information to a web-based delivery format, all lectures and tutorials can be referenced at any time and can be used and reused by students when they need information to solve a problem. This increases the student's motivation for understanding the material, and helps students proceed through the material at a pace that is individually appropriate.

In addition, more than 30 separate studies reveal that interactive technologies such as web-based training reduce learning time requirements by an average of 31% and in some cases up to 50%, while simultaneously increasing retention by as much as 70%. This timesavings and increased retention rate are a result of several factors:

- Self-paced instruction encourages students to take the most efficient path to content mastery. They can skip areas of strength while investing more time in areas of weakness.
- Immediate interaction and feedback provides constant, highly effective reinforcement of concepts and content.
- Personalized instruction accommodates different learning styles to maximize learning efficiency. Some students can complete the course in an extremely short period of time.

In addition, web-based training increases student access to information. Students can reference a part of a training class, an entire training class, or a specific topic again and again when they need it. Students also have increased motivation to learn the material and not simply "keep up with the class" because they can proceed at a pace most comfortable for them while receiving responsive, personalized feedback from the software. The feedback is personalized in the fact that it is provided to the students in direct response to their actions. Students do not have to wait for an instructor to return a test or quiz to determine their level of mastery of the information being presented.

Following is a list of key benefits that any organization will receive by automating their training process. This list comes from industry expert Brandon Hall's newsletter "Multimedia and the Internet Training Newsletter." Brandon Hall, Ph.D. has been interviewed by the *New York Times*, *Fortune*, *Training*, *Training and Development* and other periodicals for his knowledge in the area of interactive training.

Hall spends his time monitoring the use of technology in the field of training and then disseminating that information to others within the field. His list of benefits follows:

- More frequent learner interaction leads to faster learning and improved retention.
- Reduces and/or eliminates travel time and expense.
- Privacy of the experience supports more risk-taking and trail-and-error by learner.
- Learning is self-paced and adapted to learner strengths and weaknesses
- Learning time is reduced by as much as 50%.
- Interactive video simulations ensure skill competency and mastery.
- Training is consistent time after time.
- Measures and tracks an individual's skill levels for review, analysis, and prescription.
- Can be used as reinforcement for previously conducted training.
- Training doesn't have to wait for assembly of a "class." One new employee can get going with training right away.
- e-Learning can cover the basics — the trainer can focus on coaching and application in the classroom environment.[7]

Hall also states that e-learning can provide "the most efficient delivery of information because of its ability to be accessible from anywhere, anytime, and to disseminate a standardized, updateable version to multiple users."[8]

Clearly, there are many benefits to be gained by combining the e-learning concept with LRP.

## e-Learning/LRP Connection

The enterprisewide approach of LRP, complete with built-in evaluations and the classification of the type of information to be learned, lends itself to the application of automated training. LRP and e-learning are both about knowledge acquisition. The goal is for individuals within the organization to gain the knowledge necessary to effectively operate and interpret the information within the ERP system. A merger of the two provides a powerful tool for the initial and continuous training of a workforce.

LRP software is needed in the manufacturing and training industries. Many powerful tools are available to help trainers, performance technologists, and knowledge managers in virtually every aspect of training management and delivery. A combination of these tools would make the development and delivery of an online LRP not only feasible but highly effective.

The advent of intranets, universal databases, and drill-down capabilities in software make it possible to automate the LRP process. This automation process will bring together different elements of training and e-learning within an organization. The learner can enter into the LRP process within the company through what is called a "Learning Portal."

A LRP Learning Portal would be a "one-stop shop" on a corporation's intranet, allowing employees to gain access to all of the training opportunities within their organization and to see how those learning opportunities tied directly into the learning objectives and strategic objectives of the organization.[9]

The LPR Learning Portal could be programmed to recognize an individual's "profile" and provide him or her with exactly the type of training needed according to both content and employee learning style as determined in the Diagnosis step of LRP. The "profile" would consist of the employee's job title, required skills for their current position, what they needed to know for the ERP implementation, and any skills required for them to move to up within the organization. The information within the profile could be matched to corporate ERP e-learning offerings and the individual could receive a customized listing of the course he or she should take to support the ERP implementation effort.

The ability to tie all corporate ERP training needs together in one place provides a powerful tool for helping to implement an ERP system within an organization. It is possible to program all of the ERP learning goals into a corporate learning portal and then allow the employees direct access to the training that specifically meets the needs of their roles before, during, and after the ERP implementation right from their desktops. This "just-in-time" approach to ERP training provides a tremendous advantage to an organization in terms of the effectiveness, timeliness, and relevance of the training received by employees.

In addition, a properly programmed LRP system allows a corporate manager to drill-down on corporate learning goals and determine how close the organization is to being trained in the areas critical to the corporation's strategic goals. The system would display the organization's net learning requirements and progress made toward meeting its learning needs. The visibility of the learning goals would help to focus the organization on learning.

The creation of LRP e-learning software would allow an organization to post information and status reports online for the entire organization to monitor. LRP and e-learning can share technology to provide a powerful tool for educating an organization to transform from a manufacturing into a learning organization through an ERP system implementation.

## Summary

As ERP vendors and client organizations maximize their effectiveness through the application of e-learning, employees are finding training readily available. The idea of anytime, anywhere ERP training is an incentive for organizations to put an e-learning plan in action. The LRP process can be supported through e-learning because of the potential for it to use the technology of the web to provide interconnected information through databases and drill-down software features.

While a comprehensive LRP software package does not currently exist, the potential for an ERP vendor or third-party training vendor to develop such a package is imminent. An automated, systematic manufacturing management system like ERP requires a systematic, automated training management system to help implement it. The framework of LRP has been developed. The next evolution will be automated LRP based on today's e-learning technology.

## References

1. Wheatley, M., ERP training stinks, *CIO Magazine* [online], http://www2.cio.com/archive/060100_erp_content.html, June 2000.

2. Horton, W., *Designing Web-Based Training*, John Wiley & Sons, New York, 2000, chap. 1.
3. Driscoll, M., *Web-Based Training*, Jossey-Bass, Pfeiffer, San Francisco, 1998, chap. 8.
4. Driscoll, M., *Web-Based Training*, Jossey-Bass, Pfeiffer, San Francisco, 1998, chap. 7.
5. Hall, B., *Web-Based Training Cookbook*, John Wiley & Sons, New York, 1997, chap. 1.
6. Hall, B., *Web-Based Training Cookbook*, John Wiley & Sons, New York, 1997, chap. 6.
7. Hall, B., Benefits of interactive training, Multimedia Internet Training Newsletter, 4(5), 9, 1997.
8. Hall, B., *Web-Based Training Cookbook*, John Wiley & Sons, New York, 1997, p. 19.
9. Mantyla, K., Learning portals: online e-learning options, in *The ASTD 2000/2001 Distance Learning Yearbook*, Mantyla, K., Ed., McGraw-Hill, New York, 2000, p. 15.

# 11 Conclusion

## Introduction

In Chapter 4, discussing the Analysis process, Marshall Manufacturing was a company in trouble. Inventory levels were through the roof, nobody knew what inventory was needed or when, the sales department was furious about late delivery, and the entire company was dreading the ERP implementation date that was quickly approaching.

The president of Marshall knew that there were fundamental problems that needed to be solved before the ERP implementation could be successful. He also knew that he wanted to use the ERP implementation as a catalyst to transform the organization from its old habits to a new, competitive presence in the market. The president of this fictitious company decided to implement the Learning Requirements Planning process to achieve ERP implementation success and to become a learning organization. The following are the results of that effort.

## Marshall Revisited

Imagine walking into Marshall Manufacturing and seeing a well-run organization. Production employees of Marshall are commenting that inventory items are available right when they need them and in the location they expected to find them. Raw material seems to be arriving just when it is needed. The purchasing manager has been heard saying, "I only purchase what we need ... and now we know exactly what we need and when we need it." He smiles as the visitors walk past. There are no shortages, raw materials inventory keeps getting smaller and smaller, and safety stock is virtually a "thing of the past," as the inventory manager likes to say.

WIP inventory is being reduced as well. It is still higher than the manufacturing manager would like but he is able to see a definite trend where WIP is reducing. The shipping department no longer disassembles items to get parts for urgent orders. They now clearly have visibility of upcoming orders. The expediters still occasionally appear on the floor, but they are all being retrained and shifted to other positions as their role has been quickly diminishing. The manufacturing manager has been heard saying, "In all my years of manufacturing, I've never seen a place run like this; WIP is being reduced, employees are getting properly trained, and the darn computer system is actually helping me do my job."

The shop floor has been cleared of all excess inventory and employees can now move from one area of the plant to another without fear of running into some piece of inventory just lying on the floor. The inventory manager has begun a cycle-counting program and is meeting with a high level of success. Employees now willingly store materials in their proper places even though it "takes some extra time."

The sales department manager now actively participates in the weekly Sales and Operations Planning meetings and is beginning to understand the negative impact of selling just to sell. The sales and production staff are working together so that promotions and special deals do not adversely impact the entire organization. Monthly sales quotas have been changed to weekly goals to help level production. Pricing discounts are not based on a single order but orders over a yearly period. Sales is now trying to develop long-term relationships with customers to deliver a little bit of product every week instead of some huge quantity delivered at unpredictable intervals.

Marshall has given some of its key vendors access to its manufacturing schedule via a secured Internet connection. These vendors are able to support Marshall's production because they can now anticipate demand. The vendors deliver smaller quantities to Marshall on a weekly basis. This has resulted in fewer stock-outs of key materials and has actually begun to reduce purchasing costs because premium freight and vendor expediting costs have been reduced. Marshall hopes to expand its vendor relationship program to more vendors and is considering holding a yearly vendor's conference.

In addition to having access to manufacturing information at Marshall, the key vendors are also able to take the same e-learning training programs that Marshall employees are taking. This means that the vendors and the purchasing employees at Marshall are both approaching purchasing from a common background using common terminology.

The accounting department knows how much inventory is in stock, what the actual and planned costs are for jobs and, for the first time in 12 months, profits are above expectations. The accounting manager is receiving reports containing detailed tracking of labor and materials against work orders.

The employees on the shop floor are shipping material on time and recording every labor and inventory transaction as it occurs. The company no longer needs to conduct year-end inventory counts because it is cycle-counting on a daily basis. When problems arise, the counting team identifies the root cause of those problems and quickly makes adjustments. The adjustments are then written into corporate procedures and the counting of those items is repeated to make sure the adjustments provided the desired outcome.

The company is thrilled that in just 12 months (only a little longer than originally anticipated) the company has turned itself around, successfully implemented its new ERP system, and has achieved record levels of profitability. Marshall is even considering have a local manufacturing professional society tour their facility because of their success.

## The Difference at Marshall

What is the difference between the Marshall Manufacturing company on the verge of bankruptcy in Chapter 4 and the Marshall we are standing in today? The answer is Learning Requirements Planning.

Marshall has a successful ERP implementation because they used a systematic program that works. Marshall concentrated on education, training, and actual corporate needs. Employees could focus on the problem because they understood the ERP system, their roles in the organization, the education they needed to achieve success, how they could best learn that information, and how to make ERP work.

Marshall is not unlike many small, medium, or large manufacturing organizations. Executives first believed that implementing LRP would be a difficult and time-consuming process. The manager of manufacturing thought the process was too linear and would require too much effort. Today he will look you straight in the eye and tell you he was wrong.

The process of carefully conducting an analysis of organization objectives was a process the executive team at Marshall was familiar with, but not comfortable conducting. It took the intervention of an outside consultant familiar with learning theory and business operations to make the process successful.

The executive team made it through the analysis process with a few problems, but nothing insurmountable. The most interesting part of the analysis process was that when Marshall executives discussed developing learning objectives that was the first time the executive ever discussed, as a group, the educational needs of the organization. While the team had said they supported developing human resources, this process was the first time they actually put plans into place to make their employees successful through education and training. Marshall, like many other organizations, had never before had a formal, systematic approach for meeting the training needs of its employees.

The next step, Diagnosis, took place with the assistance of the local university's psychology department. A couple of graduate students and a professor took a week and administered a short test to employees to help them identify their learning styles. The group from the university explained the implication of the various learning styles and provided the employees with some insight into how they could learn best now that they were aware of their preferred method of learning. The employees enjoyed the educational experience and several mentioned that they would apply what they know to learning about their interests outside of work as well.

The upfront investment in Analysis and Diagnosis has paid rich dividends for the personnel and for the entire organization. The emphasis on a careful plan with feedback of information into the plan has worked well for Marshall. The implementation was not always easy and setbacks occurred from time to time, but the employees were ready because they were educated on the ERP implementation process — the ERP system did not happen to them, they made ERP happen.

The design step provided challenges to Marshall as well. Marshall did not have the money to totally design an ERP implementation curriculum from scratch. Instead, they pieced together the elements they needed from APICS materials, classes provided by the ERP vendor, and classes conducted by a local manufacturing consultant. Once one or two people internally gained knowledge of the ERP system, they assisted others with their training needs.

This method of "designing" the ERP implementation curriculum was successful for Marshall because the implementation team took the time to determine what materials were needed to meet the needs of the employees and the organization. Employees could choose from a wide variety of materials and instructional methods. Most employees opted for the training classes, a few chose the e-learning classes, and a smaller number chose to learn the system "on their own" with only an occasional question of clarification from instructors or other employees.

The key to Marshall's ultimate ERP implementation success was the use of LRP. The first step in the implementation process was the establishment and training of the implementation team. The implementation team consisted of six core members who were trained in communication skills, sales skills, and technical skills. Each of the core team members understood the flow of the ERP system and the impact each module had on the other modules by the time the ERP implementation team training was concluded.

In addition, the ERP implementation team received training in the various methods of "going live." The implementation team chose to use a pilot approach. Using this approach, the ERP system was put through it paces by the implementation team and users prior to implementing the system. This gave employees within the company an opportunity to review the functionality of the system before it was released companywide and become part of their daily routine.

This method allowed the users to become familiar and comfortable with the system. Complications that arose during the pilot were identified and addressed long before the system was expected to be actually supporting the organization. Problems with the system still arose during the first week of production. However, the users were comfortable with the system and generally did not panic when a problem arose. A roaming "fix-it squad" was available to answer any questions the users had and to address a software or procedural issue as soon as it was identified.

Another key to success was helping all the employees of the company understand the general flow of information through the ERP system. Many classroom sessions and work on the pilot system provided an overview of the ERP process to the employees. This process was facilitated by interactive group role-play exercises in which employees from different parts of the organization assumed roles of other employees. The employees were then given a scenario and a production problem and told to solve the problem in line with their assigned role. The employee didn't know it at the time, but each scenario was carefully chosen to reflect typical problems that occur during an ERP implementation.

The employees were coached through the process by the outside consultant as well as internal "assistants" who were trained by the consultant to conduct the role-play exercise. Eventually, the consultant was not needed and the assistants conducted the role-plays themselves. This was successful because many unspoken agenda items or biases were addressed during this session and each person gained an understanding of the responsibilities of their counterparts in other departments in terms of the ERP system.

Each of the training events was evaluated for its effectiveness and modified if it was determined to be "not effective." The implementation team took the time to review the level 1 evaluations, make corrections to the course material, and then deliver the course to new students using the revised materials. The method worked well and the employees generally liked the ERP training and understood why it was necessary.

Marshall did conduct some testing at the end of the training session but, because of union issues, did not record individual employee scores. Instead, employees self-scored their own tests and then, based on the results, either borrowed remedial materials, signed up for a web-based version of the course, or received assistance from one of the internal system mentors.

The implementation team conducted follow-ups with a subset of employee managers to determine if the training impacted attitudes and behaviors. These follow-ups got mixed reviews. The majority of trainees did exhibit some noticeable differences in terms of being able to perform functions they never could before as related to ERP. However, some employees with negative attitudes were still negative after the training. Unfortunately, in one case, the employee was asked to leave the company.

Marshall has made a concentrated effort to continue with training and education now that the system is up and running. Many times, lunchtime educational and training sessions are held to inform the employees of unique features and functions of the system that are not commonly known or used. The employees are also given a chance to conduct the internal sessions themselves. This helps to spread knowledge through the company and also helps employees to gain confidence and experience in presenting their ideas to others.

## Impact of LRP

Marshall Manufacturing is not unlike other manufacturing companies. Implementing ERP is not its primary concern. The primary motivator here is to produce product on time, deliver it on time and to maintain a profit level. ERP enables this process to occur. ERP is a means to an end.

The six steps of LRP, Analysis, Diagnosis, Design, Implementation, Evaluation, and Continuation, is a model for implementing the ERP system on time and within budget. The model is not hard to follow or understand but its effective implementation can be difficult. Implementing any new methodology, process, or software system at the enterprise level is difficult.

In spite of the difficulties, a successful implementation leads to profit, increased employee morale, and a better position within the marketplace. As global competition increases and goods and services are available from anywhere in the world, one of the remaining sustainable competitive advantages is the ability to learn faster than competitors.

LRP is a process for enabling that learning. Not only can LRP be used for ERP implementation, but following the LRP steps can enhance the implementation of any e-technology. The model is based on sound educational principles that are supported by empirical research as well as anecdotal evidence. Learning is the forgotten element in many organizational strategies — the element that, if ignored, won't impact the company in the short term, but in the long term will literally cripple its operations.

The learning cannot be limited to shop floor or office employees, the learning must also occur continuously at the executive level. Many companies have failed because the executives no longer understood the market or were not able to learn about new technologies that their competitors had employed. A lust for learning needs to permeate the organization to ensure survival.

Organizational learning is about adapting to change. Charles Darwin once said, "It is not the strongest of the species nor the smartest that survive, but those most adaptive to change." LRP is about adapting to change continuously through learning.

The LRP process makes the implementation of the ERP system more than the installation of software; instead, LRP serves as a catalyst to transform the company into a learning organization that will have an unprecedented advantage over competitors.

# Glossary

**ABCD Objective Format:** This is a format for developing learning objectives that are measurable and testable. The letters represent different requirements of the written objective. The A represents the *audience* who will receive the training for the objective, B represents the desired *behavior* the employee will exhibit as a result of the training, C represents the *condition* under which the desired behavior will be triggered, and D represents the *degree* of accuracy, correctness, or frequency that is required for the objective to be successfully met.

**ARCS Motivation Model:** A systematic method for designing motivational instruction for learners developed by John Keller. Keller proposed a four-step model. The steps of the model are *Attention, Relevance, Confidence,* and *Satisfaction* and the model is known as the ARCS model of motivation. Each element of the model must be present for motivative instruction to occur.

**Affective Domain:** One of the three domains of learning. The affective domain deals with teaching attitudes, values, and respect. Since change can be intimidating, the implementation team should spend time designing instruction to meet the emotional needs of the employees. The taxonomy for the affective domain within an ERP implementation includes, *Ignoring, Receiving, Responding, Valuing, Organizing,* and *Championing.* This affective taxonomy moves from simply paying attention to what is being taught at the *Ignoring* level, all the way to *Championing* the implementation and incorporating the ideas into the employee's basic belief system.

**Bill of Learning (BOL):** A BOL is a hierarchy of enabling learning objectives that must be achieved by an organization to support a strategic goal. The lowest level of the hierarchy contains learning objectives supporting the objectives on the next higher level which, in turn, supports the objective to the next higher level of the hierarchy. This logic continues until the hierarchy terminates at the strategic organizational level.

**Benchmarking:** Benchmarking is a systematic process of comparing a company's products, services, costs, processes, and procedures against those of its competitors. Benchmarking can also involve comparing an organization's processes to those considered best-in-class regardless of industry. There are two types of benchmarking — performance benchmarking and process benchmarking. Performance benchmarking involves tracking and monitoring measurable product characteristics. Process benchmarking goes outside of an industry to look at true best practices.

**Chief Learning Officer (CLO):** A person appointed to ensure that the learning needs of the organization are implemented in a manner that is congruent with the ERP implementation and other corporate initiatives. The job of the CLO is to monitor internal training practices, position training to support the strategic direction of the company, participate in planning the education of the organization's workforce for ERP, and champion organizational learning and employee growth and development.

**Cognitive Domain:** One of the three domains of learning. The cognitive domain covers information, knowledge, naming, solving, predicting, and other intellectual aspects of learning. The cognitive domain classifies information in the form of various taxonomies with knowledge at the lowest level, while higher mental abilities are classified into increasingly greater intellectual levels. The levels in LRP are labeled *Names, Jargon, Facts And Acronyms, Concepts, Rules, Procedures, Problem Solving,* and *Soft Skills.*

**ERP Software System:** This is an integrated computer system designed to handle all of the operations of an organization from order entry to final shipment of product to the customers. An ERP system can be examined from five perspectives. The first is that of a data management system. The second is that all the software modules in the organization are sharing the same database. The third is that of a manufacturing philosophy. The fourth is that of a business philosophy communication tool. Finally, ERP can be viewed as a knowledge management system. However, in the final analysis, it is the people who make or break the ERP system.

**Explosion Logic:** This is the method that LRP uses to ensure that all the learning objectives within an organization are being addressed. The BOL is an explosion of corporate learning objectives into discrete measurable learning objectives for specific skill sets that support the corporate strategic direction. The explosion process ensures that the educational initiatives within a company are tied directly to the strategic direction of the company.

**Formative Evaluation:** A formative evaluation is a series of mechanisms and techniques for measuring the effectiveness of the training development process. Formative evaluation can be divided into four different types. They are *Subject Matter Expert (SME)*, *One-on-One*, *Small-Group*, and *Field Trail* evaluations. Formative evaluation shapes and molds the training so that it meets the needs of the users, is easy to understand, and helps employees learn.

**Gross-to-Net Logic:** The act of comparing the existing skills and knowledge within the organization with the skills and knowledge required to obtain its stated ERP or strategic goals.

**Human Resources Analysis (HRA):** A Systems Thinking tool. A Human Resource Analysis involves answering a series of questions related to learning with the organization. The questions include: Does anyone in the organization have the word "learning" in his or her job description? and Is "learning" in the corporate mission statement? The HRA technique includes a review of job descriptions, productivity records, employee interviews, observation of how employees are performing, and focus group discussions of organizational human resource issues.

**Learning Organization:** A group of people who have woven a continuous, enhanced capacity to learn into the corporate culture — an organization in which learning processes are analyzed, monitored, developed, and aligned with competitive goals. A learning organization generates knowledge and learning faster than its competitors and turns that learning into a strategic advantage to outmarket, outmanage, and outsell competition.

**Learning Portal:** A "one-stop shop" on a corporation's intranet that allows individual employees to gain access to all of the online training opportunities within their organization. The portal can be programmed to recognize an individual's profile and provide him or her with exactly the type of training needed. The profile consists of the employee's job title, required skills for the current position and any skills required to move up within the organization. The information within the profile can be matched to corporate ERP training offerings.

**Learning Requirements Planning (LRP):** A formal, enterprise-wide ERP implementation process that is time phased to meet the long- and short-term learning objectives of an organization. LRP uses the concepts of "explosions," Bills of Learning, Master Learning Schedules, and Gross-to-Net Logic combined with a macro-level view of instructional design. The five steps of the model consist of Analysis, Diagnosis, Implementation, Evaluation, and Continuation. The LRP logic is simple and the results are dramatic.

**e-Learning:** The presentation of training materials, information, and content via the Internet or through an intranet.

**Level 1:** A training and education evaluation tool. A level 1 evaluation is conducted by handing out questionnaires at the end of an instructor-led training session or electronically at the end of an e-learning lesson. The Level 1 evaluation answers questions like: Was the presenter knowledgeable? Did the presenter carry himself well? Were the ERP concepts explained adequately? Were the MRP formulas easy to understand? At this level of evaluation, initial customer satisfaction is being measured.

**Level 2:** A training and education evaluation tool. A level 2 evaluation tests employee learning. At this level, the evaluation includes feedback indicating what was learned, and what was not learned. This is in the form of a test or assessment instrument completed by the employee who attended the learning session. The idea is to see if the employee can pass a test demonstration of what he or she learned. Level 2 evaluations can be paper-and-pencil exams or hands-on performance-based tests.

**Level 3:** A training and education evaluation tool. A level 3 evaluation checks to see if the skills taught in the training are actually being used on the job. Level 3 evaluates the transfer of learning from the learning experience to the job. Supervisory Reports, On-the-Job Peer Surveys, Action Plan Reports, Observation, and Self-Reports can assess this level of learning.

**Level 4:** A training and education evaluation tool. A level 4 evaluation attempts to measure the bottom-line result of the training. Did the training positively impact the ERP implementation? Is the implementation faster and more effective because of the type of training supplied to the employees? This level of evaluation can be obtained by conducing a ROI analysis and a benefit/cost analysis.

**Master Learning Schedule (MLS):** An MLS is a time-phased view of all the educational and training efforts undertaken within an organization. In many organizations, no comprehensive plan exists to view all of the objectives being taught. The MLS is an attempt to add visibility both to the courses or classes being offered and to the objectives being taught with the classes (or other forms of training delivery).

**Net Learning Requirements:** Skills and knowledge needed within an organization that are not currently available within the organization and cannot easily, quickly, or efficiently be purchased or developed.

**Psychomotor Domain:** Of the three domains of learning, the third domain is the psychomotor domain. This domain deals with learning physical movements. Keyboarding and mouse manipulation are two skills that fall under the psychomotor domain. Other skills in this domain include lifting, driving, and performing any type of coordinated physical activity.

**Soft Skills:** Soft skills deal with the development of communication, leadership, and team building skills. The need for soft skills training is critical for implementation success. The interrelationship between people is what makes an ERP system function effectively.

**Strategic Goal:** A strategic goal is the direction and vision of where a company wants to go. It is typically stated in terms of corporate direction. The intent is to create a goal for employees to strive toward. Top management must develop the strategic goal and then empower the employees to achieve the goal.

**Strategic Learning Goal:** A strategic learning goal is a high-level objective established by an organization stating the types of learning that must occur for it to successfully compete within its chosen industry.

**Summative Evaluation:** This level of evaluation determines if the instruction accomplished the goals for which it was developed or delivered. "Was the instruction effective?" is the question answered by a summative evaluation. Summative evaluation is used to quantify the impact that the training program had on the ERP implementation process. It puts cold, hard numbers to the often vague and fuzzy concept of corporate learning. Summative evaluation uses a four-level framework for evaluating the effectiveness of training. The levels are simply named *level 1*, *level 2*, *level 3*, and *level 4*.

**Systems Loop Diagram:** A Systems Thinking tool. The systems loop diagram provides visualization, typically in the form of a circle, of the cause and effect of interrelated problems within a manufacturing organization. The purpose of the diagram is to visually depict problems and the cause of those problems. Development of the diagram involves three steps. The first step is to list all of the individual events that are symptoms of the problem. The second step is to look for actions and reactions that relate the seemingly independent events to each other. The third step is to map the items onto a circular diagram. The Systems Loop Diagram provides a "picture" of problems and clearly identifies the interrelationships of the various elements within the organization. The management team can then determine which items in the loop need to be broken to stop the unproductive cycle.

**Systems Thinking:** Is a focus on the whole, as opposed to the parts. It is a method for thinking about and understanding the forces and interrelationships existing between the different functional areas within a manufacturing organization. Systems Thinking helps manufacturers see how to change their organizations to act more in tune with the larger processes of the economic environment in which they function.

**Visionweb:** A visionweb provides a visual representation of all the items contributing to a corporate vision. Creating a visionweb begins by recording, in the center of a chalkboard, flipchart, or piece of paper, a central point or idea that represents the ultimate vision and then drawing lines that extend from the center. Each line contains a future area of focus for the company. From each line, other lines can be drawn to show extensions of thought on various ideas. In addition, dotted lines are drawn to illustrate the interrelatedness of various items to each other.

# Appendix A:
# LRP Implementation Checklist

This appendix contains complete lists of all the tasks required to implement Learning Requirements Planning to support the ERP implementation process.

|  | Completed | | |
| --- | --- | --- | --- |
| *Analysis Tasks* | *Yes* | *No* | *Date* |

**General Tasks**

1. Explained the need for careful analysis of the organization to top managers.
2. Conveyed importance of the analysis step to all employees.

**Systems Thinking**

3. Taught concept of Systems Thinking to management.
4. Developed a systems loop to address problems within the manufacturing organization.
5. Examined the organization as an integrated system through a series of thought-provoking questions.
6. Conducted a Human Resources Analysis.
7. Conveyed the concept, through effective education to managers and employees, that ERP software is a system and should be treated as such.

**Benchmarking**

8. Conducted performance benchmarking.
9. Conducted process benchmarking.
10. Developed strategic goals for the organization.
11. Developed strategic goals for the ERP implementation.

| Analysis Tasks (Continued) | Completed | | |
|---|---|---|---|
| | Yes | No | Date |
| 12. Conducted a SWOT analysis. | ___ | ___ | ___ |
| 13. Developed strategic learning goals based on the strategic goals of the organization. | ___ | ___ | ___ |

**Analysis of Key Processes**

| | | | |
|---|---|---|---|
| 14. Chose symbols for process diagramming. | ___ | ___ | ___ |
| 15. Diagrammed key processes. | ___ | ___ | ___ |
| 16. Reach consensus on desired process. | ___ | ___ | ___ |
| 17. Walked key processes. | ___ | ___ | ___ |
| 18. Used Fishbone analysis for difficult-to-solve problems or difficult-to-understand process problems. | ___ | ___ | ___ |

**Bills of Learning**

| | | | |
|---|---|---|---|
| 19. Created a Bill of Learning for key Learning Objectives. | ___ | ___ | ___ |
| 20. Compared learning objectives across the various bills of learning. | ___ | ___ | ___ |

| Diagnosis Tasks | Completed | | |
|---|---|---|---|
| | Yes | No | Date |

**Gross-To-Net Learning Requirements**

| | | | |
|---|---|---|---|
| 21. Identify currently needed skills and knowledge. | ___ | ___ | ___ |
| 22. Identify new skills needed for new initiatives. | ___ | ___ | ___ |
| 23. Identify existing skills and knowledge. | ___ | ___ | ___ |
| 24. Identify easily purchasable skills and knowledge. | ___ | ___ | ___ |
| 25. Calculate net learning requirements. | ___ | ___ | ___ |
| 26. Prioritize net learning requirements appropriately. | ___ | ___ | ___ |

**Employee Learning Styles**

| | | | |
|---|---|---|---|
| 27. Introduce topic of learning styles to executives and upper management. | ___ | ___ | ___ |
| 28. Introduce topic to employees. | ___ | ___ | ___ |
| 29. Assess employee learning styles. | ___ | ___ | ___ |
| 30. Educate employees on the implications of their identified learning style. | ___ | ___ | ___ |
| 31. Design instruction to include multiple learning styles | ___ | ___ | ___ |

**Maslow's Hierarchy of Needs**

| | | | |
|---|---|---|---|
| 32. Identify if any employees have "physiological" needs. | ___ | ___ | ___ |
| 33. Address the physiological needs. | ___ | ___ | ___ |

|  | Completed | | |
| --- | :---: | :---: | :---: |
| *Diagnosis Tasks (Continued)* | *Yes* | *No* | *Date* |
| 34. Identify if any employees have "safety" needs. | ___ | ___ | ___ |
| 35. Address the safety needs. | ___ | ___ | ___ |
| 36. Identify any "social" needs. | ___ | ___ | ___ |
| 37. Address any social needs | ___ | ___ | ___ |
| 38. Identify any "self-esteem" needs. | ___ | ___ | ___ |
| 39. Address any self-esteem needs. | ___ | ___ | ___ |
| 40. Identify any "self-actualization" needs that can possibly be impacted by the implementation. This will require input from employees. | ___ | ___ | ___ |
| 41. Help employees who have identified a self-actualization need associated with the implementation to satisfy their need. | ___ | ___ | ___ |

|  | Completed | | |
| --- | :---: | :---: | :---: |
| *Design Tasks* | *Yes* | *No* | *Date* |

**Identify Types of Classes and Learning Events Needed**

| | | | |
| --- | :---: | :---: | :---: |
| 42. Basic Manufacturing Training. | ___ | ___ | ___ |
| 43. ERP Integration Training. | ___ | ___ | ___ |
| 44. Soft Skills Training. | ___ | ___ | ___ |
| 45. Basic Computer Literacy Training. | ___ | ___ | ___ |
| 46. ERP Set Up Training. | ___ | ___ | ___ |
| 47. ERP System Functionality Training. | ___ | ___ | ___ |

**Identify Delivery Strategy for Classes and Learning Events**

| | | | |
| --- | :---: | :---: | :---: |
| 48. Instructor-Led Training. | ___ | ___ | ___ |
| 49. Informal Lunch Meeting Training. | ___ | ___ | ___ |
| 50. Conference Room Pilot Training. | ___ | ___ | ___ |
| 51. e-Learning Training. | ___ | ___ | ___ |

**Develop Instructional Strategies and Tactics for Teaching**

| | | | |
| --- | :---: | :---: | :---: |
| 52. Employees Names, Jargon, Facts, and Acronyms. | ___ | ___ | ___ |
| 53. Conceptual Information Related to ERP. | ___ | ___ | ___ |
| 54. ERP-Related Rules that Must Be Followed. | ___ | ___ | ___ |
| 55. ERP-Related Procedures that Must Be Followed. | ___ | ___ | ___ |
| 56. Problem-Solving Techniques and Strategies. | ___ | ___ | ___ |
| 57. Metacognition Strategies (thinking about thinking). | ___ | ___ | ___ |
| 58. Soft Skills (communication, leadership, teamwork). | ___ | ___ | ___ |

| | Completed | | |
|---|---|---|---|
| *Design Tasks (Continued)* | *Yes* | *No* | *Date* |

59. Emotional or Affective Domain Materials (what overall message does the company want to send concerning the ERP implementation). 　　__　__　__

60. Psychomotor Skills (mousing and keyboarding). 　　__　__　__

61. Motivational Techniques to Implementation Team.
   a. Gain Attention of Employee Being Trained. 　　__　__　__
   b. Establish Relevance of ERP Training. 　　__　__　__
   c. Allow Employee to Gain Confidence. 　　__　__　__
   d. Show how ERP Knowledge leads to Satisfaction. 　　__　__　__

**Develop Learning Objectives**

62. Write Objectives Using the ABCD Format.
   a. Establish Audience for Training. 　　__　__　__
   b. Determine Desired Behavior of Employee. 　　__　__　__
   c. Establish the Conditions which Elicit Behavior. 　　__　__　__
   d. Determine Criteria for the Degree of Behavior. 　　__　__　__

| | Completed | | |
|---|---|---|---|
| *Implementation Tasks* | *Yes* | *No* | *Date* |

**Identify Attributes of ERP Appealing to User Base**

63. Relative Advantage. 　　__　__　__
64. Compatibility. 　　__　__　__
65. Complexity. 　　__　__　__
66. Trialability. 　　__　__　__
67. Observability. 　　__　__　__

**Identify Employees on Technology Adoption Continuum**

68. Technology Enthusiasts. 　　__　__　__
69. Visionaries. 　　__　__　__
70. Pragmatists. 　　__　__　__
71. Conservatives. 　　__　__　__
72. Skeptics. 　　__　__　__
73. Opinion Leaders. 　　__　__　__

**Identify Method of Determining Opinion Leaders**

74. Organizational Survey. 　　__　__　__
75. Interview Key Players. 　　__　__　__
76. Self-Designating Survey. 　　__　__　__

| Implementation Tasks (Continued) | Completed | | |
|---|---|---|---|
| | Yes | No | Date |

### Identify Employees for Implementation Team

77. Choose Representatives from Appropriate Functional Areas. ___ ___ ___

78. Choose Representatives from Appropriate Technology Adoption Continuum Location. ___ ___ ___

79. Choose an Opinion Leader. ___ ___ ___

### Provide Team Training

80. Give Team-Building Training to Implementation Team. ___ ___ ___

81. Give Team-Building Experiences to Implementation Team. ___ ___ ___

82. Allow Team Time to Work to Maximum Effectiveness Prior to Starting Implementation. ___ ___ ___

### Consider Pros and Cons of Each Go-Live Method

83. Parallel. ___ ___ ___

84. Phased. ___ ___ ___

85. Big Bang. ___ ___ ___

86. Pilot. ___ ___ ___

87. Choose Go-Live Method. ___ ___ ___

| Evaluation and Measurement Tasks | Completed | | |
|---|---|---|---|
| | Yes | No | Date |

### Conduct a Formative Evaluation

88. Subject Matter Expert Review of Training Materials. ___ ___ ___

89. One-on-One Review of Training Materials. ___ ___ ___

90. Small-Group Review of Training Materials. ___ ___ ___

91. Field Trial Review of Training Materials. ___ ___ ___

### Conduct a Level 1 Summative Evaluation of Training

92. Develop Evaluation Criteria. ___ ___ ___

93. Distribute Evaluation Sheets to Trainees. ___ ___ ___

94. Review and Quantify the Results. ___ ___ ___

95. Use Results to Strengthen Training. ___ ___ ___

### Conduct a Level 2 Summative Evaluation of Training

96. Determine if Paper-and-Pencil or Performance Test. ___ ___ ___

97. Develop Test Questions or Performance Tasks. ___ ___ ___

| Evaluation and Measurement Tasks (Continued) | Completed | | |
|---|---|---|---|
| | Yes | No | Date |
| 98. Construct Test with Easier Questions/Tasks First. | ___ | ___ | ___ |
| 99. Administer the Test. | ___ | ___ | ___ |
| 100. Review and Quantify the Results. | ___ | ___ | ___ |
| 101. Use Results to Strengthen Training. | ___ | ___ | ___ |

**Conduct a Level 3 Summative Evaluation of Training**

| | | | |
|---|---|---|---|
| 102. Determine what Behaviors Should Be Observed. | ___ | ___ | ___ |
| 103. Solicit Supervisory Reports. | ___ | ___ | ___ |
| 104. Conduct On-the-Job Peer Surveys. | ___ | ___ | ___ |
| 105. Review Trainee's Action Reports. | ___ | ___ | ___ |
| 106. Observe Trainees Back on the Job. | ___ | ___ | ___ |
| 107. Solicit Trainee Self-Reports. | ___ | ___ | ___ |
| 108. Review and Quantify the Results. | ___ | ___ | ___ |
| 109. Use Results to Strengthen Training. | ___ | ___ | ___ |

**Conduct a Level 4 Summative Evaluation of Training**

| | | | |
|---|---|---|---|
| 110. Send Training Costs to Manager, Ask for Estimation. | ___ | ___ | ___ |
| 111. Develop a Benefit/Cost Ratio for the Training. | ___ | ___ | ___ |
| 112. Calculate ROI for the Training. | ___ | ___ | ___ |
| 113. Review and Quantify the Results. | ___ | ___ | ___ |
| 114. Use Results to Strengthen and Justify Training. | ___ | ___ | ___ |

| Continuation Tasks | Completed | | |
|---|---|---|---|
| | Yes | No | Date |

**Planning Tasks**

| | | | |
|---|---|---|---|
| 115. Determine best method of conveying desired message to employees. | ___ | ___ | ___ |
| 116. Develop formal methods of conveying training message to employees (training classes, meetings). | ___ | ___ | ___ |
| 117. Encourage the development of informal methods of conveying training message to employees (pictures, impromptu events). | ___ | ___ | ___ |
| 118. Hire a Chief Learning Officer (CLO). | ___ | ___ | ___ |
| 119. Develop a Master Learning Plan (MLP). | ___ | ___ | ___ |
| 120. Develop a corporate learning infrastructure. | ___ | ___ | ___ |

**Resource Tasks**

| | | | |
|---|---|---|---|
| 121. Make training and learning a corporate priority. | ___ | ___ | ___ |

|  | Completed | | |
| :--- | :---: | :---: | :---: |
| *Continuation Tasks (Continued)* | *Yes* | *No* | *Date* |
| 122. Allocate time for employee training. | — | — | — |
| 123. Allocate time for employee thinking. | — | — | — |
| 124. Allocate the space necessary for classroom training. | — | — | — |
| 125. Allocate a space and equipment necessary for online learning. | — | — | — |
| 126. Allocate the necessary money to support continuous learning. | — | — | — |

**Rewards and Incentives**

| | | | |
| :--- | :---: | :---: | :---: |
| 127. Consider cross-training the majority of the workforce. | — | — | — |
| 128. Consider instituting a pay-for-skills program. | — | — | — |
| 129. Develop nonmonetary methods of recognition. | — | — | — |

**Learning Disciplines**

| | | | |
| :--- | :---: | :---: | :---: |
| 130. Put incentive program into place to encourage employees to reach the discipline of Personal Mastery. | — | — | — |
| 131. Develop a process for examining the Mental Models present within the organization. | — | — | — |
| 132. Implement a program to provide a Shared Vision within the entire company. | — | — | — |
| 133. Initiate a program to develop a focus on Team Learning and teamwork within the organization. | — | — | — |
| 134. Initiate a program to develop Systems Thinking at all levels of the organization. | — | — | — |

# Appendix B:
# Example of a Learning
# Diagnosis Chart

| Learning Objective | Domain of Learning | How Assessed | Personnel with Mastery |
|---|---|---|---|
|  |  |  |  |
|  |  |  |  |

**Figure B1    Learning Diagnosis Chart Format.**

# Appendix C:
# Job Description for a
# Chief Learning Officer

## Position

Manufacturing firm seeks a dynamic individual with excellent interpersonal skills for the position of Chief Learning Officer (CLO). This new position reports directly to the president of the company and is responsible for the design, development, and delivery of an entire training curriculum to support the implementation of an ERP system. This individual must have experience in the application of the instructional systems design process to large-scale strategic initiatives.

## Responsibilities

Responsibilities include:

- Managing the informal and formal learning events within the organization.
- Overseeing the human resource interests of the organization and sitting in on executive-level discussions concerning R&D commercialization, new product development, the strategic vision of the company, ERP implementation, and increasing shareholder value.
- Monitoring internal training practices, positioning training to support the ERP implementation, participating in planning the education of

the organization's workforce, championing organizational learning and employee development during and after the ERP implementation.

■ Developing, administering, and monitoring the Master Learning Plan. The MLP projects future training needs and is used to coordinate major educational initiatives with major improvement efforts within the organization.

■ Reviewing the MLP monthly with operations personnel as well as senior-level management.

■ Planning and developing an internal learning infrastructure to support the various learning efforts throughout the organization.

■ Conducting cost analysis to determine the amount of ROI derived from training efforts.

■ Lead the organization in the area of e-learning.

## Experience

Qualifications required:

■ Knowledge of manufacturing environment (APICS Certification preferred).

■ Ability to gather, analyze, and synthesize information.

■ Excellent written and oral communication skills.

■ Ability to evaluate existing training programs.

■ Ability to implement new training programs.

■ 10–12 years of executive level experience dealing with human resource issues.

# Index

## A

ABCD format for learning objectives, 158
Abstract conceptualization learning, 131
Accommodator, 132
Accountability
  implementation team, 215
  training, 242
Acronym mnemonics, 163
Action plan, 253
Action reports, 259
Active experimentation learning, 131
Activity-based costing (ABC), 38–39, 75
Adult learners, 264
Advanced planning and scheduling module, 37
Affective domain, 156
Amazon.com, 89, 94
Amoco Corporation (BP Amoco), 223
Analogies, fact-based learning, 164, 166
Analysis, 69–107
  new skills needed, 117
  practicality, 103
  processes, 96–99, 299
  questions, 246
Andragogy, 181
APICS, 13, 121
  basic manufacturing concepts classes, 145
  field trials, 237
  learning organization, 263

SME, 234
summative evaluation, 251
Application questions, 246
Application sharing, 285
ARCS model, 180
Assessment, *see* Evaluation, Testing
Assessment pool, 243
Assimilator, 132
Assumptive errors, 44
ASTD, 268
Asynchronous learning, 286, *see also* e-learning
Attention, 180, 181
Attitude taxonomy, 156
Attitudinal learning, 57, 175–179
Audience (learning objectives), 158
Auditory learner, 127, *see also* Learning styles

## B

Baan, 280
Backflushing methods, 36
Bannister, Roger, 176
Barden Corporation, 7
Barnes & Noble, 94
Basic computer literacy classes, 149
Basic manufacturing classes, 145–146
  go-live training pyramid, 145
Behavior (learning objectives), 158

# D

Deductive learner, 126, *see also* Learning
   styles
Degree (learning objectives), 158, 159
Demand planning, 25
Deming, W. Edwards, 75
Design, LRP, 54
Detailed capacity planning module, 33
Diagnosis, 109–140, *see also* LRP, diagnosis
Diffusion, 189–190, 193
Discrete manufacturing environment, 36
Distance education, *see* e-learning
Distance learning, *see* e-learning
Distribution Requirements Planning (DRP),
   21
Diverger, 132
Domains of learning, 152
Do-or-die, 22
Drill and practice, 164
Drill-down, 293
Drop-dead date, 215, *see also* Go live
Dynamic data, 31

# E

e-commerce, 27
e-commerce modules, 41
EDI, 27
Educational needs, 109
Educational Society for Resource
   Management, *see* APICS
Eduneering, 121
e-learning, 64–66, 279–285, 300, *see also*
   Online learning, Intranet training,
   Web-based learning
  application sharing, 285
  asynchronous learning, 286
  benefits, 291
  Blackboard software, 243
  CD-ROM, 280
  Centra Symposium, 285
  chat rooms, 281
  compared to traditional training, 288
  defining, 281
  distance training, 280
  information access, 292

  Internet training, 280
  InterWise, 285
  lag time before go-live, 289
  learning portal, 293
  learning time requirements, 291
  LRP connection, 293
  Marshall Manufacturing, 298
  PeopleSoft, 285
  SAP, 285
  synchronous, 284–285
  testing, 284
  threaded discussions, 281
  traditional training, problems, 287
  web-based training, 280, 281
  web-cast, 283
  whiteboard, 283
Electronic data interchange, *see* EDI
Employee interviews (HRA), 84
Employee retention, 40
  training, 267, 273
Employees, motivating, 136
Empowerment, implementation team, 213
End-of-course evaluation, 240
Engineering BOM, 39
Engineering modules, 39
Enterprise Resource Management, *see* ERP
  advanced planning and scheduling (APS)
   module, 37
  as a system, 85
  assumptive errors, 44
  benchmarking implementation, 89
  business and strategic planning module,
   23
  compared to MRP, 86
  content errors, 43
  costing modules, 38
  customer relationship management
   module, 26
  data, 17
  defined, 13, 15
  detailed capacity planning module, 33
  e-commerce modules, 41
  engineering modules, 39
  executive decision support module, 24
  failure, 5–6, 58, 73, 78, 181, 187
  financial modules, 38
  forecasting module, 26
  history, 18–22
  human resources module, 40

# H

Habitat for Humanity, 176
Half-life of learning, 270
Hall, Brandon, 292
Hands-on performance tests, 248
Hard skills, 148
Hershey Foods, Inc., 5, 224
Hewlett-Packard, 267
HR analysis (HRA), 79, 83–85
HR module, 40
Human resources, see HR

# I

Images, fact-based learning, 164
Implementation
    affect of training, 238
    drop-dead date, 215
    ERP, 57
    failures, avoiding, 58
Implementation approaches, 58–59,
        217–227
    Amoco Corporation (BP Amoco), 223
    big bang, 59, 221–224
    conference room pilot, 222, 223
    Hershey Foods, Inc., 224
    little bangs, 223
    parallel, 218–219
    phased, 59, 219–221
    pilot, 59, 224–226
    pilot areas, choosing, 225
    play database, 222
    quick slice, 224
    scheduling, 222
    Westell Technologies, 220
Implementation methods, see
        Implementation approaches
Implementation model, 48
Implementation problems, undermining the
        system, 200
Implementation strategies, see
        Implementation approaches
Implementation task lists, 47
Implementation team, 10, 190, 200, 203, 300
    accountability, 215

as champions of system, 204
authority, 213
characteristics, 205
commitment, 213, 214
communication, 211
company culture, 216
developing as effective, 204
drop-dead date, 215, 216
empowerment, 213
exit plan, 216
function and purpose, 203–204
incremental goals, 214
job descriptions, 206
member involvement, 212
mission, 214
noncontributing members, 212
process, 210
project leader, 205, 206–208
project manager, 205
project recorder, 208–209
purpose, 205
rate of technological adoption, 191
roles, 205
roles and responsibilities, table, 206
simulations, 204
superusers, 217
team champion, 205, 210
team facilitator, 205, 209
technological, 193, 196
technology adoption continuum, 195
trust, 216
upper management commitment, 214
working rules, 210
Implementation training, field trial, 236
Implementation Triangle, 189
Incentives, 263, 271–272, 277
Incremental goals, 214
Inductive learner, 126, see also Learning
        styles
Influence, informal, 202, see also Opinion
        leaders
Informal influence, 202
Informal learning, 263
Information access, 292
    teaching, 169
Information types, 160
    conceptual learning, 165
    problem solving, 170